To the Instructor

Thank you for your interest in the Townsend Press vocabulary series—so successful that it now appears in a Fourth Edition. Our goal in this series has been to produce nothing less than excellent books at nothing more than reasonable prices.

About the Book

Notice that the introduction to students (page 1) immediately makes clear to them just why vocabulary study is important. Students are motivated to learn by the four compelling kinds of evidence for word study. The back cover as well convinces students that "a solid vocabulary is a source of power."

Next, you may want to look at the preface, starting on page vii, which describes in detail the nine distinctive features of the book.

There are thirty chapters in the book, divided into six units. You'll note that while each chapter takes up only six pages, those pages contain a great deal of hands-on practice to help ensure that students master each word. And you'll find that the practice materials themselves are far more carefully done, and more appealing, than the run-of-the-mill items you typically find in a skills text. The quality and interest level of the content will help students truly learn the words, without either boring them or insulting their intelligence.

Supplements to the Book

Adding to the value of *Groundwork for a Better Vocabulary* is the quality of the supplements:

- An **Instructor's Edition**, which you hold in your hand. The *Instructor's Edition* is identical to the student text except that it includes the answers to all of the practices and tests.

- A combined **Instructor's Manual and Test Bank**, free with adoptions of 20 or more copies. This supplement contains a general vocabulary placement test as well as a pretest and a posttest for the book and for each of the six units in the text. It also includes teaching guidelines, suggested syllabi, an answer key, and an additional mastery test for each chapter as well as a related-words activity for each chapter.

- **PowerPoint presentations and a Blackboard cartridge.** These may be downloaded from the "Supplements" area for instructors at **www.townsendpress.com**.

- **Online exercises,** available at **www.townsendpress.com**, which provide a general placement test and two additional tests for each vocabulary chapter in the book. These exercises contain a number of user- and instructor-friendly features, including actual, audible pronunciations of the words; brief explanations of answers; a sound option; frequent mention of the user's first name; a running score at the bottom of the screen; and a record-keeping file.

Adopters of *Groundwork for a Better Vocabulary* can obtain the print supplements by calling our toll-free number, 1-800-772-6410, or by e-mailing Customer Service at **cs@townsendpress.com**.

(Continues on next page)

New Features of the Book

Among the changes in this Fourth Edition of *Groundwork for a Better Vocabulary* are the following:

- **A full-color design.** Color has been carefully used throughout, not as window dressing but to add clarity and readability to the different parts of each chapter and the different sections of the book.

- **Additional multicultural names and repeated words.** To broaden both the appeal and the effectiveness of the practice materials, ethnic names have been used more frequently, and even more vocabulary words have been repeated.

- **Revised and updated practice items.** As always, a number of practice items throughout the book have been revised or updated to ensure that each item works as clearly and effectively with students as possible.

A Comprehensive Vocabulary Program

There are nine books in the Townsend Press vocabulary series:

- *Vocabulary Basics* (reading level 4–6)
- *Groundwork for a Better Vocabulary* (reading level 5–8)
- *Building Vocabulary Skills* (reading level 7–9)
- *Building Vocabulary Skills, Short Version* (reading level 7–9)
- *Improving Vocabulary Skills* (reading level 9–11)
- *Improving Vocabulary Skills, Short Version* (reading level 9–11)
- *Advancing Vocabulary Skills* (reading level 11–13)
- *Advancing Vocabulary Skills, Short Version* (reading level 11–13)
- *Advanced Word Power* (reading level 12–14)

Note that the short versions of the *Building*, *Improving*, and *Advancing* books are limited to 200 words, as opposed to the 260 words and 40 word parts in each of the long versions. For some students and classes, the short versions of the books will provide an easier, more manageable approach to vocabulary development.

Groundwork for a Better Vocabulary

Fourth Edition

Beth Johnson
Janet M. Goldstein

TP

Townsend Press Reading Series

Groundwork for College Reading with Phonics
Groundwork for College Reading
Ten Steps to Building College Reading Skills
Ten Steps to Improving College Reading Skills
Ten Steps to Advancing College Reading Skills
Ten Steps to Advanced Reading

Townsend Press Vocabulary Series

Vocabulary Basics
Groundwork for a Better Vocabulary
Building Vocabulary Skills
Building Vocabulary Skills, Short Version
Improving Vocabulary Skills
Improving Vocabulary Skills, Short Version
Advancing Vocabulary Skills
Advancing Vocabulary Skills, Short Version
Advanced Word Power

Supplements Available for Most Books

Instructor's Edition
Instructor's Manual and Test Bank
Online Exercises
PowerPoint Presentations
Blackboard Cartridges

ISBN-13 (Student Edition): 978-1-59194-223-8
ISBN-10 (Student Edition): 1-59194-223-3
ISBN-13 (Instructor's Edition): 978-1-59194-224-5
ISBN-10 (Instructor's Edition): 1-59194-224-1

Send book orders and requests for desk copies or supplements to:

Townsend Press Book Center
439 Kelley Drive
West Berlin, New Jersey 08091

For even faster service, contact us in any of the following ways:

By telephone: 1-800-772-6410
By fax: 1-800-225-8894
By e-mail: cs@townsendpress.com
Through our website: www.townsendpress.com

Contents

NOTE: For ease of reference, the titles of the selections that close each chapter are included.

Unit Four

Unit Five

Unit Six

Appendixes

Preface: To the Instructor

The problem is all too familiar: *students just don't know enough words*. Reading, writing, and content teachers agree that many students' vocabularies are inadequate for course demands. Weak vocabularies limit students' understanding of what they read and the clarity and depth of what they write.

The purpose of *Groundwork for a Better Vocabulary* and the other books in the Townsend Press vocabulary series is to provide a solid, workable answer to the vocabulary problem. In the course of 30 chapters, *Groundwork for a Better Vocabulary* teaches 300 important basic words. Here are the book's distinctive features:

1 **An intensive words-in-context approach.** Studies show that students learn words best by reading and using them repeatedly in different contexts, not through rote memorization. The book gives students an intensive in-context experience by presenting each word in **eight** different settings. Each chapter takes students through a productive sequence of steps:

- Students infer the meaning of each word by considering two sentences in which it appears and then choosing a brief definition from multiple-choice options.
- On the basis of their inferences, students identify each word's meaning in a matching activity. They are then in a solid position to deepen their knowledge of a word.
- Finally, they strengthen their understanding of a word by applying it in five different words-in-context passages, including sentence-completion activities and high-interest fill-in-the-blank passages.

Each encounter with a word brings it closer to becoming part of the student's permanent word bank.

2 **Abundant practice.** Along with extensive practice in each chapter, there are a crossword puzzle and a set of unit tests at the end of every five-chapter unit. The puzzle and tests reinforce students' knowledge of the words in each chapter. In addition, Chapters 2 through 30 reuse words from earlier chapters (such repeated words are marked with small circles, like this°), allowing for more reinforcement. Last, there are supplementary tests in the *Instructor's Manual and Test Bank* and the online exercises that accompany the book. All this practice means that students learn in the surest possible way: by working closely and repeatedly with each word.

3 **Controlled feedback.** The opening activity in each chapter gives students three multiple-choice options to help them decide on the meaning of a given word. The multiple-choice options also help students complete the matching exercise that is the second activity of each chapter. A limited answer key at the back of the book then provides answers for the third activity in the chapter. All these features enable students to take an active role in their own learning.

4 **Focus on essential words.** A good deal of time and research went into selecting the 300 words featured in the book. Word frequency lists were consulted, along with lists in a wide range of vocabulary books. In addition, the authors and editors each prepared their own lists. A computer was used to help in the consolidation of the many word lists. A long process of group discussion then led to final decisions about the words that would be most helpful for students reading at a basic level.

5 Appealing content. Dull practice materials work against learning. On the other hand, meaningful, lively, and at times even funny sentences and passages can spark students' attention and thus enhance their grasp of the material. For this reason, a great deal of effort was put into creating sentences and passages with both widespread appeal and solid context support. We have tried throughout to make the practice materials truly enjoyable for teachers and students alike. Look, for example, at the selections on page 15 that serve as the Final Check in Chapter 1.

6 Clear format. The book has been designed so that its very format contributes to the learning process. Each chapter consists of three two-page spreads. In the first two-page spread (the first such spread is on pages 10–11), students can easily refer to all ten words in context while working on the matching activity, in which they must choose a clear meaning for each word. The other two-page spreads allow students to see the words in a variety of contexts as they work through the activities.

7 Supplementary materials.

a A convenient *Instructor's Edition* is available at no charge to instructors using the book. It is identical to the student book except that it contains answers to all of the activities and tests.

b A combined *Instructor's Manual and Test Bank* is also offered at no charge to instructors who have adopted the book. This supplement contains a general vocabulary placement test, along with a pretest and a posttest for the entire book as well as for each of its six units. It also includes teaching guidelines, suggested syllabi, and an answer key, as well as a "Related Words" activity and an additional mastery test for each chapter.

c *PowerPoint presentations and a Blackboard cartridge* are available for the book and may be downloaded from the "Supplements" area for instructors at www.townsendpress.com.

d *Online exercises,* available in the Online Learning Center at www.townsendpress.com, also accompany the book. These exercises consist of two to four additional tests for each vocabulary chapter in the book. The program includes a number of user- and instructor-friendly features: brief explanations of answers; a sound option; frequent mention of the user's first name; a running score at the bottom of the screen; a record-keeping file; and actual, audible pronunciations of the words.

Probably in no other area of reading instruction is the computer more useful than in reinforcing vocabulary. These online exercises take full advantage of the computer's unique capabilities and motivational appeal. Here's how the program works:

● Students are tested on the ten words in a chapter, with each word in a sentence context different from any in the book itself.

● After students answer each question, they receive immediate feedback: The program states that the answer is right or wrong and why, frequently using the student's first name and providing a running score.

● When they complete each test, students receive their scores. If they repeat the test, they then receive a new score, labeled "R" on the scores report, with a number following the "R" indicating how many times they have taken the same test. What is so valuable about this, of course, is that the program gives students immediate additional practice with the words they need to review.

- In addition, the online exercise program offers a second, more challenging "Word Definitions" test in which students must identify the meanings of the chapter words without the benefit of context. This test is a final check that students have really learned the words. And, again, there is the option of a retest, with its own score.

    Once students complete these exercises, their knowledge of each word in the chapter will have been carefully reinforced. And this reinforcement will be even more effective for having occurred in an electronic medium that especially engages today's students.

To obtain a copy of either the *Instructor's Edition* or the *Instructor's Manual and Test Bank*, instructors may contact Customer Service at 1-800-772-6410 or at cs@townsendpress.com.

8 Realistic pricing. As with the previous editions, the goal has been to offer the highest possible quality at the lowest possible price. While *Groundwork for a Better Vocabulary* is comprehensive enough to serve as a primary text, its modest price also makes it an inexpensive supplement.

9 One in a sequence of books. The most fundamental book in the Townsend Press vocabulary series is *Vocabulary Basics*. It is followed by *Groundwork for a Better Vocabulary* (a slightly more advanced basic text) and then by the three main books in the series: *Building Vocabulary Skills* (also a basic text), *Improving Vocabulary Skills* (an intermediate text), and *Advancing Vocabulary Skills* (a more advanced text). The most advanced book in the Townsend Press vocabulary series is *Advanced Word Power*. There are also short versions of the *Building, Improving,* and *Advancing* books. Suggested reading levels for the books are included in the *Instructor's Manual.* Together, the books can help create a vocabulary foundation that will make any student a better reader, writer, and thinker.

Notes on the Fourth Edition

A number of changes have been made in the fourth edition of *Groundwork for a Better Vocabulary:*

- **A full-color design.** Color has been carefully used throughout, not as window dressing but to add clarity and readability to the different parts of each chapter and the different sections of the book.

- **Additional multicultural names and repeated words.** To broaden both the appeal and the effectiveness of the practice materials, ethnic names have been used more frequently, and even more vocabulary words have been repeated.

- **Revised and updated practice items.** As always, a number of practice items throughout the book have been revised or updated to ensure that each item works as clearly and effectively with students as possible.

Acknowledgments

We are grateful for the enthusiastic comments provided by users of the Townsend Press vocabulary books over the life of the first three editions. We appreciate as well the work done on earlier editions by Terri Amici, Lisa Barsky, George Jiang, and, in particular, Carole Mohr. We would also like to thank Kathryn Bernstein, Denton Cairnes, and Rick Moore for design, editing, and proofreading assistance with the fourth edition. And we owe special thanks to Barbara Solot, whose full-color text design is as clear as it is inviting. The result of her artistry is a strikingly attractive book that both students and teachers will enjoy. All of these talented colleagues have helped us make *Groundwork for a Better Vocabulary* even more effective and user-friendly than before.

Beth Johnson   Janet M. Goldstein

Introduction

Why Vocabulary Development Counts

You have probably often heard it said, "Building vocabulary is important." Maybe you've politely nodded in agreement and then forgotten the matter. But it would be fair for you to ask, "*Why* is vocabulary development important? Provide some evidence." Here are four compelling kinds of evidence.

1. Common sense tells you what many research studies have shown as well: **vocabulary is a basic part of reading comprehension.** Simply put, if you don't know enough words, you are going to have trouble understanding what you read. An occasional word may not stop you, but if there are too many words you don't know, comprehension will suffer. The content of textbooks is often challenge enough; you don't want to work as well on understanding the words that express that content.

2. **Vocabulary is a major part of almost every standardized test**, including reading achievement tests, college entrance exams, and armed forces and vocational placement tests. Test developers know that vocabulary is a key measure of both one's learning and one's ability to learn. It is for this reason that they include a separate vocabulary section as well as a reading comprehension section. The more words you know, then, the better you are likely to do on such important tests.

3. Studies have indicated that **students with strong vocabularies are more successful in school.** And one widely known study found that **a good vocabulary, more than any other factor, was common to people enjoying successful careers in life.** Words are in fact the tools not just of better reading, but of better writing, speaking, listening, and thinking as well. The more words you have at your command, the more effective your communication can be, and the more influence you can have on the people around you.

4. **In today's world, a good vocabulary counts more than ever.** Far fewer people work on farms or in factories. Far more are in jobs that provide services or process information. More than ever, words are the tools of our trade: words we use in reading, writing, listening, and speaking. Furthermore, experts say that tomorrow's workers will be called on to change jobs and learn new skills at an ever-increasing pace. The keys to survival and success will be the abilities to communicate skillfully and learn quickly. A solid vocabulary is essential for both of these skills.

Clearly, the evidence is overwhelming that building vocabulary is crucial. The question then becomes, "What is the best way of going about it?"

Words in Context: The Key to Vocabulary Development

Memorizing lists of words is a traditional method of vocabulary development. However, you are likely to forget such memorized lists quickly. Studies show that to master a word, you must see and use it in various contexts. By working actively and repeatedly with a word, you greatly increase the chance of really learning it.

The following activity will make clear how this book is organized and how it uses a words-in-context approach. Answer the questions or fill in the missing words in the spaces provided.

Inside Front Cover and Contents

Turn to the inside front cover.

- The inside front cover provides a _____pronunciation guide_____ that will help you pronounce all the vocabulary words in the book.

Now turn to the table of contents on pages v–vi.

- How many chapters are in the book? ___30___

- Four sections follow the last chapter. The first of these sections provides a limited answer key, the second gives helpful information on using _____the dictionary_____, the third contains _____topics for discussion and writing_____, and the fourth is a list of the 300 words in the book.

Vocabulary Chapters

Turn to Chapter 1 on pages 10–15. This chapter, like all the others, consists of seven parts:

- The **first part** of the chapter, on pages 10–11, is called _____Ten Words in Context_____.

The left-hand column lists the ten words in the chapter. Under each **boldfaced** word is its _____pronunciation_____ (in parentheses). For example, the pronunciation of *challenge* is _____chăl´ĭnj_____. For a guide to pronunciation, see the inside front cover as well as "Dictionary Use" on pages 243–244.

Below the pronunciation guide for each word is its part of speech. The part of speech shown for *challenge* is ___noun___. The vocabulary words in this book are mostly nouns, adjectives, and verbs. **Nouns** are words used to name something—a person, place, thing, or idea. Familiar nouns include *boyfriend, city, hat,* and *truth.* **Adjectives** are words that describe nouns, as in the following word pairs: *former* boyfriend, *large* city, *red* hat, *whole* truth. All of the **verbs** in this book express an action of some sort. They tell what someone or something is doing. Common verbs include *sing, separate, support,* and *imagine.*

To the right of each word are two sentences that will help you understand its meaning. In each sentence, the **context**—the other words in the sentence—provides clues you can use to figure out the definition. There are four common types of context clues: examples, synonyms, antonyms, and the general sense of the sentence. Each is briefly described on the pages that follow.

Common Context Clues

1 Examples

A sentence may include examples that reveal what an unfamiliar word means. For instance, take a look at the following sentence from Chapter 2 for the word *category*:

> When Jasmine was in high school, she didn't seem to fit into any **category**. She wasn't an athlete, a scholar, or a rebel.

The second sentence gives three examples of *category*—being "an athlete, a scholar, or a rebel." To figure out what *category* means, think about those examples. What is the speaker saying that Jasmine doesn't fit into? Look at the choices below, and in the space provided, write the letter of the answer you think is correct.

   _C_ *Category* means   A. goal.   B. feeling.   C. group.

Since the speaker is talking about the types of groups in high school, you may have correctly guessed that answer *C* is the right choice.

2 Synonyms

Synonyms are words that mean the same or almost the same as another word. For example, the words *joyful, happy*, and *pleased* are synonyms—they all mean about the same thing. A synonym serves as a context clue by stating the meaning of an unknown word that is nearby. For instance, the sentence below from Chapter 1 includes a synonym clue for the vocabulary word *peculiar*.

> My brother thinks my chip-and-dip sandwiches are **peculiar**, but I don't think they're as strange as the peanut-butter-and-tuna sandwiches he eats.

Rather than repeat *peculiar* in the second part of the sentence, the author used a synonym. Find that synonym, and then, from the choices below, write in the letter of the meaning of *peculiar*.

   _B_ *Peculiar* means   A. attractive.   B. unusual.   C. innocent.

In the sentence from Chapter 1, *strange* is used as a synonym for *peculiar*. Since another word for *strange* is *unusual*, the correct answer is *B*.

3 Antonyms

Antonyms are words with opposite meanings. For example, *help* and *harm* are antonyms, as are *work* and *rest*. Antonyms serve as context clues by stating the opposite meaning of a nearby unknown word. The sentence below from Chapter 2 provides an antonym clue for the word *deliberate*.

> Manny's pushing me was quite **deliberate**; it wasn't accidental at all.

To make a point, the author used an antonym of *deliberate*. Find the antonym, and use it to help you figure out what *deliberate* means. Then write in the letter of the meaning you choose.

   _C_ *Deliberate* means   A. easy.   B. fair.   C. planned.

(Continues on next page)

The sentence suggests that "deliberate" pushing and "accidental" pushing are very different things. So we can guess that *deliberate* means the opposite of *accidental*. Another word that is the opposite of *accidental* is *planned*, so *C* is the correct answer—*deliberate* means "planned."

4 General Sense of the Sentence

Even when there is no example, synonym, or antonym clue in a sentence, most of the time you can still figure out the meaning of an unfamiliar word. For example, look at the sentence from Chapter 1 for the word *surplus*.

More and more restaurants are donating their **surplus** food to homeless people.

After thinking carefully about the context, you should be able to figure out what kind of food restaurants would be giving to homeless people. Write the letter of your choice.

_B_ *Surplus* means   A. strange.   B. extra.   C. main.

From the general sense of the sentence from Chapter 1 plus your own common sense, you probably guessed that the restaurants are donating "extra" food. Answer *B* is correct.

By looking closely at the pair of sentences provided for each word, as well as the answer choices, you should be able to decide on the meaning of a word. As you figure out each meaning, you are working actively with the word. You are creating the groundwork you need to understand and to remember the word. *Getting involved with the word and developing a feel for it, based upon its use in context, is the key to word mastery.*

It is with good reason, then, that the directions at the top of page 10 tell you to use the context to figure out each word's _____meaning_____. Doing so deepens your sense of the word and prepares you for the next activity.

● The **second part** of the chapter, on page 11, is titled _____Matching Words with Definitions_____.

According to research, it is not enough to see a word in context. At a certain point, it is important to look at the actual meaning of a word. The matching activity provides that meaning, but it also makes you look for and think about that meaning. In other words, it continues the active learning that is your surest route to learning and remembering a word.

Note the caution that follows this activity. Do not go any further until you are sure that you know the correct meaning of each word as used in context.

Keep in mind that a word may have more than one meaning. In fact, some words have quite a few meanings. (If you doubt it, try looking up the word *make* or *draw* in a dictionary.) In this book, you will focus on one common meaning for each vocabulary word. However, many of the words have additional meanings. For example, in Chapter 1, you will learn that *challenge* means "a test of one's abilities," as in the sentence "My new job is a real challenge." If you then look up *challenge* in the dictionary, you will discover that it has other meanings. For example, it can also mean "a call to take part in a contest or fight," as in "Ted never turns down a challenge to play any kind of game." After you learn one common meaning of a word, you will find yourself gradually learning its other meanings in the course of your school and personal reading.

● The **third and fourth parts** of the chapter, on page 12, are titled _____Check 1_____ and _____Check 2_____.

The first check consists of ten sentences that give you an opportunity to test your understanding of the ten words. After filling in the words, check your answers in the limited answer key at the back of the book. (But be sure to use the answer key as a learning tool only. Doing so will help you to master the words and to prepare for the remaining activities and the unit tests, for which answers are not provided.) The second check on page 12 then gives you another chance to deepen your understanding of the words.

- The **fifth part** of the chapter, on page 13, is titled _____ Word Work _____.
  The practices on this page will make the meanings of the words come more alive through the use of vivid examples. Chances are you may find this activity to be one of the most enjoyable in the book.

- The **sixth part** of the chapter, on page 14, offers practice in one of three areas: word parts, synonyms and antonyms, or analogies. Each is explained below.

Word Parts, Synonyms-Antonyms, and Analogies

Word Parts

The first and third chapters in each unit contain practice with word parts.

Word parts are building blocks used in many English words. Learning word parts can help you to spell and pronounce words, unlock the meanings of unfamiliar words, and remember new words.

This book covers twenty-four word parts. You will learn two types: prefixes and suffixes. A **prefix** is a word part that is found at the *beginning* of a word. When written separately, a prefix is followed by a hyphen to show that something follows it. For example, the prefix *sur* is written like this: *sur-*. *Sur-* can mean "beyond" or "additional," as in *surpass* (to go beyond) and *surcharge* (an additional charge).

A **suffix** is a word part that is found at the end of a word. To show that something always comes before a suffix, a hyphen is placed at the beginning. For instance, the suffix *ly* is written like this: *-ly*. One common meaning of *-ly* is "in a certain way," as in the words *gratefully* (in a grateful way) and *angrily* (in an angry way).

Each word-part practice begins with the meaning of a word part and examples. Fill-in items then help you recognize and remember the word parts. To see what these items are like, try the one below from Chapter 1 for the word part *sur*. On the answer line, write the word that best completes the sentence.

surcharge   surface   surpass   surplus   surtax

_____ surtax _____ In addition to the usual taxes, people who earn more than a certain amount will have to pay a ___.

The sentence suggests that people who earn more than a certain amount will have to pay an additional tax. Since you now know that *sur-* can mean "additional," you probably wrote the correct word on the line: *surtax* (an additional tax).

(There is a third type of word part—a root. You will not be working with roots in this book. **Roots** are word parts that carry the basic meanings of words. For example, one common root is *vis*, which means "to see," as in the words *visit* and *vision*.)

(Continues on next page)

Synonyms and Antonyms

The second and fourth chapters in each unit contain synonym-antonym practices. You have already learned in this introduction that a **synonym** is a word that means the same or almost the same as another word, and that an **antonym** is a word that means the opposite of another word. These practices will deepen your understanding of words by getting you to think about other words with the same or opposite meanings.

To see what the synonym questions are like, do the example below. Write the letter of the word that most nearly means the **same** as the first word, *hard*.

   B   **hard**
- A. new
- B. difficult
- C. far
- D. bad

Since *difficult* is another way of saying *hard*, the correct answer is *B*.

Now, to see what the antonym questions are like, do the sample item below. Write in the letter of the word that most nearly means the **opposite** of *kind*.

   D   **kind**
- A. silly
- B. busy
- C. young
- D. cruel

The opposite of *kind* is *cruel*, so *D* is the correct answer.

Analogies

The last chapter in each unit contains an analogy practice, which is yet another way to deepen your understanding of words. An **analogy** is a similarity between two things that are otherwise different. Doing an analogy question is a two-step process. First you have to figure out the relationship in a pair of words. Those words are written like this:

LEAF : TREE

What is the relationship between the two words above? The answer can be stated like this: A leaf is a part of a tree.

Next, you must look for a similar relationship in a second pair of words. Here is how a complete analogy question looks:

LEAF : TREE ::
- A. pond : river
- B. foot : shoe
- C. page : book
- D. beach : sky

And here is how the question can be read:

   C   LEAF is to TREE as
- A. *pond* is to *river.*
- B. *foot* is to *shoe.*
- C. *page* is to *book.*
- D. *beach* is to *sky.*

To answer the question, you have to decide which of the four choices has a relationship similar to the first one. Check your answer by seeing if it fits in the same wording as you used to show the relationship between *leaf* and *tree:* A ___ is part of a ___. Which answer do you choose?

The correct answer is *C*. Just as a leaf is part of a tree, a page is part of a book. On the other hand, a pond is not part of a river, nor is a foot part of a shoe, nor is a beach part of the sky.

We can state the complete analogy this way: *Leaf* is to *tree* as *page* is to *book.*

(Continues on next page)

Here's another analogy question to try. Begin by figuring out the relationship between the first two words.

_D_ COACH : PLAYER ::

   A. soldier : military   C. actor : famous
   B. infant : baby   D. boss : worker

A coach and a player have different responsibilities in an organization: a coach gives orders to a player. So you need to look at the other four pairs to see which has a similar relationship. When you think you have found the answer, check to see that the two words you chose can be compared in the same way as *coach* and *player*: a ___ gives orders to a ___.

In this case, the correct answer is *D*; a boss gives orders to a worker. (In other words, *coach* is to *player* as *boss* is to *worker*.)

By now you can see that there are basically two steps to doing analogy items:

1 Find out the relationship of the first two words.

2 Find the answer that expresses the same type of relationship as the first two words have.

Now try one more analogy question on your own. Write the letter of the answer you choose in the space provided.

_A_ SWING : BAT ::

   A. drive : car   C. catch : bat
   B. run : broom   D. fly : butterfly

If you chose answer *A,* you were right. "Swing" is what we do with a bat, and "drive" is what we do with a car.

Here are some other relationships often found in analogies:

● **Synonyms:** freedom : liberty (*freedom* and *liberty* mean the same thing)

● **Item to category:** baseball : sport (baseball is one kind of sport)

● **Item to description:** school bus : yellow (*yellow* is a word that describes a school bus)

● **Producer to product:** singer : song (a singer is the person who produces a song)

● **Time sequence:** January : March (January occurs two months before March)

● The **seventh part** of the chapter, on page 15, is titled _____ Final Check _____. Here you are given two interesting passages where you can practice applying the words in context. The first two such passages, on page 15, are titled _____ "Johnny Appleseed" _____ and _____ "The Lovable Leech?" _____.

Final Notes

1   You now know how to proceed with the words in each chapter. Make sure that you do each page very carefully. Remember that as you work through the activities, you are learning the words.

How many times will you use each word? If you look, you'll see that each chapter gives you the opportunity to work with each word at least seven times. Each time that you work with a word adds to the likelihood that the word will become part of your active vocabulary. You will have further opportunities to use the word in the crossword puzzle and tests that end each unit. The online exercises that are available in the Online Learning Center at **www.townsendpress.com** will give you even more practice.

In addition, many of the words are used again in later chapters of the book. Such repeated words are marked with small circles, like this°. For example, which words from Chapter 1 are repeated in the Final Check passages on page 21 of Chapter 2?

| _transform_ | _challenge_ | _preference_ |

Sometimes words related to the vocabulary words are used in the word-parts activities. Those words are also marked with the small circle (°). For example, in Chapter 2, *deliberate* is defined as "Done on purpose; carefully planned." In the Word Parts section of Chapter 3, you will see that *deliberately* means "in a deliberate way" (or, in other words, "in a purposeful way").

2   At the bottom of the last page of each chapter is a "Check Your Performance" box, where you can enter your scores for four of the practices. Note that these scores should also be entered into the vocabulary performance chart located on the inside of the _____back_____ cover.

To get your score, count the number of items that you answered correctly in each section. Then add a zero. For example, if you got seven questions right in Check 2, you would write "70%" in the blank.

3   The facts are in. A strong vocabulary is a source of power. Words can make you a better reader, writer, speaker, thinker, and learner. They can dramatically increase your chances of success in school and in your job.

But a strong vocabulary will not be yours without effort. Words must be learned in a program of regular study. If you commit yourself to learning words, and you work actively and honestly with the chapters in this book, you will not only enrich your vocabulary—you will enrich your life, as well.

Unit One

Chapter 1

challenge	principal
dependent	solitary
fertile	suitable
peculiar	surplus
preference	transform

Chapter 2

analyze	deliberate
attitude	excessive
category	fragile
contrast	frustration
critical	indicate

Chapter 3

accompany	improper
desperate	preserve
determine	pursue
dispose	rejection
evident	restore

Chapter 4

abundant	distinct
betray	exaggerate
comparison	inhabit
demonstrate	neutral
dispute	reduction

Chapter 5

aggravate	intentional
cease	interference
coincide	obnoxious
considerable	unstable
humane	utilize

challenge	principal
dependent	solitary
fertile	suitable
peculiar	surplus
preference	transform

Ten Words in Context

In the space provided, write the letter of the meaning closest to that of each **boldfaced** word. Use the context of the sentences to help you figure out each word's meaning.

1 challenge
(chăl′ənj)
- *noun*

● Ginny enjoys rock climbing. It's a difficult **challenge**, but she feels very proud after making a climb.

● When the babysitter arrived, he stared at the four active little boys he was expected to watch. "This will be quite a **challenge**," he sighed.

_C_ *Challenge* means   A. reason.   B. something boring.   C. something requiring effort.

2 dependent
(dĭ-pĕn′dənt)
- *adjective*

● Some animals can take care of themselves as soon as they are born, but human babies are **dependent** upon their parents for years.

● Tyrone's father said to him, "You are still much too **dependent** on me. It's about time you got a job and supported yourself."

_A_ *Dependent* means   A. relying.   B. leading.   C. puzzling.

3 fertile
(fûr′tl)
- *adjective*

● Because its soil is so **fertile**, Iowa has many farms.

● Our pet hamsters were so **fertile** that we ended up selling many baby hamsters back to the pet store.

_C_ *Fertile* means   A. common.   B. large.   C. able to produce.

4 peculiar
(pĭ-kyōōl′yər)
- *adjective*

● Jack didn't know why people were giving him **peculiar** looks until he realized there was a food stain on his shirt.

● My brother thinks my chip-and-dip sandwiches are **peculiar**, but I don't think they're as strange as the peanut-butter-and-tuna sandwiches he eats.

_B_ *Peculiar* means   A. attractive.   B. unusual.   C. innocent.

5 preference
(prĕf′ər-əns)
- *noun*

● There are Chinese, Italian, and Indian restaurants nearby. What's your **preference** for dinner tonight?

● What is your color **preference** for the living room? Do you like cool blues and greens, or warm oranges and yellows?

_A_ *Preference* means   A. choice.   B. skill.   C. effect.

6 principal
(prĭn′sə-pəl)
- *adjective*

● The **principal** cause of most success is hard work, not luck or talent.

● The queen of England has no real power. The **principal** leader of England is the prime minister.

_C_ *Principal* means   A. most recent.   B. false.   C. chief.

7 solitary
(sŏl′ĭ-tĕr′ē)
- *adjective*

- After taking a **solitary** vacation in a cabin for two weeks, Ned was ready to return to the company of other people.
- In the mood to be by herself, Melba looked forward to spending the evening in such **solitary** activities as reading and taking a long bubble bath.

C *Solitary* means   A. friendly.   B. proper.   C. done alone.

8 suitable
(sōō′tə-bəl)
- *adjective*

- Sharon asked her mother if her blue dress was **suitable** for a funeral, or if she had to wear black.
- Because the prices and food are so good, the team decided that the Red Lion Inn would be **suitable** for its annual banquet.

A *Suitable* means   A. right.   B. too expensive.   C. important.

9 surplus
(sûr′pləs)
- *adjective*

- More and more restaurants are donating their **surplus** food to homeless people.
- The Barkleys had more kitchen supplies than they needed, so they gave their **surplus** pots and pans to their son, who had just gotten his own apartment.

B *Surplus* means   A. strange.   B. extra.   C. main.

10 transform
(trăns-fôrm′)
- *verb*

- My sister plans to **transform** this messy attic into an attractive office.
- The magician seemed to **transform** a chicken's egg into an egg the size of a basketball.

C *Transform* means   A. to accept.   B. to repeat.   C. to change.

Matching Words with Definitions

Following are definitions of the ten words. **Print** each word next to its definition. If you look closely at each word in context, you will be able to figure out its meaning.

1. _____fertile_____   Producing or able to produce much fruit, large crops, or many children

2. _____principal_____   Most important; main; leading

3. _____dependent_____   Relying on others for aid or support

4. _____surplus_____   Extra; more than what is used or needed

5. _____peculiar_____   Odd; strange

6. _____challenge_____   A test of one's abilities; anything that calls for a special effort

7. _____solitary_____   Happening or done alone

8. _____transform_____   To change in form or appearance

9. _____suitable_____   Right for a certain purpose; proper; fitting

10. _____preference_____   A choice; first choice; something preferred

CAUTION: Do not go any further until you are sure the above answers are correct. Then you can use the definitions to help you in the following practices. Your goal is eventually to know the words well enough so that you don't need to check the definitions at all.

Check 1

Using the answer lines, complete each item below with the correct word from the box.

| A. **challenge** | B. **dependent** | C. **fertile** | D. **peculiar** | E. **preference** |
| F. **principal** | G. **solitary** | H. **suitable** | I. **surplus** | J. **transform** |

_____transform_____ 1. Just one can of spinach ___s Popeye from a weakling into a hero.

_____fertile_____ 2. If land is always planted with the same crop, it will become less ___. Changing crops from one year to the next keeps the soil rich.

_____preference_____ 3. Although Al's ___ is for a daytime job, he will work at night if necessary.

_____surplus_____ 4. An Army-Navy Store in our town sells ___ military products such as survival gear, tents, and boots. It offers great bargains on items the Army or Navy doesn't need.

_____peculiar_____ 5. I can't imagine what that ___ odor is from. It's like a mixture of burning tires and freshly cut grass.

_____solitary_____ 6. A man lived by himself in a cave most of his life. He had a ___ life.

_____principal_____ 7. I know you have reasons for quitting your job. What's the ___ reason?

_____challenge_____ 8. Juggling two balls is easy enough, but juggling three or more is a greater ___.

_____suitable_____ 9. My neighbors are looking for ___ homes for the eight puppies their collie gave birth to. They want homes where the pups will be well cared for.

_____dependent_____ 10. Sometimes Estela felt like giving up, but she knew she couldn't because she had three young children and an elderly mother who were ___ on her.

NOTE: Now check your answers to these items by turning to page 239. Going over the answers carefully will help you prepare for the remaining practices, for which answers are not given.

Check 2

Using the answer lines, complete each item below with **two** words from the box. Use each word once.

_____preference_____
_____solitary_____ 1–2. When I'm not feeling well, my ___ is to have lots of company, but when my husband is sick, he would rather be ___.

_____transform_____
_____principal_____ 3–4. In the last year, our neighbors have ___ed their unattractive yard into something beautiful. The ___ change they made was to put in some lovely flowering plants; all of the other changes were small ones.

_____suitable_____
_____dependent_____ 5–6. Ben is happy to live at home, pay no rent, and use his mother's car, but I don't think it's ___ for a grown man to be so ___ on his parents.

_____fertile_____
_____challenge_____ 7–8. Our tomato plants are almost too ___. It is a ___ to use or give away all the tomatoes before they spoil.

_____peculiar_____
_____surplus_____ 9–10. We had so many tomatoes that we ended up inventing some ___ recipes to use up the ___ fruit; perhaps the strangest was "Peanut Butter Tomato Pie."

Word Work

A. In the space provided, write the letter of the choice that best completes each item.

___C___ 1. A boy who is too **dependent** on his friends
   A. pays little attention to them.
   B. is too bossy with them.
   C. won't make a decision without asking what they think.

___B___ 2. Someone who enjoys **solitary** work would probably like a job
   A. selling a product that he or she believed in.
   B. working in a one-person office, rarely seeing other people.
   C. meeting people and answering their questions.

___C___ 3. We knew for sure that our dog was **fertile** when she
   A. bit the mailman.
   B. did very well in training class.
   C. had puppies.

___A___ 4. Most people would think it was **peculiar** if a teacher
   A. came into class dressed as Bozo the Clown.
   B. punished a student for cheating.
   C. dropped a piece of chalk on the floor.

___A___ 5. If a friend came to you and sadly said, "My grandfather just died," what would be the most **suitable** response for you to make?
   A. "That's awful. I'm really sorry."
   B. "That's nothing; wait until you hear about my day."
   C. "Can you lend me some money?"

B. In the space provided, write the letter of the word that most closely relates to the situation in each item.

___A___ 6. I like Pepsi more than I like Coca-Cola.

   A. preference   B. fertile   C. transform

___B___ 7. The weightlifter is going to try to beat her own best record.

   A. dependent   B. challenge   C. surplus

___C___ 8. Cream is the main ingredient in butter.

   A. challenge   B. dependent   C. principal

___A___ 9. These pieces of cloth were left over after I made myself a shirt.

   A. surplus   B. fertile   C. preference

___C___ 10. Cinderella's fairy godmother will change her rags into a beautiful gown, a pumpkin into a carriage, and mice into horses.

   A. solitary   B. principal   C. transform

Word Parts

A. The prefix *trans-* can mean "across" or "change to."

Examples: *translate* — to change from one language to another
              transport — to take from one place across to another

On each answer line, write the word from the box that best completes the item.

A. **transatlantic**	B. **transform**	C. **translate**
D. **transplant**	E. **transportation**	

translate   1. Trina's job is to ___ business letters from Spanish into English.

transform   2. You can ___ a room simply by painting it a different color.

transplant   3. The doctor ___ed one of Malik's kidneys into his sister.

transportation   4. Since my grandmother doesn't drive and there is no public ___ in her area, she depends on Dad to take her shopping.

transatlantic   5. The ship will cross the Atlantic Ocean next week. The ship's ___ trip begins in New York City and ends in England.

B. The prefix *sur-* means "over," "upon," "beyond," or "additional."

Examples: *surcharge* — an overcharge;   *surpass* — to go beyond
                   extra amount charged   *surtax* — an additional tax

On each answer line, write the word from the box that best completes the item.

F. **surcharge**	G. **surface**	H. **surpass**
I. **surplus**	J. **surtax**	

surface   6. I like to protect and shine the ___s of my wooden tables with wax.

surplus   7. Our garden produced so much zucchini that we gave big bagfuls of ___ squash to all our neighbors.

surtax   8. In addition to the usual taxes, people who earn more than a certain amount will have to pay a ___.

surpass   9. The drive to raise money for the children's hospital was so successful that the money raised ___ed the goal that was set.

surcharge   10. Because our luggage weighed more than fifty pounds, we had to pay the airline a ___.

Final Check

Read the passages carefully. Then fill in each blank with the word that best fits the context.

A. Johnny Appleseed

A. **fertile**	B. **peculiar**	C. **solitary**	D. **surplus**	E. **transform**

John Chapman, who is known to the world as Johnny Appleseed, must have been a strange sight. His (1)_____peculiar_____ clothing included cloth sacks for shirts and a tin pot for a hat.

In western Pennsylvania, where Johnny lived, many people grew apples. But there weren't any apples in the lands further west, which were just then being cleared and settled. So Johnny wandered among his neighbors, asking them for their (2)_____surplus_____ apple seeds. During his lifetime, Johnny walked thousands of miles, making many long trips from his home to the valleys of Ohio and Indiana. Everywhere he went, he scattered seeds. Many of those seeds fell on (3)_____fertile_____ ground and grew into strong trees.

Johnny often wandered through areas where Native Americans fought with the white settlers. Since Johnny was a loner, his travels were always (4)_____solitary_____. He carried no weapon, yet he was never harmed. The Indians believed that the Great Spirit especially loved people like Johnny, who was not like other people. In his own quiet way he (5)_____transform_____ed the American wilderness, filling it with thousands of flowering, fruit-filled trees.

B. The Lovable Leech?

F. **challenge**	G. **dependent**	H. **preference**	I. **principal**	J. **suitable**

As highly developed as we human beings like to think we are, the fact is that we are still (6)_____dependent_____ upon many lower forms of life. The (7)_____principal_____ way that this is true, of course, is that we use meat for food and skins for clothing. But there are other ways, sometimes strange ways, that we rely on other creatures. Take, for example, the leech. It would be a (8)_____challenge_____ for anyone to really like a leech. It is a disgusting-looking worm that lives in freshwater ponds and streams. As many people have discovered when they've gone swimming, a leech's (9)_____preference_____ for dinner is human blood. It loves to attach itself to a swimmer's foot and sink in its teeth—as many as three hundred of them. The bite does not cause any pain. But the leech can suck out eight times its own weight in blood. "How disgusting," you are probably thinking. But listen to this. In recent years, doctors have found that leeches are the most (10)_____suitable_____ way to remove extra blood from a person after an injury, especially around the eyes. Yes, leeches are honored guests in many modern hospitals.

Scores	Check 2 _____%	Word Work _____%	Word Parts _____%	Final Check _____%

analyze	deliberate
attitude	excessive
category	fragile
contrast	frustration
critical	indicate

Ten Words in Context

In the space provided, write the letter of the meaning closest to that of each **boldfaced** word. Use the context of the sentences to help you figure out each word's meaning.

1 analyze
(ăn′ə-līz)
- *verb*

- Someone in the laboratory will **analyze** the blood sample to see if the patient has an illness.
- Before we can suggest solutions, we must carefully **analyze** the city's money problems.

<u>B</u> *Analyze* means   A. to plan.   B. to study.   C. to create.

2 attitude
(ăt′ĭ-tood′)
- *noun*

- Athletes need to have a positive **attitude**. Even if they have lost the previous game, they need to come into the next one ready to win.
- Rudy came to the party with a poor **attitude**; he was sure that he'd be bored and wouldn't have any fun.

<u>C</u> *Attitude* means   A. set of rules.   B. background.   C. way of thinking.

3 category
(kăt′ĭ-gôr′ē)
- *noun*

- When Jasmine was in high school, she didn't seem to fit into any **category**. She wasn't an athlete, a scholar, or a rebel.
- The small store had many jazz and rock recordings, but not much in the **category** of country music.

<u>C</u> *Category* means   A. goal.   B. feeling.   C. group.

4 contrast
(kŏn′trăst′)
- *noun*

- Everyone is surprised to see that there's a **contrast** between Peggy's eyes. One eye is brown, and the other is green.
- I was struck by the **contrast** between the fancy houses west of Main Street and the poor neighborhoods to the east.

<u>C</u> *Contrast* means   A. disappointment.   B. place.   C. difference.

5 critical
(krĭt′ĭ-kəl)
- *adjective*

- My boss can be very **critical** of me when I don't do my best work, but she's also quick to praise me when I do well.
- My aunt is **critical** of her neighbors. She calls them lazy because their house needs painting and their yard is overgrown with weeds.

<u>A</u> *Critical* means   A. faultfinding.   B. jealous.   C. proud.

6 deliberate
(dĭ-lĭb′ər-ĭt)
- *adjective*

- Manny's pushing me was quite **deliberate**; it wasn't accidental at all.
- I'm sure our neighbor knew that the tall tree he was planting would keep the sun from our flowers. It was a **deliberate** dirty trick.

<u>C</u> *Deliberate* means   A. easy.   B. fair.   C. planned.

7 excessive
(ĭk-sĕs′ĭv)
- *adjective*

- **Excessive** speed caused the accident; the truck driver was going nearly eighty miles an hour.
- Mrs. Hill's concern about her little boy's health is **excessive**. She rushes him to the doctor every time he gets the sniffles or scrapes his knee.

<u>A</u> *Excessive* means   A. overly great.   B. off and on.   C. normal.

8 fragile
(frăj′əl)
- *adjective*

- The lamp is **fragile**, so when you pack it, please put it in a deep box with plenty of newspaper around it.
- Our bones become more **fragile** with age. That is why elderly people often break their hips when they fall.

<u>C</u> *Fragile* means   A. broken.   B. strong.   C. breakable.

9 frustration
(frŭ-strā′shən)
- *noun*

- As Dan studied the instructions for setting up his computer, a look of **frustration** crossed his face. "I'll never figure this out!" he groaned.
- Elaine felt great **frustration** when she failed her driving test for the third time.

<u>B</u> *Frustration* means   A. relief.   B. discouragement.   C. pleasure.

10 indicate
(ĭn′dĭ-kāt′)
- *verb*

- Jeff's frown seemed to **indicate** that he was unhappy with our plan.
- The parking-lot attendant pointed to **indicate** that Lonnie should drive the car all the way up to the fence.

<u>B</u> *Indicate* means   A. to hide.   B. to show.   C. to plan.

Matching Words with Definitions

Following are definitions of the ten words. **Print** each word next to its definition. If you look closely at each word in context, you will be able to figure out its meaning.

1. _frustration_   A feeling of anger and helplessness that comes from bad luck, defeat, or failure; disappointment

2. _attitude_   A point of view; state of mind; way of thinking or feeling

3. _category_   A group of people or things having something in common; type

4. _excessive_   Too much; more than is reasonable

5. _deliberate_   Done on purpose; carefully planned

6. _contrast_   An obvious difference

7. _critical_   Disapproving; tending to find fault

8. _fragile_   Easily broken or damaged

9. _analyze_   To examine carefully; study closely

10. _indicate_   To show; serve as a sign or signal

CAUTION: Do not go any further until you are sure the above answers are correct. Then you can use the definitions to help you in the following practices. Your goal is eventually to know the words well enough so that you don't need to check the definitions at all.

Check 1

Using the answer lines, complete each item below with the correct word from the box.

A. **analyze**	B. **attitude**	C. **category**	D. **contrast**	E. **critical**
F. **deliberate**	G. **excessive**	H. **fragile**	I. **frustration**	J. **indicate**

__frustration__   1. To avoid the ___ of failing the driving test again, Elaine has decided to take driving lessons.

__deliberate__   2. A planned action is ___.

__Excessive__   3. ___ eating during the holidays led to my gaining three pounds.

__indicate__   4. A road sign with a picture of a leaping deer ___s that deer often cross the road at that spot.

__attitude__   5. After losing every game last season, the soccer players began training this year with a poor ___. If their mind-set doesn't improve, they will have another losing season.

__fragile__   6. Something that is ___ can be easily damaged.

__category__   7. Which ___ of movie do you prefer, comedy or action-adventure?

__analyze__   8. When Maggie ___d her reasons for wanting to marry Joe, she realized that they were not good ones.

__critical__   9. Many teenagers feel their parents are too ___ of their clothing, music, and friends.

__contrast__   10. I was surprised by the ___ between kind, gentle Bill and his impatient, bad-tempered brother.

NOTE: Now check your answers to these items by turning to page 239. Going over the answers carefully will help you prepare for the remaining practices, for which answers are not given.

Check 2

Using the answer lines, complete each item below with **two** words from the box. Use each word once.

__contrast__
__category__   1–2. There is a large ___ between things that fit in the ___ of junk food and those foods needed for basic nutrition.

__attitude__
__critical__   3–4. When a child is learning to play a musical instrument, parents should have an encouraging ___. Rather than being ___ of the child, parents should find things to praise.

__deliberate__
__fragile__   5–6. When we broke three glasses while washing the dishes, it wasn't ___. They were just too ___.

__frustration__
__excessive__   7–8. Marina is feeling ___ at her mother-in-law's ___ advice. "She means well," Marina says, "but her constant suggestions make me angry."

__analyze__
__indicate__   9–10. When we ___ the citywide election returns, they will ___ how each neighborhood voted.

Word Work

A. In the space provided, write the letter of the choice that best completes each item.

_C_ 1. A piano teacher who was very **critical** of a child's playing would

   A. not pay attention.   B. praise the child.   C. point out every mistake.

_A_ 2. When the boss advised Jim to improve his **attitude**, he meant that Jim should

   A. have a better   B. be neater.   C. speed up his typing.
   outlook about work.

_C_ 3. If a rash **indicates** an allergy, the rash

   A. has nothing to do   B. causes the allergy.   C. is a sign of the allergy.
   with the allergy.

_A_ 4. My grandmother's lace wedding veil is too **fragile** for me to wear at my own wedding. The veil

   A. might get torn.   B. is too old-fashioned. C. is stained.

_B_ 5. There is a big **contrast** in the twins' personalities. Their personalities
   A. are very much alike.   B. are very different.   C. aren't very pleasant.

B. In the space provided, write the letter of the word that most closely relates to the situation in each item.

_B_ 6. The fire that destroyed the store was no accident. Someone set it on purpose.

   A. category   B. deliberate   C. uncritical

_A_ 7. Did the murdered man's coffee contain poison? The police laboratory will examine a sample of the coffee to find out.

   A. analyze   B. contrast   C. attitude

_B_ 8. When the swimming class was divided into sections, I was put with the "beginners."

   A. excessive   B. category   C. fragile

_C_ 9. The little girl can't get her snow boots off. She pulls and tugs, pulls and tugs, and finally bursts into tears.

   A. deliberate   B. contrast   C. frustration

_B_ 10. The servings at the restaurant are much too large. Plates are heaped with more food than anyone could eat.

   A. indicate   B. excessive   C. fragile

Synonyms and Antonyms

A. Synonyms. Write the letter of the word or phrase that most nearly means the **same** as each boldfaced word.

_B_   1. **analyze**
      A. remember
      B. examine
      C. find fault with
      D. use

_B_   2. **attitude**
      A. height
      B. outlook
      C. knowledge
      D. skill

_A_   3. **category**
      A. group
      B. purpose
      C. reaction
      D. problem

_D_   4. **critical**
      A. absent
      B. frightened
      C. nervous
      D. disapproving

_C_   5. **indicate**
      A. plan
      B. conceal
      C. show
      D. disappoint

B. Antonyms. Write the letter of the word or phrase that most nearly means the **opposite** of each boldfaced word.

_D_   6. **contrast**
      A. difference
      B. environment
      C. enjoyment
      D. sameness

_A_   7. **deliberate**
      A. accidental
      B. harmful
      C. helpful
      D. fortunate

_B_   8. **excessive**
      A. not real
      B. not enough
      C. unexpected
      D. required

_B_   9. **fragile**
      A. damaged
      B. unbreakable
      C. unnecessary
      D. beautiful

_C_   10. **frustration**
      A. showing ignorance
      B. feeling hatred
      C. being satisfied
      D. expressing surprise

Final Check

Read the passages carefully. Then fill in each blank with the word that best fits the context.

A. Finding Fault

A. **attitude**	B. **category**	C. **critical**	D. **excessive**	E. **frustration**

Are you one of those people who are constantly finding fault with others? Are you very (1)_____*critical*_____ of everyone else's mistakes? If the washing machine or the DVD player breaks down, is your reaction (2) _____*excessive*_____ anger and (3)_____*frustration*_____? If so, beware! Too much bad temper and discouragement could be harming your health. Scientists say that faultfinders and those who are often angry actually seem to have more heart attacks. So if you fall into this (4)_____*category*_____ of people, try to transform° your outlook. Learn to take things more calmly; learn to be more patient when someone or something disappoints you. If your (5)_____*attitude*_____ improves, your health may improve, too.

B. What Do Your Hobbies Reveal about You?

F. **analyze**	G. **contrast**	H. **deliberate**	I. **fragile**	J. **indicate**

Mira, Pat, and Celia are sisters, very close in age and very similar in looks—but what a huge (6)_____*contrast*_____ there is in their leisure activities! Mira loves an exciting challenge° and often takes (7)_____*deliberate*_____ risks. She has mastered the skateboard, she drives in stock-car races, and she's even tried boxing. In fact, she says she'd go skydiving if only she could afford it. Pat is a collector. She spends her spare time searching for old crystal and china—and taking care of it. She never minds the hours it takes her to wash and dust her precious, (8)_____*fragile*_____ treasures. Then there's Celia, whose preference° is to spend every possible minute reading—that's all she wants to do! You've never met Mira, Pat, and Celia, but doesn't this tell you a lot about them? If we (9)_____*analyze*_____ how people spend leisure time, their interests and hobbies can reveal a great deal about their personalities. What do you think your hobbies and other activities would (10)_____*indicate*_____ about you?

Scores   Check 2 _____%   Word Work _____%   Synonyms and Antonyms _____%   Final Check _____%

Enter your scores above and in the **Vocabulary Performance Chart** on the inside back cover of the book.

CHAPTER

3

accompany	improper
desperate	preserve
determine	pursue
dispose	rejection
evident	restore

Ten Words in Context

In the space provided, write the letter of the meaning closest to that of each **boldfaced** word. Use the context of the sentences to help you figure out each word's meaning.

1 accompany
(ə-kŭm′pə-nē)
- *verb*

- Mr. and Mrs. Myers asked my sister to **accompany** them to the seashore to help take care of their young children.
- In popular music, words usually **accompany** the tune. In much classical music, there are no words to go with the notes.

_C_ *Accompany* means   A. to go before.   B. to go after.   C. to go with.

2 desperate
(dĕs′pər-ĭt)
- *adjective*

- Extremely ill people may be so **desperate** for a cure that they will try anything.
- The earthquake victims are **desperate** for food and clothing.

_B_ *Desperate for* means   A. harmed by.   B. in great need of.   C. surprised by.

3 determine
(dĭ-tûr′mĭn)
- *verb*

- The doctor looked at the x-ray and **determined** that Chen's ankle was sprained, not broken.
- Using a calculator, I **determined** that the "super-giant" box of laundry soap was a better buy than the "family economy" box.

_C_ *Determine* means   A. to regret.   B. to remember.   C. to discover.

4 dispose
(dĭ-spōz′)
- *verb*

- The sign said, "Lungs at work. Please **dispose** of all cigarettes, cigars, and pipes before entering."
- After losing forty pounds, Herb decided to **dispose** of all the clothes that reminded him of his old size. He never wanted to see them again.

_A_ *Dispose of* means   A. to get rid of.   B. to pay for.   C. to use up.

5 evident
(ĕv′ĭ-dənt)
- *adjective*

- The fact that my aunt dyes her hair is **evident**—her gray roots show.
- To make it **evident** that she didn't want to go out with James again, Crystal sent him back all his letters and gifts.

_B_ *Evident* means   A. useful.   B. easy to see.   C. unlikely.

6 improper
(ĭm-prŏp′ər)
- *adjective*

- A bathing suit is fine for the beach, but it's **improper** for church.
- Movies are rated PG-13 if they contain material that is **improper** for young children.

_C_ *Improper* means   A. common.   B. useful.   C. wrong.

7 preserve
(prĭ-zûrv′)
- *verb*

● Steps are being taken to **preserve** the remaining giant redwood trees of California and Oregon for future generations.

● To **preserve** its valuable old fabrics, the museum keeps them away from bright lights and extreme temperatures.

A *Preserve means*   A. to keep safe.   B. to sell off.   C. to seek.

8 pursue
(pər-sōō′)
- *verb*

● After raising her children, my sister returned to college to **pursue** a degree in art education. She then taught art in an elementary school.

● Victor plans to **pursue** an acting career in New York City. His goal is to become a great actor, not a great star.

B *Pursue means*   A. to avoid.   B. to work toward.   C. to replace.

9 rejection
(rĭ-jĕk′shən)
- *noun*

● My brother was upset when he received a letter of **rejection** from a college he wanted to attend.

● Nita wasn't too disturbed when she didn't get the job she had interviewed for. "If you can't handle **rejection**, you have some growing up to do," she said.

B *Rejection means*   A. respect.   B. not being accepted.   C. bad taste.

10 restore
(rĭ-stôr′)
- *verb*

● During the 1980s, the Statue of Liberty was **restored**. The damaged torch and the 1,600 iron bands that hold the copper skin to the frame were replaced.

● Surprisingly, there have been cases where a bump on the head has **restored** the sight of a blind person.

A *Restore means*   A. to fix.   B. to harm.   C. to give away.

Matching Words with Definitions

Following are definitions of the ten words. **Print** each word next to its definition. If you look closely at each word in context, you will be able to figure out its meaning.

1. ____evident____ Obvious; clear

2. ____determine____ To find out exactly; figure out

3. ____dispose____ To throw or give away; get rid of

4. ____desperate____ Having a great need or desire

5. ____improper____ Not in good taste; not right for a situation; not suitable°

6. ____restore____ To bring back to a normal or former condition; repair

7. ____preserve____ To protect; keep in good condition

8. ____rejection____ The act of saying "no" (to a request or desire); refusal

9. ____pursue____ To try to get or succeed in; seek

10. ____accompany____ To go along with; be together with

CAUTION: Do not go any further until you are sure the above answers are correct. Then you can use the definitions to help you in the following practices. Your goal is eventually to know the words well enough so that you don't need to check the definitions at all.

Check 1

Using the answer lines, complete each item below with the correct word from the box.

A. accompany	B. desperate	C. determine	D. dispose of	E. evident
F. improper	G. preserve	H. pursue	I. rejection	J. restore

desperate   1. If you are ___ for food, that means you are in great need of it.

evident   2. When we say that something is ___, we mean that it can be clearly seen or clearly understood.

accompany   3. Do you like ketchup to ___ your French fries, or do you prefer them plain?

improper   4. At some fancy restaurants, it's considered ___ for a man to show up without a jacket and a tie.

dispose of   5. There are several ways to ___ things you no longer want: put them in the garbage, recycle them, or give or sell them to someone who can use them.

rejection   6. The opposite of "acceptance" is "___."

preserve   7. To ___ a piece of furniture, protect it from too much heat, sun, and moisture.

determine   8. You can always ___ which twin is which because Beth wears glasses, but her sister Lisa doesn't.

pursue   9. Many athletes ___ an Olympic medal by practicing hours a day for years, but only a few athletes can actually win one.

restore   10. To ___ an old table, you must first remove all the old varnish and paint.

NOTE: Now check your answers to these items by turning to page 239. Going over the answers carefully will help you prepare for the remaining practices, for which answers are not given.

Check 2

Using the answer lines, complete each item below with **two** words from the box. Use each word once.

evident
preserve   1–2. It is ___ that this old movie theater has been very well taken care of. The original seats and wallpaper have been ___d since 1924.

pursue
improper   3–4. Jill can't ___ the scholarship offered by that company. Her father is on the committee that decides who wins the award, so it would be ___ for her to apply.

desperate
determine   5–6. The woman was ___ for money, so she decided to sell her grandmother's diamond ring. She was disappointed when the jeweler ___d that the diamond was a cheap imitation.

restore
dispose of   7–8. The owners of the old car are trying to decide if they will ___ it with new parts and a lot of body work, or ___ it by giving it away.

accompany
rejection   9–10. I offered to ___ my friend to the tryout for the play, thinking that if she did not get the part, she might need help in dealing with the ___.

Word Work

A. In the space provided, write the letter of the choice that best completes each item.

_A_ 1. **Dispose** of clothes that
   A. are old and no longer fit.
   B. you just bought.
   C. you will wear next summer.

_C_ 2. Ernie experienced **rejection** when he
   A. was invited to a party.
   B. moved into a new house.
   C. was turned down for a date.

_B_ 3. Yelling, screaming, and jumping up and down would be **improper** behavior at
   A. a baseball game.
   B. a movie.
   C. an amusement park.

_C_ 4. You could **restore** an old piano with
   A. a large truck.
   B. beautiful music.
   C. new keys, strings, and woodwork.

_A_ 5. You might feel **desperate** if you were
   A. stuck on a desert island.
   B. wearing attractive new clothes.
   C. standing in a long line at the supermarket.

B. In the space provided, write the letter of the word that most closely relates to the situation in each item.

_C_ 6. Keep your wedding gown carefully wrapped in plastic and stored in a box.
   A. restore   B. determine   C. preserve

_A_ 7. In my opinion, waffles go best with butter and maple syrup.
   A. accompany   B. restore   C. dispose

_B_ 8. It was clear where the missing brownie went—the little boy's face was smeared with chocolate.
   A. desperate   B. evident   C. preserve

_C_ 9. To find out what was wrong with his patient, the doctor had to do several tests.
   A. dispose of   B. accompany   C. determine

_B_ 10. Annamarie worked hard to reach her goal—owning her own restaurant.
   A. preserve   B. pursue   C. evident

Word Parts

A. One meaning of the suffix *-ly* is "in a certain way."

Examples: desperate — in great need   grateful — thankful
             desperately — in a way that shows great need   gratefully — in a thankful way

On each answer line, write the word from the box that means the same as the *italicized* words.

| A. **angrily** | B. **deliberately°** | C. **desperately** |
| D. **excessively°** | E. **skillfully** | |

___deliberately___   1. Eva *in a deliberate° way* stuck her foot out as her little brother came by. As he fell, he yelled, "Hey, you did that on purpose!"

___skillfully___   2. If the wound is sewed up *in a skillful way,* it won't even leave a scar.

___excessively___   3. I guess I have been watching TV *in an excessive way* recently. I know the characters on my favorite programs better than I know my family members.

___desperately___   4. Many neighbors stayed up all night, searching *in a desperate way* for the missing child.

___angrily___   5. The principal said to the class *in an angry way,* "There's no good reason for such rude behavior toward a substitute teacher."

B. One meaning of the prefix *re-* is "back."

Examples: recall — to call back to mind; remember   repay — to pay back
             reflect — to bend light back   restore — to bring back to a former condition

On each answer line, write the word from the box that best completes the item.

| F. **recall** | G. **reflect** | H. **remove** |
| I. **repay** | J. **restore** | |

___restore___   6. To ___ this old lamp, you'll need to put in new electrical wiring.

___repay___   7. My brother is constantly asking me for loans, promising he will ___ me when he gets his allowance.

___recall___   8. I remember the man's face, but I cannot ___ his name.

___reflect___   9. According to legend, when a vampire looks in the mirror, he sees nothing. The mirror doesn't ___ his image.

___remove___   10. Before you hold the baby, you'd better ___ your long earrings. He might grab them.

Final Check

Read the passages carefully. Then fill in each blank with the word that best fits the context.

A. Fixing Up Furniture

| A. **determine** | B. **dispose** | C. **evident** | D. **preserve** | E. **restore** |

I feel proud when I can fix up furniture that other people have (1)_____*dispose*_____d of. Instead of spending a lot of money on new furniture, I'll recycle an old chair thrown out by a relative or an ugly bureau I've found in a neighbor's trash pile. I like the challenge° of trying to (2)_____*restore*_____ them to their original condition. I often find a beautiful piece of furniture hidden under many coats of paint or varnish. At first it is hard to (3)_____*determine*_____ how good or bad the piece underneath really is. I must carefully remove the old paint or varnish. If it becomes (4)_____*evident*_____ that the quality of the piece of furniture is good, I sand it until it is smooth. Then I stain it to bring out the wood's natural lines and colors. Finally, I apply new varnish to (5)_____*preserve*_____ the wood from damage by water or excessive° heat. Fixing other people's "junk" has been an inexpensive way for me to get some beautiful furniture.

B. Barbara's Date with Her Cousin

| F. **accompany** | G. **desperate** | H. **improper** | I. **pursue** | J. **rejection** |

Barbara can finally laugh about the time twenty years ago when she was so (6)_____*desperate*_____ for a date that she paid her cousin twenty-five dollars to go with her to the senior prom. She admits that she had very few dates in high school. However, when the prom tickets first went on sale, Barbara hoped that some suitable° fellow would fall for her charms and ask her to the prom, and maybe even ask her to go steady. It didn't happen.

Back then, people didn't think it was very "ladylike" behavior to actively (7)_____*pursue*_____ a date with a boy. But Barbara wanted to go to the prom so badly that she didn't care if her actions seemed (8)_____*improper*_____. Despite her fear of (9)_____*rejection*_____, she got up her nerve to ask Gary. He already had a date. So she asked Emilio and then Chuck. They also said no.

One week before the prom, she called her cousin. He said, "Okay, but it will cost you." He wanted ten dollars to (10)_____*accompany*_____ her to the dance and another fifteen dollars not to tell anyone at the prom that they were related.

| Scores | Check 2 _____% | Word Work _____% | Word Parts _____% | Final Check _____% |

abundant	distinct
betray	exaggerate
comparison	inhabit
demonstrate	neutral
dispute	reduction

Ten Words in Context

In the space provided, write the letter of the meaning closest to that of each **boldfaced** word. Use the context of the sentences to help you figure out each word's meaning.

1 abundant
(ə-bŭn′dənt)
- *adjective*

- Our apple tree bore such an **abundant** crop this year that we'll have plenty of applesauce all winter.
- Mom's energy is so **abundant** that the rest of us can't keep up with her. After a day's work, she'll bike ten miles and then say, "Let's shoot a few baskets before dinner!"

__B__ *Abundant* means   A. different.   B. great.   C. reasonable.

2 betray
(bĭ-trā′)
- *verb*

- The prisoners of war refused to **betray** their country by telling its secrets.
- I didn't mean to **betray** my brother by telling our parents he was using drugs. I wanted to help him.

__A__ *Betray* means   A. to turn against.   B. to give aid to.   C. to argue with.

3 comparison
(kəm-păr′ĭ-sən)
- *noun*

- LaTanya decided which car to buy after making a **comparison** of all the cars in her price range.
- A **comparison** between Tim's and Eric's rooms makes it clear that Tim is the neater of the two boys.

__A__ *Comparison* means   A. check of what is alike and different.   B. argument.   C. explanation.

4 demonstrate
(dĕm′ən-strāt′)
- *verb*

- I asked the salesman to **demonstrate** how to use the camera, but it was clear he didn't know how.
- When the new copying machine arrives in our office, someone who knows how to use it will **demonstrate** how all its features work.

__C__ *Demonstrate* means   A. to remember.   B. to imagine.   C. to show.

5 dispute
(dĭ-spyo͞ot′)
- *noun*

- My **dispute** with my brother about who would get the last piece of pie was settled when our father ate it.
- Business at the store was so slow that the salespeople had a **dispute** over who would get the next customer.

__B__ *Dispute* means   A. answer.   B. disagreement.   C. explanation.

6 distinct
(dĭ-stĭngkt′)
- *adjective*

- The faces of the people in the faded old photo were not **distinct**. We couldn't identify anyone.
- Although the two bowls of onion dip looked the same, there was a **distinct** difference in their taste.

__A__ *Distinct* means   A. definite.   B. healthy.   C. hard to notice.

7 exaggerate
(ĭg-zăj′ə-rāt′)
- *verb*

- Dad, reminding us not to stretch the truth, always jokes, "I've told you a million times never to **exaggerate**!"
- I didn't **exaggerate** when I called Randall a musical genius. He really does play the guitar amazingly well.

<u>B</u> *Exaggerate* means   A. to ask questions.   B. to overstate.   C. to explain.

8 inhabit
(ĭn-hăb′ĭt)
- *verb*

- More than six and a half billion people **inhabit** the Earth.
- Bats often **inhabit** the attics of houses, barns, and other buildings.

<u>B</u> *Inhabit* means   A. to show.   B. to live in.   C. to check.

9 neutral
(noo′trəl)
- *adjective*

- If you ever go to a marriage counselor, don't expect him or her to agree with just you or just your spouse. A counselor must remain **neutral**.
- Switzerland has been a **neutral** country since 1648. It doesn't participate in wars or support one country against another.

<u>B</u> *Neutral* means   A. clear.   B. not taking sides.   C. not loyal.

10 reduction
(rĭ-dŭk′shən)
- *noun*

- When the company offered to pay workers for sick time they didn't use, there was a sudden **reduction** in the number of sick days taken.
- It seems everyone who runs for public office promises a **reduction** in taxes.

<u>C</u> *Reduction* means   A. order.   B. quarrel.   C. cut.

Matching Words with Definitions

Following are definitions of the ten words. **Print** each word next to its definition. If you look closely at each word in context, you will be able to figure out its meaning.

1. _____inhabit_____   To live in

2. _____abundant_____   Very plentiful; more than enough

3. _____comparison_____   The act of checking or judging how two or more things are alike or different

4. _____exaggerate_____   To say that something is larger or greater than it really is; overstate

5. _____distinct_____   Clear; obvious; easy to see or notice

6. _____neutral_____   Not taking sides in a quarrel

7. _____dispute_____   An argument; a quarrel

8. _____betray_____   To be disloyal to; turn against

9. _____reduction_____   A decrease; cutback

10. _____demonstrate_____   To explain or teach by showing

CAUTION: Do not go any further until you are sure the above answers are correct. Then you can use the definitions to help you in the following practices. Your goal is eventually to know the words well enough so that you don't need to check the definitions at all.

Check 1

Using the answer lines, complete each item below with the correct word from the box.

A. **abundant**	B. **betray**	C. **comparison**	D. **demonstrate**	E. **dispute**
F. **distinct**	G. **exaggerate**	H. **inhabit**	I. **neutral**	J. **reduction**

reduction 1. If someone's new job pays less than the old job, he or she has taken a ___ in pay.

betray 2. Benedict Arnold was an American officer who secretly helped the British enemy during the American Revolution; he is remembered as a man who ___ed his country.

exaggerate 3. You ___ a point when you overstate it, as in saying, "I'm dying of hunger."

abundant 4. We had such an ___ crop of tomatoes this year that we had enough to give some to our neighbors.

neutral 5. If you want to remain friends with two people who are quarreling, it is best to stay ___ and keep out of the fight.

comparison 6. A ___ of our backgrounds and interests revealed we had a lot in common.

demonstrate 7. The uncooperative salesman refused to ___ how to use the TiVo system, saying, "Just read the manual and figure it out yourself."

distinct 8. Even though I was only three years old at the time, I have a ___ memory of the first time I saw the ocean.

inhabit 9. The people who ___ Canada are called Canadians.

dispute 10. When we say that two people had a ___, we mean that their fight consisted of words, not punches.

NOTE: Now check your answers to these items by turning to page 239. Going over the answers carefully will help you prepare for the remaining practices, for which answers are not given.

Check 2

Using the answer lines, complete each item below with **two** words from the box. Use each word once.

dispute
neutral 1–2. My family is having a ___ over whether to paint the kitchen yellow or tan. I'm remaining ___; I don't care what color it is.

reduction
comparison 3–4. There has been a ___ in crime in our city this year. In ___ with last year, far fewer crimes were committed.

abundant
exaggerate 5–6. I'll admit that ants were ___ at our picnic, but let's not ___. There really were not a trillion of them.

demonstrate
distinct 7–8. Although I'd never sent a text message on a phone before, Corey ___d how it works so clearly that I now have a ___ idea of how to do it myself.

inhabit
betray 9–10. Homeless people secretly ___ed the abandoned building, but when someone ___ed them and told the police, they were thrown out.

Word Work

A. In the space provided, write the letter of the choice that best completes each item.

___B___ 1. Polar bears **inhabit**
    A. fish.
    B. the North Pole.
    C. white fur.

___C___ 2. The neighbors had a **dispute**
    A. to celebrate a birthday.
    B. because they got along so well together.
    C. over where the property line between them was supposed to be.

___C___ 3. The king's most trusted advisers **betrayed** him by
    A. giving him a surprise party.
    B. checking to be sure his food was safe.
    C. planning to kill him.

___A___ 4. During the car dealership's "The Boss Is Out Of Town" sale, prices on new cars were **reduced** by 10 percent. The prices were
    A. lowered.
    B. raised.
    C. kept the same.

___B___ 5. In a **comparison** at the supermarket, Annie learned that
    A. it takes her forty-five minutes to shop.
    B. Wheatsies cereal is a better buy than Oatsies.
    C. her friend Cara shops at the same store.

B. In the space provided, write the letter of the word that most closely relates to the situation in each item.

___C___ 6. "My grandchildren are the smartest youngsters in the world, and as for their behavior—they're perfect, that's all. They're angels."
    A. neutral   B. betray   C. exaggerate

___B___ 7. In the woods and fields around my hometown, blueberries grow everywhere. You can pick them by the bucketful.
    A. neutral   B. abundant   C. betray

___C___ 8. The view of the moon through the new telescope was extremely clear and sharp.
    A. abundant   B. reduction   C. distinct

___A___ 9. "When my husband and I have an argument," Naomi said, "my mother-in-law never takes sides."
    A. neutral   B. demonstrate   C. abundant

___B___ 10. To show the new soldiers how to take a rifle apart and put it together again, the instructors go through the whole process themselves.
    A. inhabit   B. demonstrate   C. neutral

Synonyms and Antonyms

A. Synonyms. Write the letter of the word or phrase that most nearly means the **same** as each boldfaced word.

___D___ 1. **betray**

    A. encourage   C. escape

    B. annoy   D. be disloyal

___B___ 2. **comparison**

    A. thoughts and feelings   C. questions and answers

    B. ways things are alike or different   D. time and effort

___A___ 3. **demonstrate**

    A. show   C. entertain

    B. confuse   D. judge

___A___ 4. **dispute**

    A. argument   C. fact

    B. agreement   D. condition

___C___ 5. **inhabit**

    A. go away from   C. live in

    B. approach   D. explore

B. Antonyms. Write the letter of the word or phrase that most nearly means the **opposite** of each boldfaced word.

___A___ 6. **abundant**

    A. not enough   C. lucky

    B. effective   D. great

___D___ 7. **distinct**

    A. quiet   C. large

    B. not constant   D. not clear

___C___ 8. **exaggerate**

    A. admire   C. understate

    B. destroy   D. defend

___B___ 9. **neutral**

    A. unusual   C. frightened

    B. favoring one side over another   D. possible

___B___ 10. **reduction**

    A. comment   C. agreement

    B. increase   D. answer

Final Check

Read the passages carefully. Then fill in each blank with the word that best fits the context.

A. The Vacuum-Cleaner Salesman

| A. **abundant** | B. **demonstrate** | C. **distinct** | D. **exaggerate** | E. **reduction** |

I'll never forget the day a salesman (1)____demonstrate____d his vacuum cleaner on my living-room rug. I know some salespeople (2)____exaggerate____ their product's good qualities, so I didn't believe everything he said. But I let him show me what his machine could do.

The first thing he did was deliberately° wipe his muddy feet on my rug. Next, he dumped an (3)____abundant____ amount of ashes onto it. Then he vacuumed the mess up. In no time, there was a contrast° between the rest of the rug and the part he had dirtied and then cleaned. A clear light stripe now ran down the middle of my rug. The machine was great. He told me how lucky I was to have a chance to buy it then, because of a great (4)____reduction____ in the price. Sadly, I had to tell him that even the lower price was too high for me. He then quickly thanked me and left.

Then I realized that he hadn't finished cleaning up all of the mess he had made. So I used my own vacuum cleaner, which did not do a very good job. As a result, I'm reminded of the frustration° of that day every time I walk through my living room. It still has a (5)____distinct____ light stripe right down the middle.

B. Peace at Last

| F. **betray** | G. **comparison** | H. **dispute** | I. **inhabit** | J. **neutral** |

My new apartment is so nice and quiet in (6)____comparison____ with my last one. In my old building, the people who (7)____inhabit____ed the apartments on both sides of me were always having (8)____dispute____s. For example, the woman in 401 and the man in 403 would argue all the time about politics. Once she yelled that she had trusted him to keep her secrets, but that he had (9)____betray____ed her by telling everyone in the building about her so-called "improper"° behavior. He then loudly insisted that she was the one with the big mouth. In addition, his wife sometimes screamed at the woman for leaving her trash bags in the hall. Although they tried to get me to take sides, I remained completely (10)____neutral____. I don't know who was right or wrong. I just know that the excessive° number of noisy arguments was too much for me to bear, and I'm glad to be out of there.

Scores   Check 2 _____%   Word Work _____%   Synonyms and Antonyms _____%   Final Check _____%

Enter your scores above and in the **Vocabulary Performance Chart** on the inside back cover of the book.

aggravate	intentional
cease	interference
coincide	obnoxious
considerable	unstable
humane	utilize

Ten Words in Context

In the space provided, write the letter of the meaning closest to that of each **boldfaced** word. Use the context of the sentences to help you figure out each word's meaning.

1 aggravate
(ăg′rə-vāt′)
- *verb*

- If you walk on your sprained ankle, you'll only **aggravate** the injury. The pain and swelling will get worse.
- My boss is already annoyed at me for losing some important papers, so I don't want to **aggravate** the situation by asking her for a day off.

B *Aggravate* means   A. to make use of.   B. to make worse.   C. to create.

2 cease
(sēs)
- *verb*

- After the police warned him twice, our landlord **ceased** burning trash in the backyard, an illegal activity in our town.
- When the snowfall finally **ceased**, we went out to shovel the driveway.

C *Cease* means   A. to repeat.   B. to start.   C. to stop.

3 coincide
(kō′ĭn-sīd′)
- *verb*

- My best friend and I have moved to different states. We try to make our visits to our hometown **coincide** so that we can see each other.
- Our neighbor is getting married on the same day as my cousin. I wish the weddings were not going to **coincide** because I'd really like to go to both.

A *Coincide* means   A. to happen at the same time.   B. to be stopped.   C. to be interesting.

4 considerable
(kən-sĭd′ər-ə-bəl)
- *adjective*

- After two hours and **considerable** effort, I finally found Vernon's apartment.
- Elena loves gardening, so she spends a **considerable** amount of time caring for flowers, vegetables, and herbs.

C *Considerable* means   A. too little.   B. gentle.   C. quite a bit.

5 humane
(hyoo-mān′)
- *adjective*

- When our cat developed a fatal blood disease, we didn't want her to suffer. We felt it was more **humane** to have her painlessly "put to sleep."
- In the past, zoo animals were usually kept in bare concrete cages. In an attempt to be **humane**, many zoos have built more natural, comfortable animal housing.

C *Humane* means   A. wasteful.   B. fast.   C. caring.

6 intentional
(ĭn-tĕn′shə-nəl)
- *adjective*

- The police believe the fire was **intentional**, although they don't know why someone would purposely burn down the movie theater.
- I know I'm an hour late, but it wasn't **intentional**. A huge traffic accident held me up.

B *Intentional* means   A. important.   B. planned.   C. illegal.

7 interference
(ĭn′tər-fîr′əns)
- *noun*

- Because the street workers outside our classroom window were such an **interference**, the class was moved to the library.

- My mom rarely gets involved in my arguments with my brother and sister. "You must learn to settle your problems without my **interference**," she says.

B *Interference* means   A. help.   B. getting in the way.   C. silence.

8 obnoxious
(ŏb-nŏk′shəs)
- *adjective*

- The children visiting the chicken farm held their noses because of the **obnoxious** smell.

- I won't go to the party if Lester is there. He always makes himself **obnoxious** by insulting and making fun of people.

C *Obnoxious* means   A. not interesting.   B. popular.   C. not pleasant.

9 unstable
(ŭn-stā′bəl)
- *adjective*

- The ladder felt so **unstable** that I was afraid to climb any higher than the third step.

- The young man's personality was **unstable**. One minute he seemed quiet and satisfied, and the next minute he was angry about something.

A *Unstable* means   A. not steady.   B. useful.   C. secure.

10 utilize
(yo͞ot′l-īz′)
- *verb*

- Don't throw bread away just because it's stale. Stale bread can be **utilized** to make bread crumbs and croutons.

- Last summer, Cindy **utilized** her swimming skills as a camp lifeguard.

C *Utilize* means   A. to sell.   B. to replace.   C. to use.

Matching Words with Definitions

Following are definitions of the ten words. **Print** each word next to its definition. If you look closely at each word in context, you will be able to figure out its meaning.

1. _____obnoxious_____ Very unpleasant; distasteful; disgusting

2. _____cease_____ To stop; discontinue; quit

3. _____unstable_____ Unsteady; wobbly; not reliable

4. _____intentional_____ Done on purpose; planned

5. _____aggravate_____ To make worse

6. _____humane_____ Kind; sympathetic; merciful; gentle

7. _____coincide_____ To happen at the same time

8. _____considerable_____ Rather great; rather large

9. _____interference_____ The act of getting in the way of something; meddling in someone else's business; something that gets in the way

10. _____utilize_____ To make use of; put to use, especially to good use

CAUTION: Do not go any further until you are sure the above answers are correct. Then you can use the definitions to help you in the following practices. Your goal is eventually to know the words well enough so that you don't need to check the definitions at all.

Check 1

Using the answer lines, complete each item below with the correct word from the box.

| A. **aggravate** | B. **cease** | C. **coincide** | D. **considerable** | E. **humane** |
| F. **intentional** | G. **interference** | H. **obnoxious** | I. **unstable** | J. **utilize** |

_____unstable_____ 1. It's no wonder the vase fell over; the flowers were so top-heavy that the whole arrangement was ___.

_____utilize_____ 2. My brother is glad he'll be able to ___ his skills as a mechanic in his new job at a garage.

_____aggravate_____ 3. Surprisingly, going to bed and taking it easy can actually ___ back pain. Gentle movement is often more helpful.

_____considerable_____ 4. A ___ amount of time is the opposite of a rather small amount of time.

_____obnoxious_____ 5. You may feel that slurping with straws is ___, but many kids don't find it disgusting at all.

_____intentional_____ 6. The young man was charged with arson—the ___ setting of a harmful fire.

_____coincide_____ 7. The two funerals will ___; that is, they will take place on the same day.

_____interference_____ 8. My nosy neighbor calls what she does just "taking a healthy interest in people's lives," but I call what she does "___."

_____humane_____ 9. It really isn't ___ to give small children chicks and baby ducks as presents. The fragile° little birds are almost sure to die soon.

_____cease_____ 10. The opposite of "begin" is ___.

NOTE: Now check your answers to these items by turning to page 239. Going over the answers carefully will help you prepare for the remaining practices, for which answers are not given.

Check 2

Using the answer lines, complete each item below with **two** words from the box. Use each word once.

_____aggravate_____
_____cease_____
1–2. "No pain, no gain" is bad advice when it comes to sports injuries. You can easily ___ an injury by playing before the pain has ___d.

_____unstable_____
_____interference_____
3–4. If a couple's marriage seems ___, family members may try to get involved. But ___ from relatives sometimes does more harm than good.

_____considerable_____
_____obnoxious_____
5–6. It may take ___ effort to get along with an ___ classmate or coworker, but learning how to deal with unpleasant people is a valuable skill.

_____utilize_____
_____humane_____
7–8. Animal-rights activists say it is not right to ___ cats, dogs, and monkeys in medical experiments. However, many researchers argue that their treatment of the animals is ___.

_____coincide_____
_____intentional_____
9–10. The vocabulary skills class and the study skills class ___ this semester. Scheduling them for the same day and time probably wasn't ___, but students who wanted to take them both are annoyed.

Word Work

A. In the space provided, write the letter of the choice that best completes each item.

_C_ 1. According to the weather report, the rain should **cease** tonight. Tonight the rain should

    A. start, after a period of dry weather.
    B. get much worse, with flooding in some areas.
    C. stop, probably after raining most or all of the day.

_B_ 2. Maria works at home, and sometimes there is a great deal of **interference** from her children. The children

    A. help her with her work.
    B. bother her when she is trying to work.
    C. leave for long periods of time.

_C_ 3. The bus strike **coincided** with a blizzard, so many offices downtown were closed. The strike

    A. took place a week after the blizzard.
    B. was called off because of the blizzard.
    C. happened at the same time as the blizzard.

_C_ 4. "If I hurt your feelings, you can be sure it was not **intentional**." I

    A. tried to hurt your feelings.
    B. have hurt you before.
    C. did not mean to hurt your feelings.

_A_ 5. The cost of getting wisdom teeth removed is **considerable**. It is

    A. quite expensive.
    B. much cheaper than expected.
    C. free.

B. In the space provided, write the letter of the word that most closely relates to the situation in each item.

_C_ 6. Mom doesn't like to dispose° of anything. She uses the comics as wrapping paper, cuts up worn-out rubber gloves to make rubber bands, and saves old stockings to use as dust cloths.

    A. interference
    B. humane
    C. utilize

_A_ 7. My grandmother took in foster children and also gave much of her time to a program for pregnant teenagers.

    A. humane
    B. aggravate
    C. obnoxious

_C_ 8. A man at the restaurant was loudly critical° of other customers and tried to start a fight.

    A. utilize
    B. coincide
    C. obnoxious

_B_ 9. Suki's allergies got much worse when she moved into a house where three cats and two dogs lived.

    A. intentional
    B. aggravate
    C. utilize

_C_ 10. Our restaurant table was distinctly° rocking back and forth, so we put a matchbook under one leg to steady it.

    A. coincide
    B. humane
    C. unstable

Analogies

Each item below starts with a pair of words in CAPITAL LETTERS. For each item, figure out the relationship between these two words. Then decide which of the choices (A, B, C, or D) expresses a similar relationship. Write the letter of your choice on the answer line. (All the repeated words in these items are from this unit.)

Note: To review analogies, see pages 6–7.

__A__ 1. AGGRAVATE : WORSEN ::

    A. improve : make better   C. heal : injure

    B. improve : make worse   D. raise : lower

__C__ 2. CEASE : BEGIN ::

    A. continue : go on   C. stop : start

    B. stop : quit   D. fertile° : soil

__D__ 3. STUDY : TEXTBOOK ::

    A. restore° : repair   C. find : lose

    B. chair : furniture   D. analyze° : problem

__C__ 4. OBNOXIOUS : PLEASANT ::

    A. harmful : unpleasant   C. annoying : nice

    B. annoying : irritating   D. pleasure : enjoyment

__D__ 5. UTILIZE : TOOL ::

    A. catch : run   C. ship : car

    B. shaky : wobbly   D. swing : bat

__B__ 6. UNSTABLE : STEADY ::

    A. large : big   C. abundant° : plentiful

    B. evident° : unclear   D. busy : happy

__A__ 7. INTENTIONAL : ON PURPOSE ::

    A. untrue : false   C. planned : prevented

    B. accidental : on purpose   D. hoped for : feared

__D__ 8. REJECTION° : ACCEPTANCE ::

    A. hour : time   C. school : college

    B. child : children   D. contrast° : similarity

__D__ 9 INTERFERENCE : ASSISTANCE ::

    A. reduction° : decrease   C. teacher : subject

    B. garbage : bag   D. dispute° : agreement

__A__ 10. VALUABLE : GOLD ::

    A. fragile° : glass   C. diamond : ruby

    B. new : old   D. excessive° : deliberate°

Final Check

Read the passages carefully. Then fill in each blank with the word that best fits the context.

A. Study Skills to the Rescue!

| A. **aggravate** | B. **coincide** | C. **considerable** | D. **interference** | E. **utilize** |

Students say that one of their biggest headaches is what to do when several exams and assignments (1)____*coincide*____; for example, when they have a test and a quiz the same week that a paper and a report are due. To deal with this situation, don't panic—that will only (2)____*aggravate*____ your problem. Instead, (3)____*utilize*____ some study skills that will make you a better manager of your time. First, you can get (4)____*considerable*____ help simply by planning well. Determine° what will take the most time; probably the test will need more study time than the quiz, and a long report might take more time than a short paper. Setting aside suitable° amounts of time will give you a sense of control. Second, be sure you get the most out of the time you've planned. Find a quiet place to work, and don't allow any (5)____*interference*____ from your friends or roommates, TV, radio, or CD player. And third? Well, try adding your own ideas to the list. The more you add, the more self-confident you'll feel.

B. Training a Puppy

| F. **cease** | G. **humane** | H. **intentional** | I. **obnoxious** | J. **unstable** |

Training a puppy is always a challenge. Although puppies are adorable creatures, their chewing and snapping can be (6)____*obnoxious*____. Their naughtiness is not (7)____*intentional*____, of course. They're just doing what comes naturally. However, in order for puppies to be good members of the household, these improper° behaviors have to (8)____*cease*____. It's up to the human owners to teach puppies good manners.

There are two important points to remember when you are training a puppy. The first is to treat the puppy in a (9)____*humane*____ manner, rather than a cruel one. For example, scold it by shaking a can of pennies at it instead of slapping it. Secondly, don't do things that confuse your dog. If you let it play tug-of-war with an old sneaker, don't be surprised when it chews up your brand-new Nikes. If your dog doesn't understand what you want of it, it is likely to develop an (10)____*unstable*____ personality instead of a calm, pleasant one.

| Scores | Check 2 _____% | Word Work _____% | Analogies _____% | Final Check _____% |

Enter your scores above and in the **Vocabulary Performance Chart** on the inside back cover of the book.

The box at the right lists twenty-five words from Unit One. Using the clues at the bottom of the page, fill in these words to complete the puzzle that follows.

Word box:

accompany
attitude
betray
cease
challenge
coincide
critical
deliberate
dispute
evident
fertile
fragile
humane
improper
indicate
inhabit
neutral
preference
preserve
reduction
rejection
solitary
surplus
unstable
utilize

ACROSS

5. To protect; keep in good condition
6. To go along with; be together with
7. To live in
10. Happening or done alone
12. To make use of; put to use, especially to good use
14. Done on purpose
16. A test of one's abilities
20. Not taking sides in a quarrel
21. The act of saying "no" (to a request or desire); refusal
22. Not in good taste; not right for a situation

DOWN

1. Kind; sympathetic; merciful; gentle
2. A decrease; cutback
3. Producing or able to produce much fruit, large crops, or many children
4. Easily broken or damaged
7. To show; serve as a sign or signal
8. An argument; a quarrel
9. To stop; discontinue
11. A point of view; state of mind; way of thinking or feeling
12. Unsteady; wobbly; not reliable
13. To be disloyal to; turn against
15. Choice; first choice; something desired
16. To happen at the same time
17. Obvious; clear
18. Extra; more than what is used or needed
19. Disapproving; tending to find fault

PART A

Choose the word that best completes each item and write it in the space provided.

_____transform_____ 1. A bucket of paint can ___ a room's looks.

  A. transform   B. accompany   C. challenge   D. utilize

_____unstable_____ 2. Jenna was afraid to touch the ___ house of cards—it looked ready to collapse.

  A. improper   B. distinct   C. neutral   D. unstable

_____deliberate_____ 3. Cho thought my not inviting her to my party was a ___ insult. In reality, her invitation slipped under a book, so it never was mailed.

  A. deliberate   B. suitable   C. humane   D. improper

_____aggravate_____ 4. Don't scratch a mosquito bite! You'll only ___ the itching and end up feeling even worse.

  A. analyze   B. aggravate   C. indicate   D. utilize

_____principal_____ 5. Julio's ___ aim in going to college is to get a good job when he graduates, but he hopes to have a good time while he's there, as well.

  A. abundant   B. obnoxious   C. principal   D. desperate

_____determine_____ 6. It took a long time for doctors to ___ what Felicia was allergic to, but they finally figured out that it was her lipstick.

  A. utilize   B. preserve   C. determine   D. restore

_____solitary_____ 7. After hours of ___ work at my desk, I am ready to spend some time with other people.

  A. abundant   B. solitary   C. humane   D. dependent

_____fragile_____ 8. My grandmother's old china doll is much too ___ to play with; it would soon be broken.

  A. fragile   B. suitable   C. distinct   D. improper

_____betray_____ 9. "Your secret is safe with me," said the handsome prince to the fair maiden. "I swear I will never ___ you!"

  A. restore   B. demonstrate   C. preserve   D. betray

_____peculiar_____ 10. The students in history class noticed a ___ odor coming from the science lab across the hall. The odor smelled like a mixture of rotten eggs and gasoline.

  A. suitable   B. humane   C. fertile   D. peculiar

(Continues on next page)

_____*evident*_____ 11. It is ___ that Wayne is interested in Shawna; he can't stop looking at her.

        A. humane   B. evident   C. dependent   D. critical

_____*inhabit*_____ 12. Animals that ___ a desert region are able to live there because they can go a long time without water.

        A. analyze   B. indicate   C. dispose of   D. inhabit

_____*demonstrate*_____ 13. I asked my stylish sister to ___ some creative ways to wear a long scarf.

        A. preserve   B. restore   C. demonstrate   D. utilize

PART B

Write **C** if the italicized word is used **correctly**. Write **I** if the word is used **incorrectly**.

_C_ 14. Suddenly, the music *ceased*, and the room was very quiet.

_I_ 15. That jigsaw puzzle is a *challenge* because it is too easy. It's meant for very young children and has only six pieces.

_C_ 16. Because of *interference* by a fan who ran onto the playing field, the game was temporarily stopped by a referee.

_I_ 17. Bullies are disliked because of the *humane* way they treat their victims.

_C_ 18. Maya's elderly parents are too *dependent* on her. They constantly call her for help and advice.

_I_ 19. The bare, dry, stony fields look very *fertile*.

_I_ 20. Raspberries are so *abundant* in our city that it's hard to find them. When you do, they cost as much as five or six dollars for a tiny box.

_I_ 21. My *preference* is to go to an Italian restaurant tonight because I dislike spaghetti and pizza.

_C_ 22. The notice in the airplane said, "Seat cushions can be *utilized* for flotation." In other words, you can use the cushions to float on if the plane crashes in water.

_I_ 23. The teenagers on the subway were especially *obnoxious*. They gave up their seats so some elderly people and a pregnant woman could sit down.

_I_ 24. It was very *improper* of you to thank Mrs. Wilson for sending you a birthday card.

_C_ 25. Teenage boys are sometimes nervous about asking a girl for a date because they fear *rejection*.

Score   (Number correct) _____ x 4 = _____%

PART A

On the answer line, write the word from the box that completes each item below. Use each word once.

A. accompany	B. analyze	C. category	D. coincide	E. comparison
F. desperate	G. dispose of	H. intentional	I. neutral	J. reduction
K. restore	L. suitable	M. surplus		

_____intentional_____ 1. The man on the bus who stepped on my foot said, "Sorry! It wasn't ___. I didn't mean to do it!"

_____surplus_____ 2. Darin's vegetable garden grew so well and produced so much that he didn't know what to do with the ___ tomatoes and zucchinis.

_____comparison_____ 3. A ___ between the two jobs didn't make it much easier for Marnie to decide; one paid better, but the other was more interesting.

_____coincide_____ 4. Why do Easter and Passover ___ in some years, while in other years they are weeks apart rather than at the same time?

_____neutral_____ 5. That child hates to fight. When his brother and sister get into a quarrel, he always stays ___.

_____reduction_____ 6. Americans think too much about weight ___. There is more to life than just losing weight!

_____analyze_____ 7. The town will ___ traffic patterns to find out if more traffic lights are needed.

_____category_____ 8. Some psychologists think there are two types of people: Type A's, who are hard-working and uptight, and Type B's, who are relaxed and easygoing. Which ___ do you belong in?

_____desperate_____ 9. If a poor man is ___ for money to buy medicine for his sick wife, do you think he should steal?

_____dispose of_____ 10. Don't ___ the comic section of the Sunday paper. Save it and use it as wrapping paper; it's colorful and fun!

_____accompany_____ 11. When Josie had a tooth pulled, she asked Mark to ___ her to the dentist and see that she got home all right afterward.

_____suitable_____ 12. Cut-off jeans might be ___ to wear to a ball game, but they would be out of place at a funeral.

_____restore_____ 13. The town wants to ___ the old firehouse instead of tearing it down and building a new one.

(Continues on next page)

PART B

Write **C** if the italicized word is used **correctly**. Write **I** if the word is used **incorrectly**.

_C_   14. Ronda has an unusual *attitude* toward weekends, vacations, and holidays; she doesn't like them much and would just as soon go to work every day of the year.

_I_   15. Theo's fame as a football player is *considerable*. Nobody has ever heard of him.

_I_   16. Imagine my *frustration* when I learned I had earned straight A's for the semester!

_I_   17. Helen is far too *critical* of her husband. She adores him and never finds fault with him no matter how inconsiderately he treats her.

_C_   18. To *preserve* the seat covers in his car, Denny had slipcovers put on. Then he put plastic over the slipcovers. Then he spread old sheets over the plastic.

_C_   19. Denny's concern for his car's seat covers seems to be *excessive*. Who ever heard of using so many layers of covers at once?

_I_   20. The old photograph was so *distinct* that the faces of the people in it were just a blur.

_C_   21. "If you get robbed on the street," said the police officer, "never try to *pursue* the thief yourself. Call us and let us do the chasing!"

_I_   22. There is a real *contrast* between the twins. They look so much alike that sometimes even their mother can't tell them apart.

_C_   23. Don't *exaggerate* when you fill out a job application. If you were a store clerk, for instance, don't say you were the manager.

_C_   24. When President Calvin Coolidge wanted to *indicate* that he was not a candidate for reelection, he said, "I do not choose to run."

_I_   25. Lupe and Jorge agree about everything, so they have one *dispute* after another.

Score   (Number correct) _____ x 4 = _____%

PART A: Synonyms

In the space provided, write the letter of the choice that is most nearly the **same** in meaning as the **boldfaced** word.

<u>D</u>   1. **accompany**   A. go   B. seek   C. figure out   D. go with

<u>C</u>   2. **analyze**   A. worry about   B. argue about   C. study   D. change

<u>C</u>   3. **attitude**   A. height   B. disappointment   C. point of view   D. skill

<u>A</u>   4. **category**   A. a type   B. a book   C. a difference
       D. a check for similarities and differences

<u>B</u>   5. **challenge**   A. quarrel   B. something needing effort   C. change   D. use

<u>C</u>   6. **coincide**   A. change   B. live in   C. happen at the same time   D. show

<u>A</u>   7. **comparison**   A. a check for similarities and differences   B. an increase
       C. a feeling of anger   D. a first choice

<u>C</u>   8. **considerable**   A. unpleasant   B. difficult   C. quite large   D. producing much

<u>C</u>   9. **critical**   A. kind   B. hard to get   C. disapproving   D. harmful

<u>A</u> 10. **demonstrate**   A. show   B. get rid of   C. turn against   D. overstate

<u>B</u> 11. **desperate**   A. relying on others   B. in great need   C. clear   D. alone

<u>C</u> 12. **determine**   A. prevent   B. explain   C. figure out   D. protect

<u>C</u> 13. **evident**   A. hard to get   B. fitting   C. clear   D. too much

<u>D</u> 14. **fertile**   A. careful   B. helpful   C. fearful   D. fruitful

<u>B</u> 15. **indicate**   A. disapprove of   B. show   C. turn against   D. protect

<u>C</u> 16. **inhabit**   A. make a habit of   B. seek   C. live in   D. leave

<u>A</u> 17. **interference**   A. getting in the way   B. difference   C. decrease   D. refusal

<u>A</u> 18. **preference**   A. first choice   B. disappointment   C. extra   D. test

<u>D</u> 19. **preserve**   A. teach   B. turn against   C. destroy   D. protect

<u>A</u> 20. **principal**   A. main   B. on purpose   C. plentiful   D. unusual

<u>B</u> 21. **pursue**   A. examine   B. chase   C. get rid of   D. stop

<u>D</u> 22. **restore**   A. remove   B. seek   C. give away   D. repair

<u>C</u> 23. **solitary**   A. rare   B. alike   C. done alone   D. not reliable

<u>C</u> 24. **transform**   A. bring back   B. send   C. change   D. end

<u>B</u> 25. **utilize**   A. protect   B. use   C. show   D. stop

(Continues on next page)

PART B: Antonyms

In the space provided, write the letter of the choice that is most nearly **opposite** in meaning to the **boldfaced** word.

_C_	26. **abundant**	A. healthy	B. unplanned	C. rare	D. unkind		
_D_	27. **aggravate**	A. attack	B. learn	C. move	D. make better		
_D_	28. **betray**	A. grow	B. be happy	C. keep	D. be loyal to		
_D_	29. **cease**	A. give	B. learn	C. ruin	D. start		
_A_	30. **contrast**	A. similarity	B. help	C. agreement	D. success		
_C_	31. **deliberate**	A. unusual	B. unclear	C. unplanned	D. unnecessary		
_A_	32. **dependent**	A. relying on oneself	B. working alone	C. knowing oneself	D. not obvious	

_B_	33. **dispose of**	A. like	B. keep	C. leave	D. remember
_B_	34. **dispute**	A. test	B. agreement	C. group	D. choice
_C_	35. **distinct**	A. helpful	B. broken	C. unclear	D. well-known
_A_	36. **exaggerate**	A. understate	B. go away from	C. think about	D. support
_B_	37. **excessive**	A. not clear	B. not enough	C. strong	D. not able
_D_	38. **fragile**	A. not proper	B. unhappy	C. unpleasant	D. unbreakable
_D_	39. **frustration**	A. failure	B. kindness	C. too much	D. satisfaction
_A_	40. **humane**	A. cruel	B. forgotten	C. important	D. too little
_D_	41. **improper**	A. well-known	B. recent	C. too little	D. in good taste
_D_	42. **intentional**	A. proper	B. done poorly	C. plentiful	D. accidental
_B_	43. **neutral**	A. paying attention	B. taking sides	C. proper	D. pleasant
_C_	44. **obnoxious**	A. approving	B. common	C. pleasant	D. intelligent
_B_	45. **peculiar**	A. difficult	B. ordinary	C. weak	D. excellent
_B_	46. **reduction**	A. last choice	B. increase	C. start	D. answer
_A_	47. **rejection**	A. approval	B. addition	C. lack	D. loss
_C_	48. **suitable**	A. improved	B. unkind	C. improper	D. immediate
_B_	49. **surplus**	A. success	B. lack	C. luck	D. trouble
_A_	50. **unstable**	A. steady	B. easy	C. usual	D. quite small

Score   (Number correct) _____ x 2 = _____ %

Enter your score above and in the **Vocabulary Performance Chart** on the inside back cover of the book.

Unit Two

CHAPTER 6

advise	minimum
current	objection
deprive	originate
hesitate	penalize
maintain	reliable

Ten Words in Context

In the space provided, write the letter of the meaning closest to that of each **boldfaced** word. Use the context of the sentences to help you figure out each word's meaning.

1 advise
(ăd-vīz′)
- *verb*

- I'd like to **advise** Alan to break up with Elaine, but I know he'll get angry if I offer my opinion.
- The park ranger said, "I **advise** you to hang your food from a tree if you don't want the bears to get it."

B *Advise* means   A. to punish.   B. to suggest to.   C. to follow.

2 current
(kûr′ənt)
- *adjective*

- Rita keeps up with fashion and buys the **current** styles, but her sister wears the same basic style, year after year.
- Doctors once suggested total bed rest after surgery. However, **current** practice is to have patients walk as soon as possible after an operation.

A *Current* means   A. up-to-date.   B. little known.   C. older.

3 deprive
(dĭ-prīv′)
- *verb*

- Isaac's mother **deprives** him of his allowance when he doesn't do his household jobs.
- Dad complains that his low-fat, low-calorie diet **deprives** him of everything he enjoys eating.

A *Deprive of* means   A. to keep from.   B. to offer to.   C. to protect from.

4 hesitate
(hĕz′ĭ-tāt′)
- *verb*

- I **hesitated** so long about answering the "Help Wanted" ad that by the time I did respond, the job was already filled.
- Rodrigo **hesitated** to ask Julie to marry him. He wasn't sure he was ready to get married.

B *Hesitate* means   A. to act quickly.   B. to be undecided.   C. to be pleased.

5 maintain
(mān-tān′)
- *verb*

- When driving, it's important to **maintain** a safe distance between your car and the car ahead of you.
- My brother must have excellent study skills. He was able to **maintain** a B average throughout college while holding a full-time job.

A *Maintain* means   A. to keep up.   B. to give up.   C. to pass up.

6 minimum
(mĭn′ə-məm)
- *adjective*

- The **minimum** number of people allowed for each bus tour is eight. If fewer people sign up, the trip will be canceled.
- What's the **minimum** price you'll take for your car? I can't afford to pay much.

C *Minimum* means   A. oldest.   B. biggest.   C. lowest.

48

7 objection
(əb-jĕk′shən)
- *noun*

- Luz had a strong **objection** to the wallpaper her husband picked out for their living room. "It looks like a doctor's waiting room," she complained.
- Granddad had a strong **objection** to boys' wearing long hair. Once when my father refused to get a haircut, Granddad cut his hair while he was asleep.

C   *Objection* means   A. interest in.   B. memory of.   C. dislike of.

8 originate
(ə-rĭj′ə-nāt′)
- *verb*

- The ice-cream cone **originated** at the 1904 World's Fair in St. Louis. An ice-cream seller ran out of cups, so he wrapped a waffle around the ice cream and sold it that way.
- Many people believe that baseball **originated** in Cooperstown, New York, in 1839. However, it must have started earlier, since the sport was mentioned in English publications as early as 1744.

B   *Originate* means   A. to continue.   B. to begin.   C. to delay.

9 penalize
(pē′nə-līz′)
- *verb*

- Whenever my parents heard I had been kept after school, they would **penalize** me again at home.
- The judge decided to **penalize** the young thief with one hundred hours of volunteer work.

C   *Penalize* means   A. to depend upon.   B. to answer.   C. to punish.

10 reliable
(rĭ-lī′ə-bəl)
- *adjective*

- Joe Sherman is a **reliable** mechanic. You can count on him to tell you the truth and to fix whatever is wrong with your car.
- The ad said, "**Reliable** store clerk needed. Don't bother to apply unless you are willing to show up on time every day."

B   *Reliable* means   A. modern.   B. able to be trusted.   C. not expensive.

Matching Words with Definitions

Following are definitions of the ten words. **Print** each word next to its definition. If you look closely at each word in context, you will be able to figure out its meaning.

1. _____objection_____   A dislike; feeling of being against something; disapproval

2. _____hesitate_____   To stop because of not being able to decide; put off acting because of feeling unsure

3. _____deprive_____   To take away from; keep from having or enjoying

4. _____minimum_____   Smallest in size or amount that is allowed or possible; least

5. _____maintain_____   To continue; carry on; keep in existence

6. _____current_____   Modern; existing now; in general use or practice today

7. _____originate_____   To come into being; start

8. _____penalize_____   To punish; cause to suffer for doing something wrong

9. _____advise_____   To give advice to; recommend

10. _____reliable_____   Able to be depended upon; trustworthy

CAUTION: Do not go any further until you are sure the above answers are correct. Then you can use the definitions to help you in the following practices. Your goal is eventually to know the words well enough so that you don't need to check the definitions at all.

Check 1

Using the answer lines, complete each item below with the correct word from the box.

| A. **advise** | B. **current** | C. **deprive** | D. **hesitate** | E. **maintain** |
| F. **minimum** | G. **objection** | H. **originate** | I. **penalize** | J. **reliable** |

_____reliable_____   1. A worker who is honest and does his job carefully would be called a ___ worker.

_____advise_____   2. My aunt is not a good patient. She rarely does what her doctor ___s her to do.

_____minimum_____   3. The opposite of the highest salary the company allows would be its ___ salary.

_____penalize_____   4. To ___ the team member who skipped practice, the coach made her do fifty pushups.

_____originate_____   5. We can say that the place where a river starts is where it ___s.

_____current_____   6. We might refer to styles that are widely worn today as ___ fashions.

_____deprive_____   7. Prisons ___ people of much of their freedom.

_____hesitate_____   8. Larry ___s to work more than ten hours a week after school. He has such difficult classes that he may need more time than usual for studying.

_____objection_____   9. I have an ___ to that comedian. His jokes often hurt other people.

_____maintain_____   10. You must keep up a B average to keep your football uniform. In other words, if you don't ___ good grades, you're off the team.

NOTE: Now check your answers to these items by turning to page 239. Going over the answers carefully will help you prepare for the remaining practices, for which answers are not given.

Check 2

Using the answer lines, complete each item below with **two** words from the box. Use each word once.

_____penalize_____
_____deprive_____   1–2. The best way to ___ my little nephew when he does something bad is to ___ him of his tricycle for a day.

_____minimum_____
_____reliable_____   3–4. The girls accepted jobs that paid the ___ wage, hoping that they would get raises once they proved they were ___ workers.

_____objection_____
_____maintain_____   5–6. My doctor has an ___ to "crash diets." Although they cause a quick reduction° in weight, they do not help the dieter ___ that new, lower weight.

_____current_____
_____advise_____   7–8. Keisha likes her hair cut in the most ___ style. Her hairdresser ___s her about the newest fashionable looks.

_____originate_____
_____hesitate_____   9–10. The fox terrier is a dog that ___d in England, where fox hunting was popular. It was valued there by hunters because it would not ___ to run into a fox's tunnel and drive the animal out.

Word Work

A. Write each word next to the examples that best match it.

| A. **advise** | B. **hesitate** | C. **originate** |
| D. **penalize** | E. **reliable** | |

penalize   1. Send a murderer to prison
Keep a teenager from a party because of poor behavior
Tell a wild four-year-old to go to her room

reliable   2. A car that always starts
A friend who is there when you need her
A bus that is never late

advise   3. Tell a good friend to try harder in school
Suggest to your sister that she should develop her musical talent
Encourage an elderly person to get a pet

hesitate   4. Being unable to decide whether to ask Gil to the dance
Stopping because of being uncertain about which way to go
Delaying the purchase of a new car because of doubt about paying so much

originate   5. Friday gets its name from "Freya," the name of a Norse goddess.
Ice-cream sundaes get their name because they were first sold only on Sundays.
Floating Ivory soap was invented accidentally when a soap-mixing machine was left on too long.

B. In the space provided, write the letter of the word that best completes each item.

_B_   6. You are likely to have an **objection** to something

   A. helpful.   B. harmful.   C. recent.

_C_   7. To **maintain** good health, you should

   A. start smoking.   B. shop.   C. exercise.

_A_   8. **Current** movies are

   A. playing now.   B. old classics.   C. comedies.

_C_   9. "When your cousin visits, he'll be sharing your room," Tim's mother announced. Tim realized he would be **deprived** of his

   A. meals.   B. relatives.   C. privacy.

_B_   10. To buy clothing at the **minimum** cost, go to

   A. department stores.   B. garage sales.   C. France.

Word Parts

A. The suffixes *-ance* and *-ence* often mean "the act, state, or quality of."

Examples: *maintain* — to keep in existence   *patient* — willing to put up with something
                   maintenance — the act of keeping   *patience* — the quality of being patient
                       in existence

On each answer line, write the word from the box that means the same as the *italicized* words.

| A. **avoidance** | B. **excellence** | C. **dependence°** |
| D. **interference°** | E. **maintenance** | |

_____interference_____   1. "I know you mean well," the woman said to her mother. "But I'm 25 now, and your *act of interfering* in how I do my job is not helpful."

_____dependence_____   2. My father's *state of depending* on caffeine is not healthy for him.

_____excellence_____   3. Takeo aims for *the quality of being excellent* in everything he does.

_____maintenance_____   4. The *act of maintaining* of good grades requires a lot of willpower.

_____avoidance_____   5. Anna's *act of avoiding* milk is easily explained—she is allergic to it.

B. The prefix *in-* often means "not," which can change words to their opposites.

Examples: *direct* — in a straight line   *humane°* — kind
                   indirect — not in a straight line   *inhumane* — not kind

On each answer line, write the word from the box that best completes the item.

| F. **incapable** | G. **inconvenient** | H. **indistinct°** |
| I. **inexpensive** | J. **inhumane°** | |

_____indistinct_____   6. The fog was so thick that the road signs were ___. In fact, I could barely see them.

_____inconvenient_____   7. I wish there were a grocery store nearby. It is ___ to have to drive all the way across town.

_____inhumane_____   8. "It's ___ to give me a ten o'clock curfew!" Claudia complained. Her father replied, "I'm sorry you think I'm unkind, but I think 10 p.m. is a perfectly reasonable time to be home."

_____incapable_____   9. Most people are ___ of wiggling their ears, but not my dad! He can make them flap like wings.

_____inexpensive_____   10. Beware of buying very ___ shoes. Because they are made with such cheap materials, they will wear out quickly in comparison° with shoes that cost a little more.

Final Check

Read the passages carefully. Then fill in each blank with the word that best fits the context.

A. Toasters

| A. **current** | B. **maintain** | C. **minimum** | D. **originate** | E. **reliable** |

Although the practice of eating toasted bread (1)____originate____d about 4,600 years ago, the pop-up electric toaster was not invented until 1919. These early pop-up toasters were not very (2)____reliable____—they broke down often. Also, they weren't able to (3)____maintain____ an even temperature, but grew hotter and hotter with each piece of bread toasted. Some poor-quality machines even popped the toast all the way across the room. Over the years, toasters have certainly improved. (4)____Current____ ones are easy to utilize°, and they give us a (5)____minimum____ number of problems with repairs and temperature control.

B. A Mean Man

| F. **advise** | G. **deprive** | H. **hesitate** | I. **objection** | J. **penalize** |

Mr. Barker says that he has no (6)____objection____ to kids—as long as they don't come into his yard, as long as they don't (7)____deprive____ him of peace and quiet, and as long as they don't grow up to be teenagers.

Neighborhood kids say he's the meanest man they ever met. Who can blame them? If he sees them choosing up sides for a ball game in the street, for example, he doesn't (8)____hesitate____ a minute. He runs right to his window and yells, "You can't do that in front of MY house!" The kids are afraid of him, but they yell back that the street belongs to everybody. "Well, I (9)____advise____ you to watch your step!" he replies. "If you kids break my window or step on my flowers, you will be (10)____penalize____d." Then he ends the dispute° by slamming his window shut. Maybe a hard life has made Mr. Barker the way he is, but it's difficult to have warm feelings for someone so obnoxious°.

| Scores | Check 2 _____% | Word Work _____% | Word Parts _____% | Final Check _____% |

Enter your scores above and in the **Vocabulary Performance Chart** on the inside back cover of the book.

abrupt	eager
astonish	endure
classify	exclaim
complex	horizontal
consent	recollect

Ten Words in Context

In the space provided, write the letter of the meaning closest to that of each **boldfaced** word. Use the context of the sentences to help you figure out each word's meaning.

1 abrupt
(ə-brŭpt′)
- *adjective*

- Seat belts in cars protect passengers from injuries caused by **abrupt** stops.
- An **abrupt** burst of laughter during the church service surprised everyone.

<u>C</u> *Abrupt* means   A. silent.   B. simple.   C. not expected.

2 astonish
(ə-stŏn′ĭsh)
- *verb*

- A magician **astonished** the audience by making seemingly impossible things happen.
- The announcement that the factory was closing forever **astonished** the employees, who had not known their jobs were in danger.

<u>C</u> *Astonish* means   A. to delay.   B. to encourage.   C. to surprise.

3 classify
(klăs′ə-fī′)
- *verb*

- The stamp collector **classified** her stamps by countries—she put all the stamps from France together, all the stamps from Spain together, and so on.
- I was surprised to learn that the sea horse is **classified** by scientists as a fish.

<u>B</u> *Classify* means   A. to lose.   B. to group.   C. to remember.

4 complex
(kəm-plĕks′)
- *adjective*

- Because income tax forms are so **complex**, many people hire professionals to prepare their tax returns.
- Our family is rather **complex**—it includes many second marriages and stepfamilies. At family reunions we spend a lot of time trying to figure out how we are all related.

<u>A</u> *Complex* means   A. hard to understand.   B. helpful.   C. small.

5 consent
(kən-sĕnt′)
- *verb*

- Only applicants who **consented** to a drug test were considered for the job.
- Enrique proposed to Anita by putting up a billboard saying, "Will you marry me?" She **consented** with her own sign that said, "Of course I will."

<u>A</u> *Consent* means   A. to say yes.   B. to listen.   C. to disagree.

6 eager
(ē′gər)
- *adjective*

- I am always **eager** to read the latest story by my favorite mystery writer.
- Our dog is **eager** to greet us when we come home. She jumps up on us and begins licking our hands before the door is even shut.

<u>C</u> *Eager* means   A. bored.   B. patient.   C. happily excited.

7 endure
(ĕn-dŏor′)
- *verb*

- We'll have to **endure** a few more weeks of cold, gray winter before spring arrives.
- Until someone finds a cure for the common cold, there's not much to do but **endure** the runny noses and sneezes.

C   *Endure* means   A. to enjoy.   B. to organize.   C. to live with unwillingly.

8 exclaim
(ĭk-sklām′)
- *verb*

- "Wow!" "Ooooh!" "Aaah!" the crowd **exclaimed** as the colorful fireworks burst in the sky.
- When a cardinal landed on the bird feeder, the little girl **exclaimed**, "Look! A red blue jay!"

C   *Exclaim* means   A. to remember.   B. to complain.   C. to call out.

9 horizontal
(hŏr′ĭ-zŏn′tl)
- *adjective*

- The surgery left a **horizontal** scar that runs from one side of my stomach to the other.
- The American flag contains red and white **horizontal** stripes.

C   *Horizontal* means   A. dirty.   B. little.   C. running from side to side.

10 recollect
(rĕk′ə-lĕkt′)
- *verb*

- Can you **recollect** much about being in first grade?
- While filling out a job application, I couldn't **recollect** my social security number. I had to dig the card out of my wallet to look at it.

B   *Recollect* means   A. to agree with.   B. to remember.   C. to arrange.

Matching Words with Definitions

Following are definitions of the ten words. **Print** each word next to its definition. If you look closely at each word in context, you will be able to figure out its meaning.

1. ____horizontal____   Lying flat; lying or extending from side to side (as opposed to going up and down)

2. ____endure____   To put up with; bear patiently

3. ____eager____   Looking forward to with great interest or desire

4. ____complex____   Not simple; not easy to understand or figure out

5. ____consent____   To agree to something

6. ____exclaim____   To speak or cry out suddenly, as from strong feelings or surprise

7. ____classify____   To arrange or organize into groups or types; place in a category°

8. ____recollect____   To remember; bring an image or idea back to mind

9. ____astonish____   To surprise greatly; amaze

10. ____abrupt____   Sudden and unexpected

CAUTION: Do not go any further until you are sure the above answers are correct. Then you can use the definitions to help you in the following practices. Your goal is eventually to know the words well enough so that you don't need to check the definitions at all.

Check 1

Using the answer lines, complete each item below with the correct word from the box.

| A. **abrupt** | B. **astonish** | C. **classify** | D. **complex** | E. **consent** |
| F. **eager** | G. **endure** | H. **exclaim** | I. **horizontal** | J. **recollect** |

_____endure_____ 1. I can't ___ the way my co-worker snaps her chewing gum. I'm going to start wearing headphones so I don't hear it.

_____classify_____ 2. Do you know that gardeners ___ the tomato as a fruit? Most people think of it as a vegetable.

_____recollect_____ 3. At age 97, Great-Grandpa does not remember the recent past, but he ___s stories from his childhood very clearly.

_____astonish_____ 4. The great magician Houdini would ___ audiences by escaping from chains, locked trunks, and even sealed coffins.

_____exclaim_____ 5. The day after Jackie had her waist-length hair cut short, nearly everyone she met ___ed, "Oh! Your hair!"

_____abrupt_____ 6. A car would probably come to an ___ stop if a dog ran out in front of it.

_____eager_____ 7. Knowing that she had done well on every test, Phyllis was ___ to see her final grade for the course.

_____complex_____ 8. The driving route to Mei Lin's house is very ___, involving highway cloverleafs, traffic circles, and bypasses. I would rather go there by train.

_____horizontal_____ 9. It's true that ___ stripes on clothing make you look wider, and stripes that go up and down make you look taller.

_____consent_____ 10. If you won the lottery, would you ___ to having your name and picture printed in the newspaper?

NOTE: Now check your answers to these items by turning to page 239. Going over the answers carefully will help you prepare for the remaining practices, for which answers are not given.

Check 2

Using the answer lines, complete each item below with **two** words from the box. Use each word once.

_____abrupt_____
_____astonish_____   1–2. In early spring, ___ changes in the weather can ___ everyone. It may be mild and sunny in the morning, then snowing by bedtime.

_____consent_____
_____endure_____   3–4. I didn't want to have dental surgery, but I decided to ___ to it rather than ___ my toothache any longer. I just want the pain to cease°.

_____horizontal_____
_____recollect_____   5–6. Lani wanted to insert a ___ line between the sections in her Word document, but she couldn't ___ which keystroke to use.

_____classify_____
_____complex_____   7–8. Scientists ___ animals in a ___ system of groupings, using features such as being warm- or cold-blooded and having feathers or scales.

<u>   eager   </u>   9–10. My kids are not exactly ___ to go to school. When I wake them every

<u>   exclaim   </u>   morning, they ___, "Oh, no! Isn't it Saturday yet?"

Word Work

A. In the space provided, write the letter of the choice that best completes each item.

<u>B</u> 1. Thelma **recollects** her neighbor's kindness. She

    A. is disappointed   B. remembers that her   C. doubts that her neighbor
       in her neighbor.   neighbor was kind.   can be kind.

<u>C</u> 2. You are likely to **exclaim**

    A. a grocery list.   B. a stamp collection.   C. an expression of surprise.

<u>B</u> 3. The rich heroine in the story announces that she wants to marry a poor woodcutter. Her father tells her, "I will never **consent** to such a marriage!" Her father means that he

    A. approves of his daughter's choice.   B. disapproves of his daughter's choice.

<u>B</u> 4. When our neighbors told us they were divorcing, we were **astonished**. Obviously, we

    A. had expected the   B. had not expected   C. were not very interested.
       divorce for a long time.   it to happen.

<u>A</u> 5. It is difficult to **endure**

    A. a terrible headache.   B. a good dinner.   C. a sunny day.

B. In the space provided, write the letter of the word that most closely relates to the situation in each item.

<u>B</u> 6. At one point on the highway, there are eight lanes of traffic, three different levels, and about twenty signs with arrows pointing every which way.

    A. eager   B. complex   C. consent

<u>A</u> 7. Len's leaving his job was very sudden; one day he just marched in and said, "I quit."

    A. abrupt   B. horizontal   C. classify

<u>C</u> 8. The trees that had fallen during the storm lay flat on the ground.

    A. recollect   B. consent   C. horizontal

<u>A</u> 9. When the doors of the store opened on the day of the big sale, shoppers rushed in, excited about finding the best bargains.

    A. eager   B. horizontal   C. consent

<u>C</u> 10. The boys sort the coins they've saved into separate piles: pennies here, nickels there, dimes next, and then quarters.

    A. endure   B. exclaim   C. classify

Synonyms and Antonyms

A. Synonyms. Write the letter of the word or phrase that most nearly means the **same** as each boldfaced word.

<u>C</u> 1. **abrupt**

    A. expected   C. sudden

    B. delayed   D. polite

<u>D</u> 2. **astonish**

    A. borrow   C. allow

    B. request   D. surprise

<u>D</u> 3. **classify**

    A. set aside for later   C. decide the value

    B. have no use for   D. organize into groups

<u>A</u> 4. **endure**

    A. bear up under   C. agree

    B. remember   D. deny

<u>B</u> 5. **exclaim**

    A. tell   C. notice

    B. call out   D. bear

B. Antonyms. Write the letter of the word or phrase that most nearly means the **opposite** of each boldfaced word.

<u>A</u> 6. **complex**

    A. simple   C. interesting

    B. true   D. wise

<u>B</u> 7. **consent**

    A. try   C. begin

    B. refuse   D. practice

<u>D</u> 8. **eager**

    A. unsteady   C. expected

    B. perfect   D. not interested

<u>C</u> 9. **horizontal**

    A. in a circle   C. straight up and down

    B. lying at a slant   D. outside

<u>A</u> 10. **recollect**

    A. forget   C. plan

    B. forgive   D. wonder

Final Check

Read the passages carefully. Then fill in each blank with the word that best fits the context.

A. A Special Memory

A. **astonish**	B. **consent**	C. **eager**	D. **horizontal**	E. **recollect**

Tony and I often did things without asking our mom to (1)_____ consent _____ to our activities—because she probably wouldn't. Besides, we loved secret projects. One summer we built a treehouse hidden among some tall trees on Mr. Leary's lot. The window was crooked, and the floor wasn't exactly (2)_____ horizontal _____, although the tilt wasn't too bad. We took Mom's ladder to use as our stairs and decorated the place with an old rug and some pillows.

One day we heard Mom yelling up to us, "So that's where my ladder went!" Then she told us that Mr. Leary had called to say that the treehouse had to come down. "You could fall and get hurt," she explained, "and he doesn't want to get sued—and he's right. That treehouse is dangerous. I advise° you to come down from there right now."

But that night, (3)_____ eager _____ to spend one last hour there, Tony and I sneaked out and headed for the treehouse. As we got near it, we were (4)_____ astonish _____ed to see a candle glowing in the crooked window. So we climbed up very quietly and peeked in. I can still (5)_____ recollect _____ the scene clearly. There was Mom, sitting on one of our pillows, smiling. Next to her were a pitcher of lemonade and three glasses. "It's about time you got here," she said. "What took you so long?"

B. Watch Your Manners!

F. **abrupt**	G. **classify**	H. **complex**	I. **endure**	J. **exclaim**

Most of us think we know how to be polite when we're with other people. But some things that Americans (6)_____ classify _____ as good manners may seem rude in other parts of the world. Every culture has its own (7)_____ complex _____ set of rules about what is and isn't acceptable.

For example, an American who went to a birthday party in Japan brought the fun to an (8)_____ abrupt _____ end by giving a clock as a present. In Japan, giving anyone a clock is a way of saying "I hope your time is running out"—in other words, "I hope you die soon." Also, Americans in China are seen as bad-tempered when they (9)_____ exclaim _____ something loudly, out of excitement or to make a point. In China, a loud voice is a sign of strong anger.

Of course, foreign visitors to the United States can also misunderstand our ways. For instance, an Arab who was a guest at a banquet in Washington later complained, "I didn't get a thing to eat." Why had he been deprived° of food? It turned out he had said, "No, thank you," each time a new dish was offered. In his country, it was good manners to refuse food several times before accepting it. His American hosts didn't know that, so they just let the poor fellow (10)_____ endure _____ his hunger.

Scores	Check 2 _____%	Word Work _____%	Synonyms and Antonyms _____%	Final Check _____%

Enter your scores above and in the **Vocabulary Performance Chart** on the inside back cover of the book.

adequate	potential
appeal	respond
awkward	vanish
customary	variety
establish	wholesome

Ten Words in Context

In the space provided, write the letter of the meaning closest to that of each **boldfaced** word. Use the context of the sentences to help you figure out each word's meaning.

1 adequate
(ăd′ĭ-kwĭt)
- *adjective*

- When I didn't have time to wash the windows, I hired a neighbor's child to do it. He did an **adequate** job—not perfect, but good enough.
- Open sandals are not **adequate** footwear for factory work. Workers should wear heavy shoes to protect their feet.

A *Adequate* means   A. OK.   B. poor.   C. popular.

2 appeal
(ə-pēl′)
- *verb*

- Every year, charities such as the American Cancer Society and the March of Dimes **appeal** to us for money to help cure disease.
- When police can't solve a crime, they sometimes **appeal** to the public for help.

C *Appeal to* means   A. to answer.   B. to run.   C. to make a request.

3 awkward
(ôk′wərd)
- *adjective*

- When I was 13, I was very **awkward**. My feet seemed too big, and I was always tripping over things.
- On her first day of ballet class, Nina felt very **awkward** in comparison° to the graceful experienced dancers.

B *Awkward* means   A. not strong.   B. not graceful.   C. kind.

4 customary
(kŭs′tə-mĕr′ē)
- *adjective*

- In some towns, it's **customary** for the "Welcome Wagon" to visit newcomers and tell them about the town.
- Americans usually eat their big meal in the evening. In Ireland, however, it is **customary** to eat a big dinner in the afternoon and a light meal at night.

B *Customary* means   A. not polite.   B. normal.   C. rare.

5 establish
(ĭ-stăb′lĭsh)
- *verb*

- The first lending library was **established** in Scotland in 1725.
- Our town plans to **establish** a food bank where people can buy groceries for very little money.

C *Establish* means   A. to leave.   B. to stop.   C. to start.

6 potential
(pə-tĕn′shəl)
- *noun*

- My grandmother had the **potential** to be a great teacher, but she couldn't afford to go to college.
- Everyone agrees that Carlos has the **potential** to be a major-league baseball player. To become that good, he must continue to work hard.

C *Potential* means   A. request.   B. memory.   C. ability.

7 respond
(rĭ-spŏnd′)
- *verb*

- You asked me a question, so why don't you stop talking for a minute so that I can **respond**?
- When very little children talk on the telephone, they sometimes don't realize they have to say "yes" or "no" out loud. They think they can **respond** to a question by nodding or shaking their heads.

<u>A</u> *Respond* means   A. to reply.   B. to repeat.   C. to leave.

8 vanish
(văn′ĭsh)
- *verb*

- The magician made the rabbit **vanish** by slipping it under a secret door.
- You gave a stranger $500 in cash to paint your house? How do you know he won't **vanish** with the money?

<u>C</u> *Vanish* means   A. to answer.   B. to begin.   C. to go out of sight.

9 variety
(və-rī′ĭ-tē)
- *noun*

- In the spring, the woods contain a **variety** of wildflowers, including bluebells, daffodils, and violets.
- Instead of being a **variety** of colors, all of Gale's clothes were lavender or purple.

<u>A</u> *Variety* means   A. mixture.   B. absence.   C. shade.

10 wholesome
(hōl′səm)
- *adjective*

- The city residents are planning a community garden where they can grow their own fresh, **wholesome** fruits and vegetables.
- We now know smoking is not **wholesome**, but early cigarette ads claimed physical and mental benefits for smokers.

<u>C</u> *Wholesome* means   A. obvious.   B. expensive.   C. healthy.

Matching Words with Definitions

Following are definitions of the ten words. **Print** each word next to its definition. If you look closely at each word in context, you will be able to figure out its meaning.

1. _____establish_____ To bring into being; set up

2. _____appeal_____ To make an important request (to someone for something)

3. _____variety_____ A number of different kinds; assortment

4. _____wholesome_____ Tending to improve the character, the mind, or the body

5. _____respond_____ To answer, either by word or by action

6. _____adequate_____ Good enough (to meet the need)

7. _____customary_____ Usual; commonly done

8. _____vanish_____ To disappear from sight

9. _____awkward_____ Clumsy; not graceful

10. _____potential_____ A natural ability that may or may not develop; possibility

CAUTION: Do not go any further until you are sure the above answers are correct. Then you can use the definitions to help you in the following practices. Your goal is eventually to know the words well enough so that you don't need to check the definitions at all.

Check 1

Using the answer lines, complete each item below with the correct word from the box.

A. adequate	B. appeal	C. awkward	D. customary	E. establish
F. potential	G. respond	H. vanish	I. variety	J. wholesome

potential   1. An acorn has the ___ to be an oak tree.

vanish   2. I looked everywhere for my car keys, but they seem to have ___ed into thin air.

variety   3. Rodney has worked in a ___ of positions, including trucker, carpenter, and rancher.

appeal   4. The signs the children put up on telephone poles ___ed to people to help find their lost cat.

wholesome   5. Starting a day with exercise is more ___ than starting the day with a cigarette. Unlike cigarettes, exercise is good for us.

adequate   6. I'd love a huge apartment, but this small one is ___; it serves my needs.

establish   7. The American Girl Scouts were ___ed in 1912.

customary   8. People's habits can be referred to as their ___ behavior.

respond   9. When asked a question, we usually ___, even if it's only to say, "I don't know."

awkward   10. On land, crocodiles seem slow and ___. However, once they are in the water, they are fast and graceful swimmers.

NOTE: Now check your answers to these items by turning to page 239. Going over the answers carefully will help you prepare for the remaining practices, for which answers are not given.

Check 2

Using the answer lines, complete each item below with **two** words from the box. Use each word once.

establish
wholesome   1–2. Parents were happy when the Youth Club was ___ed in town because it gave their kids a ___ place to go, meet friends, and have fun.

variety
adequate   3–4. The ___ of fruits and vegetables at Fresh Foods is ___, but not as good as the selection at Grocery Giant.

appeal
potential   5–6. A talent agent ___ed to Christi's parents to let her appear in commercials. He thought Christi had the ___ to be a model and make a lot of money. However, her parents had an objection° to letting a ten-year-old work.

vanish
respond   7–8. In my dream, an old woman says, "Hurry! Come with me!" But I never go with her. She ___es before I have a chance to ___.

customary
awkward   9–10. It is ___ for people in Japan to bow to one another. When Fred visited that country, he bowed, too, even though he felt ___ doing it.

Word Work

A. Write each word next to the examples that best match it.

A. **appeal**	B. **awkward**	C. **customary**
D. **variety**	E. **wholesome**	

customary   1. Ice cream and cake at a birthday party
Saying "Bless you" when someone sneezes
Saying "Hello" when answering the phone

appeal   2. Ask people to become blood donors for the Red Cross
Seek new volunteers for the public library
Call upon the public to provide tips to help the police solve a crime

wholesome   3. A teen dance that is alcohol- and smoke-free
A bowl of shredded-wheat cereal, topped with a sliced banana and skim milk
A G-rated movie

awkward   4. Bumping into someone in the doorway
Tripping over your shoelace
Spilling your coffee

variety   5. Dogs: German shepherds, cocker spaniels, Italian bulldogs
Ice cream: strawberry, peach, butter pecan
Art supplies: crayons, markers, oil paints, watercolors

B. In the space provided, write the letter of the word that most closely relates to the situation in each item.

_A_   6. The Spanish-speaking students are going to set up their own Latino Club.

    A. establish   B. vanish   C. variety

_B_   7. The wading pool is big enough for the children to splash around and cool off, even if they can't really swim in it.

    A. vanish   B. adequate   C. respond

_C_   8. After hearing Tonya singing in the hallway, the music teacher said, "You ought to try out for chorus! You have a lovely voice."

    A. variety   B. awkward   C. potential

_A_   9. Jen taught her dog to obey whenever he hears her say, "Sit!"

    A. respond   B. various   C. vanish

_B_   10. The famous pilot Amelia Earhart took off on an around-the-world flight in the summer of 1937 and was never seen again.

    A. appealed   B. vanished   C. established

Word Parts

A. The prefix *re-* often means "again."

Examples: *analyze°* — to examine carefully   *utilize°* — to make use of
                 reanalyze — to examine carefully again   *reutilize* — to make use of again

On each answer line, write the word from the box that best completes the item.

A. reanalyze°	**B. reheat**	**C. relearn**
D. relocate	**E. reutilize°**	

_____reheat_____   1. When I get home late from work, I usually find some leftovers that I can ___ for dinner.

_____relearn_____   2. It is easier to ___ something that you once knew and forgot, than to learn something for the first time.

_____relocate_____   3. Mr. Amin did not give up when a highway was built where his store had once been. He decided to ___ his business in another part of town.

_____reanalyze_____   4. After finishing a difficult math problem, I often ___ it, just to be sure I have the correct answer.

_____reutilize_____   5. After I empty plastic bags from the supermarket, I ___ them. I may use them as storage bags or even bring them back to the supermarket to use there again.

B. The prefix *un-* often means "not." It can change words to their opposites.

Examples: *intentional°* — done on purpose   *stable* — steady
                 unintentional — not done on purpose; done by accident   *unstable°* — not steady

On each answer line, write the word from the box that best completes the item.

F. unintentional°	**G. uninterested**	**H. unlucky**
I. unstable°	**J. unwholesome**	

_____uninterested_____   6. Leslie is so ___ in the current° television shows that she canceled her cable service. She now uses her TV only to watch rented movies.

_____unwholesome_____   7. Many people eat an ___ diet, filled with fried foods, fatty meats, and sugar, and lacking in vegetables and grains.

_____unintentional_____   8. "Oh, I'm sorry," said the man who bumped into me. "That was ___."

_____unlucky_____   9. Many people believe the number thirteen is ___. Some hotels won't even give a room that number.

_____unstable_____   10. Our strangely shaped dining-room chairs are so ___ that several people have fallen out of them.

Final Check

Read the passages carefully. Then fill in each blank with the word that best fits the context.

A. Big Brothers and Sisters

| A. **appeal** | B. **establish** | C. **potential** | D. **variety** | E. **wholesome** |

This week, the local Big Brother/Big Sister Agency (1)_____*appeal*_____ed to the community for volunteers. The organization is looking for men and women who are willing to (2)_____*establish*_____ a new friendship with a young boy or girl from a single-parent home. The principal° requirement for becoming a volunteer is the desire to become friends with the children—by helping them stay in school, and by choosing (3)_____*wholesome*_____ activities that will keep them out of trouble. Volunteers can do a (4)_____*variety*_____ of things with their little "brothers" or "sisters," such as taking them to the park or going out to eat. Whatever activities they choose, volunteers will play an important part in the children's lives, helping them to build their (5)_____*potential*_____ to live full lives and become good citizens.

B. Kevin's First Date

| F. **adequate** | G. **awkward** | H. **customary** | I. **respond** | J. **vanish** |

If you ask Kevin what the most embarrassing time of his life was, he will surely tell you about his first date, which was for an eighth-grade dance. He was so afraid of rejection° when he asked the girl to go with him that he almost didn't notice when she consented° to be his date.

The day of the dance was no better. Between the time he rang her doorbell and the time her father answered, he forgot his date's name—completely. He mumbled something about school (he did remember the school's name), and the girl's father let him in. The man then fired some questions at Kevin, to make sure he was an (6)_____*adequate*_____ date for his darling daughter. Kevin could barely (7)_____*respond*_____ to the questions because his nervous thirteen-year-old voice squeaked and cracked so much.

Since it was (8)_____*customary*_____ for boys to bring a corsage of flowers on this special occasion, Kevin had done so. But when his date came down the stairs in a pale pink gown and he opened the florist's box, he became even more nervous. Inside was an excessively° large flower in a bright orange color that didn't go at all with the pink dress. As he pinned the giant blossom onto the gown, he made an (9)_____*awkward*_____ movement, stuck his finger, and bled—onto the dress. The girl was so astonished° that her mouth fell open. He wanted to (10)_____*vanish*_____ from the face of the earth and never be seen again. He even considered transferring to another school. As it was, he developed such a poor attitude° about dating that he didn't ask another girl out for the next two years.

| Scores | Check 2 _____% | Word Work _____% | Word Parts _____% | Final Check _____% |

Enter your scores above and in the **Vocabulary Performance Chart** on the inside back cover of the book.

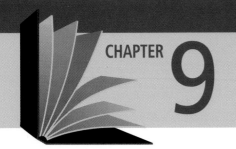

brutal	interpret
discipline	propose
eliminate	resort
emphasis	ultimate
furthermore	vague

Ten Words in Context

In the space provided, write the letter of the meaning closest to that of each **boldfaced** word. Use the context of the sentences to help you figure out each word's meaning.

1 brutal
(broot′l)
- *adjective*

- Justine's method of breaking up with her boyfriend was **brutal**. She texted him "I'm dumping you" while he was in the middle of taking a final exam.
- In the movie, the actor played a **brutal** criminal. In real life, however, he is a very kind and gentle man.

_C_ *Brutal* means   A. youthful.   B. hardly ever seen.   C. mean.

2 discipline
(dĭs′ə-plĭn)
- *verb*

- The ballplayer was put out of the game for bumping an umpire. He was also **disciplined** with a $10,000 fine.
- José wanted to teach his children to be nonviolent, so he **disciplined** them in gentle ways, such as sending them to their rooms for some quiet "time out."

_A_ *Discipline* means   A. to punish.   B. to leave.   C. to turn to for help.

3 eliminate
(ĭ-lĭm′ə-nāt′)
- *verb*

- If you hang up clothes right after the dryer stops, you can **eliminate** the need to iron many items.
- Because my father has high blood pressure, he's supposed to **eliminate** salt from his diet.

_B_ *Eliminate* means   A. to add to.   B. to remove.   C. to repeat.

4 emphasis
(ĕm′fə-sĭs)
- *noun*

- Brad's father placed a lot of **emphasis** on his son's doing well in sports but gave little attention to how Brad did in his schoolwork.
- In my Spanish class, too much **emphasis** was given to reading and not enough to speaking.

_C_ *Emphasis* means   A. delay.   B. addition.   C. importance.

5 furthermore
(fûr′thər-môr′)
- *adverb*

- "I don't believe your story about a flat tire," said Hal's boss. "And **furthermore**, I haven't believed any of your other excuses for being late."
- The Lakers will probably win because they are a talented team. **Furthermore**, they are coached well.

_C_ *Furthermore* means   A. instead.   B. later.   C. also.

6 interpret
(ĭn-tûr′prĭt)
- *verb*

- After Tarik had a dental x-ray, the dentist sat down with him to **interpret** it.
- How should I **interpret** the fact that although we were friendly yesterday, Jean refused to speak to me today?

_A_ *Interpret* means   A. to explain.   B. to suggest.   C. to discover.

7 propose
(prə-pōz′)
- *verb*

- Our little brother **proposed** buying our parents a puppy for Christmas this year, but instead we decided to give them a coffee grinder.
- Rafael was obviously too tired to study, so his mother **proposed** that he take a nap and get back to work later.

<u>C</u> *Propose* means   A. to predict.   B. to remember.   C. to suggest.

8 resort
(rĭ-zôrt′)
- *verb*

- After I'd cooked some spaghetti, I realized I didn't have any spaghetti sauce, so I **resorted** to eating it with ketchup.
- Although school was hard for Ray, he never **resorted** to cheating.

<u>C</u> *Resort to* means   A. to explain.   B. to forget about.   C. to turn to.

9 ultimate
(ŭl′tə-mĭt)
- *adjective*

- Chocolate ice cream filled with chocolate chips and topped with fudge sauce—for a chocolate-lover like me, that is the **ultimate** dessert.
- Saying they learned a lot in class is the **ultimate** compliment students can pay to a teacher.

<u>A</u> *Ultimate* means   A. greatest.   B. most interesting.   C. unknown.

10 vague
(vāg)
- *adjective*

- On the essay test, give detailed answers, not **vague** ones.
- Ben had only a **vague** idea of what yeast was. He knew it was used to make bread, but he wasn't sure what it did.

<u>A</u> *Vague* means   A. general.   B. curious.   C. wrong.

Matching Words with Definitions

Following are definitions of the ten words. **Print** each word next to its definition. If you look closely at each word in context, you will be able to figure out its meaning.

1. _____vague_____ Not clear; not exact; not definite

2. _____propose_____ To put forward for thinking over or accepting; suggest (an idea)

3. _____discipline_____ To punish; cause to suffer for doing something wrong

4. _____resort_____ To turn or go (to) for help; use for aid

5. _____brutal_____ Cruel; heartless

6. _____emphasis_____ Special attention; importance given to something

7. _____furthermore_____ In addition; besides

8. _____eliminate_____ To get rid of; do away with

9. _____interpret_____ To explain the meaning of; make sense of

10. _____ultimate_____ Greatest; highest possible

CAUTION: Do not go any further until you are sure the above answers are correct. Then you can use the definitions to help you in the following practices. Your goal is eventually to know the words well enough so that you don't need to check the definitions at all.

Check 1

Using the answer lines, complete each item below with the correct word from the box.

| A. **brutal** | B. **discipline** | C. **eliminate** | D. **emphasis** | E. **furthermore** |
| F. **interpret** | G. **propose** | H. **resort** | I. **ultimate** | J. **vague** |

discipline   1. Ms. Ramirez took her son's Wii game away for a week to ___ him after he lied to her.

ultimate   2. Your ___ goal is the highest one you hope to reach.

resort   3. When my grandmother can't think of a word in English, she ___s to saying it in Spanish.

vague   4. "When I ask my children where they're going," Sheila said, "I don't accept ___ answers. I want to know exactly where they'll be."

interpret   5. Since I didn't understand the results of my blood test, the doctor ___ed them for me.

propose   6. We encourage our children to ___ weekend activities in which the whole family can participate.

eliminate   7. People take aspirin to ___ headaches.

furthermore   8. One way to introduce an additional point is with the word "___."

emphasis   9. Your boss will put the greatest ___ on the project he or she considers most important.

brutal   10. Someone without mercy can be ___.

NOTE: Now check your answers to these items by turning to page 240. Going over the answers carefully will help you prepare for the remaining practices, for which answers are not given.

Check 2

Using the answer lines, complete each item below with **two** words from the box. Use each word once.

vague
Furthermore   1–2. "Your answers were too ___," said the teacher. "You should have made them more clear by adding details. ___, you skipped several questions."

resort
discipline   3–4. "I don't want to ___ to sending you to jail," the judge told the young lawbreaker. "Instead, I'm going to ___ you by making you do volunteer work for six weeks."

ultimate
eliminate   5–6. Liz has cut down her smoking to only three cigarettes a day, but her ___ goal is to ___ smoking from her life.

emphasis
interpret   7–8. Chu's parents had never seen an American-style report card before, so when Chu's teacher met with them, her ___ was on helping them ___ what it said.

propose

brutal

9–10. Gail ___d that we go to the movies instead of attending a boxing match because she feels that boxing is a ___ sport.

Word Work

A. In the space provided, write the letter of the word that most closely relates to the situation in each item.

__C__ 1. When I asked a passerby for directions to the post office, she pointed somewhere behind me and said, "It's over there a couple of blocks."

    A. brutal   B. discipline   C. vague

__B__ 2. Jamila hired an accountant to explain her tax forms to her.

    A. discipline   B. interpret   C. propose

__B__ 3. A citizens' group will present their idea for a community playground to the town council.

    A. emphasis   B. propose   C. eliminate

__C__ 4. The documentary contains scenes of extremely cruel, violent behavior towards animals.

    A. furthermore   B. interpret   C. brutal

__A__ 5. Because she came in so late last night, Sharon isn't allowed to go out in the evening for two weeks.

    A. discipline   B. eliminate   C. resort

B. In the space provided, write the letter of the choice that best completes each item.

__C__ 6. The **ultimate** power in a kingdom belongs to

    A. the weak.   B. the poor.   C. the king.

__B__ 7. To give **emphasis** to their words, people often

    A. stutter.   B. speak more loudly.   C. are cruel.

__C__ 8. The word **furthermore** can be useful when you want to

    A. repeat yourself.   B. change your mind.   C. add something to what you've already said.

__C__ 9. Politicians sometimes say they want to **eliminate**

    A. voters.   B. schools.   C. hunger.

__A__ 10. Many people **resort** to the personal ads for dates. They must believe that the ads are

    A. helpful.   B. harmful.   C. useless.

Synonyms and Antonyms

A. Synonyms. Write the letter of the word or phrase that most nearly means the **same** as each boldfaced word.

_D_ 1. **emphasis**

    A. flavor   C. laughter

    B. memory   D. importance

_C_ 2. **furthermore**

    A. on the other hand   C. also

    B. for instance   D. instead

_D_ 3. **interpret**

    A. punish   C. resist

    B. memorize   D. explain

_A_ 4. **propose**

    A. suggest   C. lie

    B. deny   D. pretend

_A_ 5. **resort to**

    A. turn to   C. suggest

    B. avoid   D. talk about

B. Antonyms. Write the letter of the word or phrase that most nearly means the **opposite** of each boldfaced word.

_B_ 6. **brutal**

    A. firm   C. quiet

    B. kindly   D. small

_C_ 7. **discipline**

    A. greet   C. reward

    B. interrupt   D. drop

_D_ 8. **eliminate**

    A. ignore   C. refuse

    B. hang around   D. keep

_A_ 9. **ultimate**

    A. least important   C. clear

    B. most difficult   D. medium

_B_ 10. **vague**

    A. needed   C. trusted

    B. exact   D. loud

Final Check

Read the passages carefully. Then fill in each blank with the word that best fits the context.

A. Differences in a Gym Program

| A. **emphasis** | B. **interpret** | C. **propose** | D. **ultimate** | E. **vague** |

Last spring, some parents spoke to the school board about the gym program at Walnut Street School. The parents pointed out the contrast° in programs offered to boys and girls. The boys were taught a variety° of active sports and given good equipment. They had the chance to join several teams. For girls, however, the (1)_____emphasis_____ in gym was on dancing and exercise. They had no teams and only a minimum° amount of equipment.

Why were there such big differences between the two programs? The school district's rules about physical education were (2)_____vague_____. Since they didn't say exactly what should be taught, each school (3)_____interpret_____ed the rules in its own way.

The parents (4)_____propose_____d allowing both boys and girls to use all the gym equipment at the school. And they appealed° to the school board for some sports teams to be organized for the girls. They pointed out that girls have as much potential° in sports and as much need for physical fitness as boys do. Their (5)_____ultimate_____ goal was to give all the children an equal gym experience.

B. Through a Child's Eyes

| F. **brutal** | G. **discipline** | H. **eliminate** | I. **furthermore** | J. **resort** |

Babysitting for my five-year-old nephew makes me see things in different ways. For example, last Saturday evening, I was watching an exciting action movie while he played in his room. But then he walked in and began to watch it, too. Suddenly I began to see the movie through his eyes. Instead of exciting, the movie's action seemed cruel and (6)_____brutal_____. The characters were doing things I'd never want him to (7)_____resort_____ to. They frequently demonstrated° selfish, cold-hearted behavior. (8)_____Furthermore_____, I'd certainly (9)_____discipline_____ him if he ever used language like theirs. Now, before I choose a movie to take to his house, I (10)_____eliminate_____ ones that contain violence and bad language. I'm willing to deprive° myself of a few movies in order to set a better example for him.

| Scores   Check 2 _____% | Word Work _____% | Synonyms and Antonyms _____% | Final Check _____% |

Enter your scores above and in the **Vocabulary Performance Chart** on the inside back cover of the book.

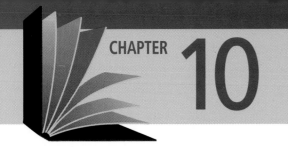

accustomed	occur
anticipate	particular
linger	reluctant
miserable	revise
misinterpret	version

Ten Words in Context

In the space provided, write the letter of the meaning closest to that of each **boldfaced** word. Use the context of the sentences to help you figure out each word's meaning.

1 accustomed
(ə-kŭs′təmd)
- *adjective*

- Although my grandfather was **accustomed** to sucking a sugar cube while he drank tea, the sugar never seemed to harm his teeth.
- After years of living in sunny Puerto Rico, Alma had trouble becoming **accustomed** to the snowy Minnesota weather.

_C_ *Accustomed to* means   A. uncomfortable with.   B. shocked by.   C. used to.

2 anticipate
(ăn-tĭs′ə-pāt′)
- *verb*

- Lee **anticipated** heavy traffic this morning, so he left for work an hour early.
- Because we **anticipated** a snowstorm, we bought extra groceries in case we couldn't get to the store for several days.

_C_ *Anticipate* means   A. to doubt.   B. to enjoy.   C. to think likely to happen.

3 linger
(lĭng′gər)
- *verb*

- My father has difficulty leaving any social event. He likes to **linger** by the door, chatting on and on with our hosts.
- After the bowling matches are over, we usually **linger** for a while to talk to our friends on the other teams.

_B_ *Linger* means   A. to stare.   B. to stay.   C. to expect.

4 miserable
(mĭz′ər-ə-bəl)
- *adjective*

- The Farrells were **miserable** on their camping trip because the green flies wouldn't stop biting them.
- Gino is sure to be **miserable** during the allergy season if he doesn't get shots.

_A_ *Miserable* means   A. very uncomfortable.   B. not proper.   C. rested.

5 misinterpret
(mĭs′ĭn-tûr′prĭt)
- *verb*

- "Tomorrow, each of you should bring in one interesting fact about Greece," the teacher said. One student **misinterpreted** her instructions and complained, "But I can't think of anything interesting about grease."
- It's clear that Jay **misinterpreted** his wife's request. He brought her flowers for a vase instead of flour for a cake.

_C_ *Misinterpret* means   A. to want.   B. to cause.   C. to understand wrongly.

6 occur
(ə-kûr′)
- *verb*

- A robbery **occurred** at the restaurant just minutes after we left.
- The first moonwalk **occurred** on July 20th, 1969, after Neil Armstrong stepped on the moon and said, "That's one small step for a man, one giant leap for mankind."

_C_ *Occur* means   A. to find.   B. to disappear.   C. to happen.

7 particular
(pər-tĭk′yə-lər)
- *adjective*

● The girl I baby-sit for has dozens of games and toys, but she insists on playing one **particular** game over and over.

● Richie didn't care where he and Elsa ate dinner, but she had a **particular** restaurant in mind, the Mexican restaurant on Fifth Street.

<u>C</u> *Particular* means   A. daily.   B. rare.   C. special.

8 reluctant
(rĭ-lŭk′tənt)
- *adjective*

● Since we're **reluctant** to have people know our phone number, we keep it unlisted.

● Although the lawyer was **reluctant** to tell his client disappointing news, he had no choice but to do so.

<u>B</u> *Reluctant* means   A. known.   B. unwilling.   C. excited.

9 revise
(rĭ-vīz′)
- *verb*

● Don't just write a paper once and hand it in. It's important to **revise** what you write until your paper is in good shape.

● Recent price increases for lumber have made it necessary for carpenters to **revise** their construction charges.

<u>B</u> *Revise* means   A. to remember.   B. to make changes in.   C. to ignore.

10 version
(vûr′zhən)
- *noun*

● The play *West Side Story* is a modern musical **version** of Shakespeare's *Romeo and Juliet*.

● There have been at least six movies about Frankenstein's monster, but the best is still the 1931 **version**, starring Boris Karloff.

<u>A</u> *Version* means   A. retelling.   B. suggestion.   C. correction.

Matching Words with Definitions

Following are definitions of the ten words. **Print** each word next to its definition. If you look closely at each word in context, you will be able to figure out its meaning.

1. _____accustomed_____   In the habit of; used to

2. _____reluctant_____   Unwilling; wanting not to do something

3. _____particular_____   Specific; separate and distinct; single

4. _____linger_____   To delay leaving; remain, especially as if unwilling to leave

5. _____miserable_____   Very unhappy or uncomfortable

6. _____anticipate_____   To expect; foresee

7. _____misinterpret_____   To understand incorrectly

8. _____version_____   One form of a basic story, song, or program

9. _____occur_____   To happen; take place

10. _____revise_____   To change in order to improve or to include new information

CAUTION: Do not go any further until you are sure the above answers are correct. Then you can use the definitions to help you in the following practices. Your goal is eventually to know the words well enough so that you don't need to check the definitions at all.

Check 1

Using the answer lines, complete each item below with the correct word from the box.

| A. **accustomed** | B. **anticipate** | C. **linger** | D. **miserable** | E. **misinterpret** |
| F. **occur** | G. **particular** | H. **reluctant** | I. **revise** | J. **version** |

_____linger_____ 1. Could you ___ for a few minutes after the meeting so I can talk privately to you?

_____anticipate_____ 2. We ___ about forty guests at our New Year's Eve party, but we're preparing food for fifty, just in case.

_____occur_____ 3. It's about time the city put up a stop sign at that corner. An accident ___s there every month or two.

_____reluctant_____ 4. Although the apartment met our needs, we were ___ to sign a long-term lease.

_____version_____ 5. Mr. Zarria's favorite magazine is the Spanish-language ___ of *Reader's Digest*.

_____particular_____ 6. When we put out a fresh bowl of jelly beans at home, one ___ kind is gone within a day. My brother eats every red one.

_____miserable_____ 7. After our dog was run over by a car, the whole family felt ___ for weeks.

_____accustomed_____ 8. For someone brought up in a warm climate, it may take time to become ___ to cold weather.

_____misinterpret_____ 9. Another word for "misunderstand" is "___."

_____revise_____ 10. Before we present our play to the third-grade class, we will ___ it so it is easier for young children to understand.

NOTE: Now check your answers to these items by turning to page 240. Going over the answers carefully will help you prepare for the remaining practices, for which answers are not given.

Check 2

Using the answer lines, complete each item below with **two** words from the box. Use each word once.

_____accustomed_____
_____misinterpret_____ 1–2. When I was in Mexico, I became ___ to having people ___ what I said because I speak Spanish so poorly.

_____anticipate_____
_____linger_____ 3–4. Joanne ___d having a boring afternoon at work, so she ___ed in the restaurant to make lunch last as long as possible. She was not at all eager° to return to the office.

_____version_____
_____particular_____ 5–6. I love my mom's ___ of chocolate chip cookies because of one ___ ingredient she adds: pecans.

_____miserable_____
_____occur_____ 7–8. No one hates arguments more than Martin; he becomes ___ whenever they ___. Unfortunately, in his household, disputes° are abundant°.

_____reluctant_____
_____revise_____ 9–10. I am ___ to show you my story until I've had a chance to ___ it. It needs considerable° changing before it will be ready for you to read.

Word Work

A. In the space provided, write the letter of the choice that best completes each item.

___B___ 1. Today you are likely to **anticipate**
   A. your birthday party last year.
   B. a phone call your friend promised to make.
   C. an argument you had yesterday.

___B___ 2. The person who is most likely to **linger** is
   A. a friend who is in a rush.
   B. a guest at a luncheon.
   C. a person about to get off a bus.

___B___ 3. A student might **revise** a paper that
   A. seems perfect.
   B. is too long.
   C. has been handed in to the teacher.

___C___ 4. A very **particular** writing assignment would be:
   A. Write a description.
   B. Write about someone you know.
   C. Write a physical description of your oldest living relative.

___A___ 5. Most people are **accustomed** to living
   A. in their houses.   B. in the future.   C. at the South Pole.

B. In the space provided, write the letter of the word that most closely relates to the situation in each item.

___B___ 6. A strange and wonderful event always happens to me in January.
   A. lingers   B. occurs   C. miserable

___C___ 7. A friend says, "Catch you later," but you think he says, "That's our waiter."
   A. anticipate   B. linger   C. misinterpret

___A___ 8. Earthquake survivors huddle in the rain, with their houses destroyed and nowhere to go.
   A. miserable   B. revise   C. particular

___C___ 9. You know you should visit Great-Uncle Lem over the holidays, but he makes you watch hours of his boring home movies, and you really don't want to go.
   A. accustomed   B. version   C. reluctant

___B___ 10. After the students read the novel *The Grapes of Wrath*, they watched the movie of the same name.
   A. linger   B. version   C. reluctant

Analogies

Each item below starts with a pair of words in CAPITAL LETTERS. For each item, figure out the relationship between these two words. Then decide which of the choices (A, B, C, or D) expresses a similar relationship. Write the letter of your choice on the answer line. (All the repeated words in these items are from this unit.)

_A_ 1. RELUCTANT : WILLING ::

    A. brutal : kind   C. anger : argument
    B. rapid : fast   D. shy : quiet

_C_ 2. MISERABLE : HAPPY ::

    A. awkward° : clumsy   C. current° : old-fashioned
    B. bright : shining   D. famous : brave

_C_ 3. LINGER : REMAIN ::

    A. purposely : accidentally   C. fix : repair
    B. complex° : simple   D. wait : depart

_D_ 4. ANTICIPATE : EXPECT ::

    A. recollect° : forget   C. explain : understand
    B. cause : effect   D. smash : break

_B_ 5. PARTICULAR : GENERAL ::

    A. unfamiliar : nervous   C. shy : quiet
    B. eager° : unwilling   D. bees : honey

_B_ 6. OCCUR : HAPPEN ::

    A. run : walk   C. shout : whisper
    B. vanish° : disappear   D. vague° : particular°

_D_ 7. REVISE : MISTAKE ::

    A. discipline° : punishment   C. sing : book
    B. write : print   D. eliminate° : error

_D_ 8. OBJECTION° : APPROVAL ::

    A. doctor : illness   C. emphasis : importance
    B. night : moon   D. argument : agreement

_A_ 9. MISINTERPRET : MISUNDERSTAND ::

    A. penalize° : punish   C. agree : disagree
    B. expect : surprise   D. discipline° : reward

_B_ 10. RECOLLECT° : EVENT ::

    A. question : answer   C. walk : exercise
    B. interpret° : message   D. establish° : destroy

Final Check

Read the passages carefully. Then fill in each blank with the word that best fits the context.

A. Knowing How to Argue

A. **linger**	B. **misinterpret**	C. **occur**	D. **particular**	E. **reluctant**

Ron and Marlene have a great marriage, and I think one reason is that they know how to argue. Many couples think arguing is bad, but I think they (1)_____*misinterpret*_____ what arguing really is. It can be a good way to settle all kinds of problems. When couples are (2)_____*reluctant*_____ to argue, they may not solve their problems, and their angry feelings can (3)_____*linger*_____ for a long time. Ron and Marlene don't hesitate° to argue and get it over with. What's good about the way they argue is that they talk only about the (4)_____*particular*_____ thing that made them angry. For example, if Marlene is angry that Ron isn't doing his share of the housework, that is all she talks about. She doesn't throw in, "And furthermore°, that new friend of yours from work is obnoxious°!" Knowing Ron and Marlene has taught me that arguments (5)_____*occur*_____ in even the best marriages, and that they can make a good relationship stronger.

B. A Change of School, A Change of Heart

F. **accustomed**	G. **anticipate**	H. **miserable**	I. **revise**	J. **version**

Matt and his family were moving, and Matt hated the whole idea. He had lived in Centerville his entire life and had always gone to school with the same group of friends. He had (6)_____*anticipate*_____d graduating from Centerville High School and then going to Centerville Community College. Now he would have to make an abrupt° change and (7)_____*revise*_____ his whole plan for the future, and he didn't like it a bit. "How can I ever become (8)_____*accustomed*_____ to a new school?" he asked his parents. "Everyone will already know each other. I'll be solitary°—I'll have no friends."

At first, it seemed that Matt was right. At his new high school, he walked around alone, not smiling or talking to anyone. Finally a friendly teacher advised° him to improve his attitude°. "I know you're feeling lonely and (9)_____*miserable*_____," he said. "But you look as though you hate this school and everyone in it. If you'll look a little friendlier, you will find new friends here." Matt decided to try. He began to talk to his classmates and take part in class. He even helped write a funny (10)_____*version*_____ of *Cinderella* that his Spanish class performed for the rest of the school. By January, Matt was able to tell his parents that he was starting to feel at home in his new school.

Scores	Check 2 _____%	Word Work _____%	Analogies _____%	Final Check _____%

*Enter your scores above and in the **Vocabulary Performance Chart** on the inside back cover of the book.*

The box at the right lists twenty-five words from Unit Two. Using the clues at the bottom of the page, fill in these words to complete the puzzle that follows.

Word Box:
- abrupt
- advise
- astonish
- awkward
- brutal
- consent
- current
- deprive
- eager
- eliminate
- endure
- establish
- linger
- miserable
- objection
- occur
- particular
- potential
- reliable
- resort
- revise
- ultimate
- vague
- vanish
- variety

ACROSS

2. Sudden and unexpected
5. Looking forward to with great interest or desire
7. To surprise greatly; amaze
8. Modern; existing now; in general use or practice today
11. To give advice to; recommend
13. To put up with; bear impatiently
15. Separate and distinct; single
17. To happen; take place
20. To bring into being; set up
21. A dislike; feeling of being against something
22. To delay leaving; remain
23. Able to be depended upon

DOWN

1. A number of different kinds; assortment
3. Cruel; heartless
4. To get rid of; do away with
6. To take away from; keep from having or enjoying
7. Clumsy; not graceful
8. To agree to something
9. Very unhappy or uncomfortable
10. A natural ability that may or may not develop; possibility
12. Not clear; not exact; not definite
14. Greatest; highest possible
16. To turn or go to for help; use for aid
18. To change in order to improve or to include new information
19. To disappear from sight

78

PART A

Choose the word that best completes each item and write it in the space provided.

_____penalize_____   1. My parents used to ___ me for misbehaving at the supper table by making me sit on the stairs, where I could hear the conversation but not take part in it.

     A. interpret   B. penalize   C. revise   D. originate

_____originated_____   2. It has been said that the practice of drinking tea ___ in China thousands of years ago when some tea leaves accidentally fell into a pot of boiling water.

     A. originated   B. misinterpreted   C. vanished   D. recollected

_____minimum_____   3. That restaurant doesn't accept reservations for small groups. The ___ number of people in your party must be five.

     A. vague   B. complex   C. current   D. minimum

_____hesitates_____   4. A beginning typist ___ often, while an experienced typist hits the keys rapidly.

     A. advises   B. hesitates   C. occurs   D. endures

_____advise_____   5. My sister-in-law knows a lot about high-definition TV sets, so I've asked her to ___ me as I decide which one to buy.

     A. exclaim   B. deprive   C. recollect   D. advise

_____maintain_____   6. I try to ___ my friendship with Sarah, but it's difficult to keep a relationship going when we're separated by so many miles.

     A. maintain   B. revise   C. respond   D. deprive

_____current_____   7. It used to be taught in schools that George Washington cut down a cherry tree with an ax and then confessed the deed to his father. However, ___ thinking is that the story was invented after Washington died.

     A. horizontal   B. reluctant   C. current   D. vague

_____objection_____   8. Garlic is delicious, but one ___ many people have to it is the way it makes their breath smell.

     A. objection   B. potential   C. version   D. variety

_____deprive_____   9. Don't put the houseplant in that dark corner. It will die if you ___ it of sunlight.

     A. resort   B. endure   C. propose   D. deprive

_____reliable_____   10. Although Leon's car is old, it is still ___; it gets him to work every day.

     A. abrupt   B. reliable   C. miserable   D. ultimate

(Continues on next page)

horizontal   11. We stared at the long brownish ___ thing floating in the river, wondering if it was a log or an alligator.

   A. horizontal   B. accustomed   C. adequate   D. wholesome

proposed   12. At the town meeting, several people had ideas about what to do with the empty supermarket building. One woman ___ that it be turned into a skating rink.

   A. vanished   B. resorted   C. endured   D. proposed

wholesome   13. Playing outdoors for hours is more ___ than watching TV for hours.

   A. reluctant   B. awkward   C. eager   D. wholesome

PART B

Write **C** if the italicized word is used **correctly**. Write **I** if the word is used **incorrectly**.

__I__   14. "To *misinterpret* my instructions," said the teacher, "listen carefully."

__I__   15. The famous ballet dancer is *awkward*; he moves so lightly his feet never seem to touch the ground.

__C__   16. It was *customary* for people to smile at each other in Laura's small town. Although she now lives in a large city, she still smiles at every stranger that she passes.

__C__   17. I think it is *brutal* to keep chickens in crowded conditions and then cut off their beaks to keep them from pecking one another.

__I__   18. If you want to gain weight, you can *eliminate* more calories in your diet by eating lots of junk food and big desserts.

__C__   19. I'm so *accustomed* to living near the fire department that whenever a siren goes off, I hardly notice.

__I__   20. The angry diner called the restaurant manager and complained that her meal had been cold, *adequate*, and too expensive.

__I__   21. Many people in town were angry when the beautiful old courthouse was *established* in order to make room for an ugly, new shopping center.

__C__   22. The directions Kim gave me to the new apartment were so *vague* that I got very mixed up on my way there.

__C__   23. Because her husband was sick and couldn't work, Corinne *appealed* to their landlady for extra time to pay the rent.

__I__   24. The *ultimate* job in a successful business career would be running errands in a large office.

__C__   25. Our store is well thought of because we put an *emphasis* on pleasing customers rather than on making as many sales as possible.

Score   (Number correct) _____ x 4 = _____%

Enter your score above and in the **Vocabulary Performance Chart** on the inside back cover of the book.

PART A

On the answer line, write the word from the box that completes each item below. Use each word once.

A. abrupt	B. anticipate	C. classify	D. consent	E. discipline
F. exclaim	G. particular	H. potential	I. recollect	J. resort
K. revise	L. vanish	M. variety		

potential   1. Every time Robert takes a girl out, he thinks about whether she has the ___ to be a good wife.

vanish   2. Wouldn't it be wonderful if dirt ___ed as easily and completely in real life as it does in the soap ads?

variety   3. The Four Corners of the World restaurant offers dishes from a ___ of countries, including France, Vietnam, Ethiopia, and Brazil.

discipline   4. To ___ him for writing on the wall of a school bathroom, the principal made Mike paint every bathroom on that floor.

resort   5. Although Ed has a hot temper, I don't think he would ever ___ to violence.

anticipate   6. Because we had ___d eight people for dinner, we were surprised when twelve showed up.

revise   7. Ronald always shows his short stories to his wife. Then he ___s them after listening to her comments.

particular   8. When I ask, "What do you need from the grocery store?" it's not helpful to say "Everything." Make me a list of the ___ items you need.

abrupt   9. The picnic came to an ___ end when a sudden thunderstorm seemed to come out of nowhere.

classify   10. In high school, students often ___ one another as belonging to an in-group or an out-group.

consent   11. "I will ___ to your getting a puppy," Mrs. Anders told her children, "if you promise that you will take care of walking, feeding, bathing, and housetraining it."

exclaim   12. Sandra didn't want to hurt her boyfriend's feelings when she unwrapped the ugly orange sweater he had bought her, so she ___ed, "Wow, it's so colorful!"

recollect   13. I was very tired last night. Although I ___ that I spoke with John, I can't remember what either of us said.

(Continues on next page)

PART B

Write C if the italicized word is used **correctly**. Write **I** if the word is used **incorrectly**.

_C_   14. When the man shook hands with the child and said, "How do you do?" the child *responded*, "How do I do **what**?"

_I_   15. Bart was sad when his best friend moved *furthermore* from his house.

_C_   16. It was fun to go to my first soccer game with Franco. He knows the sport so well that he could *interpret* everything that was happening on the field.

_I_   17. Ved didn't seem to enjoy the party. He *lingered* before most of the other guests had even shown up.

_I_   18. The students were *miserable* when their teacher said, "It's such a beautiful day. Let's forget about the math test and go outside to play softball."

_C_   19. Christmas and New Year's Eve are two holidays that *occur* in December.

_I_   20. Naturally, most people are *reluctant* to win an all-expenses-paid vacation.

_C_   21. Which *version* of The Wizard of Oz did you like better, the movie with Judy Garland or the one with Diana Ross?

_I_   22. The speaker *astonished* the audience by opening his speech with, "Good evening, ladies and gentlemen."

_C_   23. Because the novel is so *complex*, it begins with a chart that lists all the characters and shows how they are related to one another.

_C_   24. To get through exam week, I had to *endure* several nights without much sleep.

_C_   25. After hiking for miles with nothing to eat, the friends were *eager* for dinner.

Score   (Number correct) _____ x 4 = _____%

Enter your score above and in the **Vocabulary Performance Chart** on the inside back cover of the book.

PART A: Synonyms

In the space provided, write the letter of the choice that is most nearly the **same** in meaning as the **boldfaced** word.

A   1. **advise**   A. suggest   B. expect   C. praise   D. forget

D   2. **anticipate**   A. put up with   B. remember   C. dislike   D. expect

A   3. **appeal to**   A. ask   B. add to   C. disappear   D. explain

B   4. **astonish**   A. continue   B. surprise   C. refuse   D. begin

B   5. **classify**   A. praise   B. arrange by type   C. begin   D. put up with

C   6. **deprive**   A. suggest   B. turn to   C. take from   D. forget

A   7. **discipline**   A. punish   B. raise up   C. continue   D. happen

B   8. **eliminate**   A. add to   B. get rid of   C. disappear   D. make more difficult

B   9. **emphasis**   A. least   B. importance   C. retelling   D. possibility

C   10. **endure**   A. punish   B. demand   C. put up with   D. explain

B   11. **establish**   A. remain   B. start   C. turn to   D. suggest

C   12. **furthermore**   A. instead   B. later   C. in addition   D. by the way

A   13. **interpret**   A. explain   B. depend on   C. suggest   D. change

B   14. **maintain**   A. begin   B. continue   C. give up on   D. cry out

A   15. **misinterpret**   A. understand wrongly   B. argue   C. depend on   D. surprise

C   16. **occur**   A. begin   B. put off   C. take place   D. remember

C   17. **particular**   A. common   B. least   C. specific   D. important

C   18. **potential**   A. memory   B. feeling   C. possibility   D. number

D   19. **propose**   A. wait   B. make worse   C. agree   D. suggest

A   20. **resort to**   A. turn to   B. give away   C. accept as true   D. refuse

B   21. **respond**   A. disappear   B. answer   C. surprise   D. remember

D   22. **revise**   A. throw out   B. remain   C. agree   D. change

C   23. **ultimate**   A. least   B. most strange   C. greatest   D. oldest

D   24. **variety**   A. value   B. reason   C. few   D. several different kinds

A   25. **version**   A. retelling   B. dislike   C. assortment   D. penalty

(Continues on next page)

PART B: Antonyms

In the space provided, write the letter of the choice that is most nearly **opposite** in meaning to the **boldfaced** word.

A 26. **abrupt**   A. slow   B. willing   C. secret   D. scary

C 27. **accustomed**   A. not exact   B. not similar to C. not used to   D. not needed

B 28. **adequate**   A. willing   B. not enough   C. not dependable D. unhappy

D 29. **awkward**   A. up and down   B. polite   C. complicated   D. graceful

C 30. **brutal**   A. well-known   B. shaky   C. gentle   D. dark

B 31. **complex**   A. cheerful   B. simple   C. lucky   D. natural

D 32. **consent**   A. surprise   B. reward   C. appear   D. refuse

B 33. **current**   A. wise   B. old-fashioned C. unusual   D. common

D 34. **customary**   A. willing   B. most   C. clear   D. unusual

A 35. **eager**   A. not interested B. not believing C. ready   D. clear

D 36. **exclaim**   A. refuse   B. forget   C. allow   D. whisper

C 37. **hesitate**   A. ignore   B. suggest   C. rush ahead   D. reward

B 38. **horizontal**   A. careless   B. up and down   C. dark   D. square

D 39. **linger**   A. appear   B. insult   C. forget   D. hurry away

D 40. **minimum**   A. unhealthy   B. loud   C. painful   D. most

B 41. **miserable**   A. hard to understand B. happy   C. willing   D. clear

A 42. **objection**   A. approval   B. joke   C. win   D. loss

A 43. **originate**   A. end   B. explain   C. leave   D. expect

B 44. **penalize**   A. hurry   B. reward   C. give   D. appear

D 45. **recollect**   A. answer   B. ask   C. know   D. forget

D 46. **reliable**   A. not known   B. not enough   C. not usual   D. not dependable

C 47. **reluctant**   A. surprised   B. least   C. willing   D. careless

C 48. **vague**   A. lowest   B. not clumsy   C. clear   D. not exact

C 49. **vanish**   A. expect   B. keep   C. appear   D. wait

A 50. **wholesome**   A. unhealthy   B. simple   C. useful   D. old-fashioned

Score   (Number correct) _____ x 2 = _____%

Enter your score above and in the **Vocabulary Performance Chart** on the inside back cover of the book.

Unit Three

Chapter 11

assume	maximum
conscious	protest
external	remedy
incredible	spectacle
internal	verdict

Chapter 12

artificial	frequency
complicate	represent
conscience	temporary
counsel	transparent
detect	triumph

Chapter 13

agonizing	strive
energetic	substance
foresight	tolerance
interval	trait
prosper	withdraw

Chapter 14

approximately	plea
consistent	practical
cope	random
evaluate	significant
phrase	sole

Chapter 15

authentic	eligible
characteristic	harsh
concept	remote
confront	shallow
disrupt	thrive

assume	maximum
conscious	protest
external	remedy
incredible	spectacle
internal	verdict

Ten Words in Context

In the space provided, write the letter of the meaning closest to that of each **boldfaced** word. Use the context of the sentences to help you figure out each word's meaning.

1 assume
(ə-sōōm′)
- *verb*

- I **assumed** George was telling the truth, but he wasn't.
- We **assumed** the sun would shine during the outdoor wedding. What a mistake! When it comes to weather, one must not take anything for granted.

<u>C</u> *Assume* means   A. to fear.   B. to forget.   C. to believe.

2 conscious
(kŏn′shəs)
- *adjective*

- I don't think Jim is **conscious** that he sometimes seems very rude. Otherwise, he wouldn't be so ill-mannered.
- As Arlene gave her speech to the class, she was **conscious** that people were whispering in the back of the room.

<u>B</u> *Conscious* means   A. pleased.   B. aware.   C. relieved.

3 external
(ĭk-stûr′nəl)
- *adjective*

- The **external** appearances of the two houses were similar, but on the inside, the homes differed quite a bit.
- When my grandmother first came to America, she was given her very first orange. Since no one had told her to remove its **external** layer, she began to eat the peel.

<u>C</u> *External* means   A. final.   B. new.   C. outer.

4 incredible
(ĭn-krĕd′ə-bəl)
- *adjective*

- The moon landing of 1969 was an **incredible** achievement.
- It's **incredible** that a cat could survive forty-three days locked in a crate without food and water, yet it has happened.

<u>B</u> *Incredible* means   A. expected.   B. hard to believe.   C. correct.

5 internal
(ĭn-tûr′nəl)
- *adjective*

- The car looks terrific, so you'd never guess that some of its **internal** parts— the motor, brakes, and heater—need major repairs.
- A pork roast may not be safe to eat even if it looks cooked on the outside. It must have an **internal** temperature of at least 160 degrees.

<u>A</u> *Internal* means   A. inside.   B. hard.   C. light in weight.

6 maximum
(măk′sə-məm)
- *adjective*

- The safety sign in the elevator warned, "CAUTION: **Maximum** load—1500 pounds."
- Three hundred miles per hour is the **maximum** speed for this airplane; it can go no faster.

<u>A</u> *Maximum* means   A. greatest.   B. worst.   C. longest.

7 protest
(prō-tĕst′)
- *verb*

● When the builder announced plans to pack a hundred homes onto a ten-acre farm, a group called Protect Our Open Spaces showed up to **protest**.

● "Stop it," Billy's mother **protested**. "You can't pour blue food coloring into the mashed potatoes."

_C_ *Protest* means   A. to ask.   B. to suggest.   C. to complain.

8 remedy
(rĕm′ĭ-dē)
- *noun*

● Grandma's **remedy** for a cold was to wear garlic around her neck. It never cured her cold, but at least no one came close enough to her to catch it.

● There's no quick **remedy** for a broken heart; only time will heal it.

_B_ *Remedy* means   A. memory.   B. treatment.   C. main cause.

9 spectacle
(spĕk′tə-kəl)
- *noun*

● Circuses are filled with **spectacles**, from chimpanzees riding bicycles to elephants wearing party hats.

● During her temper tantrum in the supermarket, the crying little girl made a **spectacle** of herself by lying down in the middle of the checkout lane and refusing to get up.

_B_ *Spectacle* means   A. excuse.   B. unusual sight.   C. result.

10 verdict
(vûr′dĭkt)
- *noun*

● The mechanic's **verdict** was that the car was too badly damaged to fix.

● In only ninety minutes, the jury members reached their **verdict**. They found the defendant guilty.

_A_ *Verdict* means   A. decision.   B. punishment.   C. problem.

Matching Words with Definitions

Following are definitions of the ten words. **Print** each word next to its definition. If you look closely at each word in context, you will be able to figure out its meaning.

1. _____remedy_____ A cure; something that heals

2. _____incredible_____ Unbelievable; amazing; extraordinary

3. _____conscious_____ Aware (of something); noticing (that something is or was happening or existing)

4. _____external_____ Outer; located outside

5. _____protest_____ To complain; express dissatisfaction

6. _____spectacle_____ A surprising or unusual sight; a public display or scene

7. _____assume_____ To suppose to be true; take for granted

8. _____verdict_____ A decision or judgment

9. _____internal_____ Inner; located inside

10. _____maximum_____ Most; highest; largest possible

CAUTION: Do not go any further until you are sure the above answers are correct. Then you can use the definitions to help you in the following practices. Your goal is eventually to know the words well enough so that you don't need to check the definitions at all.

Check 1

Using the answer lines, complete each item below with the correct word from the box.

A. **assume**	B. **conscious**	C. **external**	D. **incredible**	E. **internal**
F. **maximum**	G. **protest**	H. **remedy**	I. **spectacle**	J. **verdict**

internal   1. The ___ part of a banana is its sweet, creamy flesh.

external   2. The ___ part of a banana is its peel.

maximum   3. The ___ speed allowed on this road is sixty-five miles an hour.

remedy   4. Do you think there will ever be a ___ for the common cold?

incredible   5. The Grand Canyon is the most ___ sight I've ever seen. It's so huge that it's hard to believe how big it is even when you're looking at it.

conscious   6. As Nikki tried to study, she became ___ of a loud "drip, drip" from the kitchen faucet.

spectacle   7. On the day the old hotel was to be knocked down, people came from miles around to watch the ___.

protest   8. If you don't like a company's policy, why not ___? For example, you could write a strong complaint letter to the company president.

assume   9. Rather than ___ it would not rain on the outdoor wedding, the bride's family rented a large tent, just in case.

verdict   10. The student smiled happily when she heard the instructor's ___ on her project. "This is excellent work," he said.

NOTE: Now check your answers to these items by turning to page 240. Going over the answers carefully will help you prepare for the remaining practices, for which answers are not given.

Check 2

Using the answer lines, complete each item below with **two** words from the box. Use each word once.

verdict
protest   1–2. After examining his room, Sean's mother's ___ was that it was too messy to live in. Sean ___ed, saying, "I know exactly where everything is!"

external
internal   3–4. Although the accident victim had only a few ___ bruises, he had serious ___ injuries, including damage to his kidneys.

incredible
remedy   5–6. It's ___ that penicillin, a ___ for various infections, was discovered by accident after some mold grew in a laboratory dish.

assume
conscious   7–8. The boss had ___d that the workers enjoyed background music, but they said they were not even ___ of it. However, once, when the music ceased°, everyone suddenly became very aware of the silence.

spectacle
maximum   9–10. College students used to enjoy arranging ___s in which they would crowd the ___ number of people possible into a phone booth.

Word Work

A. Write each word next to the examples that best match it.

| A. **assume** | B. **external** | C. **incredible** |
| D. **protest** | E. **remedy** | |

____external____ 1. Orange peel
Book covers
Gift wrapping

____remedy____ 2. Swallowing sugar to get rid of hiccups
Holding ice on a bruise to reduce swelling and pain
Taking antibiotics to clear up an ear infection

____incredible____ 3. The actual invention in 1956 of diapers for birds!
Glass and brick being made from the same main ingredient: sand!
The U.S. Army's training bats to drop bombs during World War II!

____assume____ 4. That most people in your class are right-handed
That there are lots of people named Smith in your local phone book
That your friends like pizza with sausage more than pizza with a peculiar°
topping such as anchovies

____protest____ 5. Writing letters to the White House about taxes being too high
Demanding that a nuclear-power plant be shut down
Marching in front of a courthouse with signs saying we should eliminate° the
death penalty

B. In the space provided, write the letter of the word that best completes each item.

__B__ 6. A popular **spectacle** is

    A. children arriving   B. a Fourth of July   C. a man mowing his lawn.
       at school.   fireworks display.

__C__ 7. Because the accident victim suffered **internal** bleeding, he

    A. was bleeding   B. was bleeding   C. didn't realize how much
       a great deal.   a little.   blood he had lost.

__A__ 8. The judge's **verdict** was

    A. "Guilty."   B. a black robe.   C. a courtroom.

__A__ 9. You will usually be fully **conscious** of

    A. a loud noise nearby.   B. your own breathing.   C. a small event taking place
                                  one hundred miles away.

__C__ 10. The sign on the carnival ride says, "**Maximum** weight for riders is 80 pounds." This means
that adults

    A. are the only ones   B. must go with children   C. are usually not allowed
       allowed on the ride.   on the ride.   on the ride.

Word Parts

A. The prefix *self-* often means "oneself."

Examples: *defense* — protection   *conscious* — aware
self-defense — protection of oneself   *self-conscious* — uncomfortably aware of
oneself

On each answer line, write the word from the box that means the same as the *italicized* words.

A. **self-centered**	B. **self-conscious**	C. **self-control**
D. **self-critical°**	E. **self-educated**	

self-critical   1. Ramon is so *critical of himself*. He must have a low opinion of himself.

self-control   2. It takes *control of oneself* not to eat too many warm, freshly baked chocolate-chip cookies.

self-centered   3. That writer is so *centered on himself!* After talking about himself for an hour, he said, "But enough about me. What do you think of my writing?"

self-conscious   4. Irene felt uncomfortably *conscious of herself* because of her new hair color, so she was relieved when most of her friends didn't even notice it.

self-educated   5. My grandfather was *educated by himself;* although he never even attended high school, he learned a great deal on his own.

B. The suffix *-ness* means "the quality or state of."

Examples: *wholesome°* — tending to improve the character, mind, or body
wholesomeness — the quality of tending to improve the character, mind, or body

conscious — aware
consciousness — the state of being aware

On each answer line, write the word from the box that best completes the item.

F. **awkwardness°**	G. **consciousness**	H. **eagerness°**
I. **usefulness**	J. **vagueness°**	

eagerness   6. With great ___, the excited family joined the line to enter Disneyland.

consciousness   7. The accident victim lost ___ and did not wake up for several days.

awkwardness   8. Because they are growing so rapidly, many teenagers go through a period of ___ when it seems they are always tripping over their own feet.

usefulness   9. This camping knife is famous for its ___. It provides a screwdriver, toothpick, bottle opener, magnifying glass, and tweezers.

vagueness   10. The ___ of the instructions for putting this storage box together is driving me crazy. The directions are so unclear that I don't even know which side is up.

Final Check

Read the passages carefully. Then fill in each blank with the word that best fits the context.

A. Coming Out of a Coma

A. **external**	B. **incredible**	C. **internal**	D. **remedy**	E. **verdict**

"Hi, Mom," Francis said. The effort of speaking exhausted him, and he closed his eyes again.

To his mother, these were the best words she had ever heard. The idea that her son was speaking again, after ten weeks in a coma, was (1)_____*incredible*_____. He had been gone from this world for so long that it seemed he'd never return. Those ten weeks had been difficult to endure°. Whenever Ms. King had visited Francis at the hospital, he had been completely still. There were no (2)_____*external*_____ signs that he was thinking or feeling anything. The doctor's (3)_____*verdict*_____ was that Francis would never recover. But Ms. King maintained° the hope that he still had some (4)_____*internal*_____ life. Could he, perhaps, hear her words? Could he feel her hand squeezing his? She tried desperately° to reach him in any way she could during her daily visits, when she lingered° at his bedside for hours.

Now, although Ms. King knew there was no quick (5)_____*remedy*_____ for her son's serious injuries, the simple words "Hi, Mom" gave her hope that he could, someday, live a full life again.

B. The Office Doughnut Contest

F. **assume**	G. **conscious**	H. **maximum**	I. **protest**	J. **spectacle**

"Are you telling me there are no doughnuts left? I don't believe it!" Joan said. "How could a huge supply of doughnuts be gone already?"

"I don't know how," Fran responded°. "I just know there aren't any left."

"When I brought three dozen doughnuts in this morning, I (6)_____*assume*_____d I'd get to eat at least one," Joan said. "After all, the (7)_____*maximum*_____ number of people who ever work in this place is ten. Today, Sue isn't even here. It's hard to believe that the other eight of you could eat thirty-six doughnuts in less than three hours. I even anticipated° having surplus° doughnuts for tomorrow."

Then Fran and Joan became (8)_____*conscious*_____ of laughing in the office next door. When they looked in, the fate of the missing doughnuts became evident°. They could barely believe the (9)_____*spectacle*_____ that met their eyes: Three grown men were tossing doughnuts across the room, while three other men tried to catch the doughnuts on pencils.

"I don't believe you guys!" Joan (10)_____*protest*_____ed. "Just you wait. Next time it's my turn to bring in the doughnuts, I'll bring in cream-filled and jelly-filled doughnuts, and we'll see how you play your little game then."

Scores	Check 2 _____%	Word Work _____%	Word Parts _____%	Final Check _____%

Enter your scores above and in the **Vocabulary Performance Chart** on the inside back cover of the book.

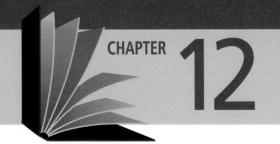

artificial	frequency
complicate	represent
conscience	temporary
counsel	transparent
detect	triumph

Ten Words in Context

In the space provided, write the letter of the meaning closest to that of each **boldfaced** word. Use the context of the sentences to help you figure out each word's meaning.

1 artificial
(är′tə-fĭsh′əl)
- *adjective*

- My uncle, who lost his left arm in an accident, was recently fitted for an **artificial** arm.
- **Artificial** flowers made of paper or silk last for years.

B *Artificial* means   A. short-term.   B. made by humans.   C. heavy.

2 complicate
(kŏm′plĭ-kāt′)
- *verb*

- Cooking for a crowd is difficult enough, so I don't **complicate** the job with fancy dishes. I keep the food simple.
- Don't **complicate** the game with too many rules.

A *Complicate* means   A. to make difficult.   B. to find.   C. to remember.

3 conscience
(kŏn′shəns)
- *noun*

- After Lena stole the earrings, her **conscience** bothered her so much that she couldn't enjoy wearing them.
- It's strange, but true, that some criminals don't have a **conscience**. They really don't believe that it is wrong to cheat, steal, or even kill.

C *Conscience* means   A. budget.   B. plan of action.   C. moral sense.

4 counsel
(koun′səl)
- *verb*

- My basketball coach **counseled** me to work at the shoe store fewer hours each week so I could have more time to study.
- I **counseled** Angela to break up with her boyfriend. "You can do better than a high-school dropout," I told her.

C *Counsel* means   A. to allow.   B. to join.   C. to suggest to.

5 detect
(dĭ-tĕkt′)
- *verb*

- If you **detect** a gas leak, leave the house immediately and call for help.
- Rachel never actually says that she dislikes Ron, but I **detect** a tone of dislike in her voice.

B *Detect* means   A. to control.   B. to notice.   C. to want.

6 frequency
(frē′kwən-sē)
- *noun*

- Luis and Adam used to visit each other once or twice a week, but since Adam got married, the **frequency** of their visits has gone down.
- I don't like to watch movies on TV because the **frequency** of ads is so great. I prefer to rent movies and see them without all the interruptions.

A *Frequency* means   A. rate.   B. cost.   C. action.

7 represent
(rĕp′rĭ-zĕnt′)
- *verb*

- Will you speak for yourself in court, or will a lawyer **represent** you?
- Tamika will **represent** her class at the Student Council meetings.

_C_ *Represent* means   A. to leave.   B. to hire.   C. to speak for.

8 temporary
(tĕm′pə-rĕr′ē)
- *adjective*

- Mimi used a **temporary** green hair dye just for St. Patrick's Day.
- A **temporary** worker will be hired to fill in for Kwan until he recovers from his injury.

_B_ *Temporary* means   A. large.   B. short-term.   C. false.

9 transparent
(trăns-pâr′ənt)
- *adjective*

- At first, I thought the glass in the door was **transparent** and that I was seeing someone on the other side. But when I got closer, I realized that it was a mirror and I was looking at myself.
- **Transparent** wrap allows you to see what's inside a container.

_A_ *Transparent* means   A. able to be seen through.   B. old.   C. thick.

10 triumph
(trī′əmf)
- *noun*

- Our football team's **triumph** over the state's first-place team was the reason for a huge party.
- My brother's good teachers, his understanding parents, and his own hard work all led to his **triumph** over a learning disability.

_C_ *Triumph* means   A. loss.   B. meeting.   C. win.

Matching Words with Definitions

Following are definitions of the ten words. **Print** each word next to its definition. If you look closely at each word in context, you will be able to figure out its meaning.

1. _transparent_   Allowing light to pass through so that objects on the other side can be seen

2. _counsel_   To give advice or guidance to; advise°

3. _frequency_   The rate at which something occurs; how often something happens

4. _detect_   To notice; discover that something exists or is present

5. _triumph_   An outstanding or very satisfying success; victory

6. _conscience_   A sense of what is right or wrong in one's behavior

7. _represent_   To act or speak for

8. _complicate_   To make difficult by adding or involving many parts or details; make complex°

9. _temporary_   Lasting or serving for a limited time only; not permanent

10. _artificial_   Made to imitate something natural

CAUTION: Do not go any further until you are sure the above answers are correct. Then you can use the definitions to help you in the following practices. Your goal is eventually to know the words well enough so that you don't need to check the definitions at all.

Check 1

Using the answer lines, complete each item below with the correct word from the box.

A. **artificial**	B. **complicate**	C. **conscience**	D. **counsel**	E. **detect**
F. **frequency**	G. **represent**	H. **temporary**	I. **transparent**	J. **triumph**

triumph   1. Beating the first-place team was a greater ___ for the players than winning over the last-place team.

artificial   2. That horror movie must have used gallons of ___ blood.

counsel   3. For how many hours a week would you ___ a student to work?

frequency   4. The ___ of our club's newsletter is about once a month.

complicate   5. If you ___ a job, you make it harder to do.

conscience   6. A person who is cruel must not have much of a ___.

temporary   7. Substitute teachers get ___ job assignments, often for only a day or two at a time.

represent   8. Elected officials are supposed to ___ the voters—in other words, do what the voters want.

transparent   9. In the winter, we put sheets of ___ plastic over our windows to help keep out the cold.

detect   10. Although Norah has lived in New York for years, I can still ___ a slight Southern accent in her voice.

NOTE: Now check your answers to these items by turning to page 240. Going over the answers carefully will help you prepare for the remaining practices, for which answers are not given.

Check 2

Using the answer lines, complete each item below with **two** words from the box. Use each word once.

frequency
counsel   1–2. To reduce the ___ of infections, people should be ___ed to wash their hands often and well. They should also be advised° to keep counters and cutting boards free of bacteria.

conscience
artificial   3–4. If your ___ won't allow you to wear real fur, choose ___ fur instead. Fake fur looks great and feels good, too!

triumph
temporary   5–6. I lost ten pounds last year. That was a great victory, but my ___ was only ___. I've gained every ounce of it back.

transparent
detect   7–8. The eyes are sometimes called "the windows of the soul," as if they were ___ and one could ___ what's inside a person's soul by looking into them.

represent
complicate   9–10. The Spruce Street Block Association worked well when it ___ed only the residents of our street. However, it has ___d matters by trying to speak for other parts of the neighborhood, as well.

Word Work

A. Write each word next to the examples that best match it.

A. **artificial**	B. **detect**	C. **frequency**
D. **temporary**	E. **triumph**	

artificial   1. Plastic grass
Wax fruit
A glass eye

triumph   2. A neighborhood basketball team wins the city championship.
A student gets all A's on a report card.
You win a citywide talent contest.

detect   3. Spot a child's chocolate fingerprints on a candy dish
Discover a thief's footprints
Notice fear in someone's voice

frequency   4. Mail delivery: once a day, six days a week
Flu shots: once a year
The Main Street bus: every half hour

temporary   5. Campers' tents set up on the shore of a lake
A place you live in until your new home is ready
Extra salespeople hired for the holiday season

B. In the space provided, write the letter of the choice that best completes each item.

_B_   6. A **transparent** dome on a stadium lets in

A. rain. B. sunlight. C. air.

_A_   7. The school would **complicate** students' lives if it

A. changed the whole class schedule at midterm. B. reduced tuition. C. installed a coffee machine in the library.

_B_   8. Because of your **conscience**, you might

A. buy a new pair of jeans. B. apologize to your brother for yelling at him. C. forget to pay back a loan.

_B_   9. You might **represent**

A. a hot summer's day. B. your neighborhood in the city council. C. a good book.

_C_   10. If you wanted to **counsel** friends who had been skipping school, you would

A. mind your own business and say nothing. B. avoid any contact with them. C. talk to them about the dangers of their behavior.

Synonyms and Antonyms

A. Synonyms. Write the letter of the word or phrase that most nearly means the **same** as each boldfaced word.

___C___ 1. **conscience**

    A. rate
                C. moral sense

    B. talent
               D. victory

___C___ 2. **counsel**

    A. win
                C. give advice to

    B. make difficult
        D. imitate

___D___ 3. **detect**

    A. act for
             C. disapprove

    B. ignore
              D. notice

___A___ 4. **frequency**

    A. how often something happens
    C. difficulty

    B. allowing light to pass through
    D. short time

___C___ 5. **represent**

    A. imitate
             C. speak for

    B. discover
          D. succeed

B. Antonyms. Write the letter of the word or phrase that most nearly means the **opposite** of each boldfaced word.

___C___ 6. **artificial**

    A. new
                C. natural

    B. easy
               D. old

___B___ 7. **complicate**

    A. lose
               C. ignore

    B. make easier
          D. pay attention to

___D___ 8. **temporary**

    A. easy
              C. important

    B. blocking out light
    D. lasting forever

___A___ 9. **transparent**

    A. blocking out light
    C. easy

    B. natural
            D. long-lasting

___B___ 10. **triumph**

    A. secret
             C. success

    B. loss
             D. game

Final Check

Read the passages carefully. Then fill in each blank with the word that best fits the context.

A. The People's Choice

A. **conscience**	B. **frequency**	C. **represent**	D. **temporary**	E. **triumph**

Suppose you are a candidate running for a particular° public office—and you win. What a (1)____triumph____! But now you have a new challenge°: What is the best way to (2)____represent____ those who voted for you? How do you know what "the people" want? Sometimes the great (3)____frequency____ of letters and phone calls makes you think you know what all the people want. Think again! For most people, interest in what their elected officials are doing is only (4)____temporary____; you will never hear from many of them again. Also, of course, the voters who don't write or call may feel differently from those who do. All right, then, you say, I'll just act according to my own (5)____conscience____ and do what I think is right. Not so fast! Remember that you're supposed to be "the people's choice." So what should you do? If you know the answer to that question, I propose° that you call the politicians in Washington immediately. They've been looking for the answer for over two hundred years.

B. The Christmas Wars

F. **artificial**	G. **complicate**	H. **counsel**	I. **detect**	J. **transparent**

Christmastime is supposed to be peaceful, but in some families it renews old battles. One is the dispute° between those who like a sweet-smelling, natural Christmas tree and those who prefer a shiny (6)____artificial____ tree, with no pine needles to mess up the floor. Another common battle goes on between parents, who seek the best places to hide the gifts until the big day, and children, who search tirelessly to (7)____detect____ clues about where those hiding places are. No matter what efforts a parent may make to (8)____complicate____ the search by shoving the gifts inside luggage or under three layers of linens, kids soon find them.

Then, of course, because the boxes and packages are not (9)____transparent____, the kids have to resort° to opening a corner of the wrapping. Or they try to determine° what's inside by shaking, bouncing, and rattling the box. Sooner or later, they make enough noise to catch an adult's attention. At this point the kids come out from behind the furnace or under the bed, trying very hard to look innocent. The parents get mad; the kids are in tears; everyone feels miserable°. Merry Christmas, everyone! It's hard to know how to (10)____counsel____ parents in this situation. Would the best advice be to ask Grandpa or Grandma to take the kids for a month or so?

Scores	Check 2 _____%	Word Work _____%	Synonyms and Antonyms _____%	Final Check _____%

Enter your scores above and in the **Vocabulary Performance Chart** on the inside back cover of the book.

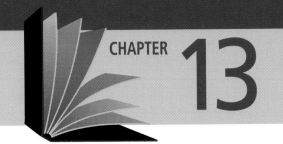

CHAPTER 13

agonizing	strive
energetic	substance
foresight	tolerance
interval	trait
prosper	withdraw

Ten Words in Context

In the space provided, write the letter of the meaning closest to that of each **boldfaced** word. Use the context of the sentences to help you figure out each word's meaning.

1 agonizing
(ăgʹə-nīʹzĭng)
- *adjective*

- After hours in the blazing sun, the hikers felt an **agonizing** thirst.
- I felt sorry for my sister as she made the **agonizing** decision to end her marriage.

_C_ *Agonizing* means   A. surprising.   B. normal.   C. very painful.

2 energetic
(ĕnʹər-jĕtʹĭk)
- *adjective*

- The **energetic** soccer game left all the players tired and hungry.
- At the age of 70, my grandmother is still **energetic** enough to go for a long, fast walk every evening after dinner.

_B_ *Energetic* means   A. short and friendly.   B. lively and active.   C. easy and pleasant.

3 foresight
(fôrʹsītʹ)
- *noun*

- Jen had the **foresight** to apply to several colleges, knowing that she might not get into the one she wanted most.
- People who are always late show a lack of **foresight**.

_A_ *Foresight* means   A. wise planning.   B. courage.   C. strength.

4 interval
(ĭnʹtər-vəl)
- *noun*

- The **interval** between Christmas and New Year's Day is only a week.
- There was an **interval** of several hours between the births of the twins—in fact, they were born on separate days.

_C_ *Interval* means   A. happiness.   B. difference in importance.   C. space.

5 prosper
(prŏsʹpər)
- *verb*

- The company is so strong that it is expected to **prosper** even though similar companies are going out of business.
- Someone who always jumps from job to job is not likely to **prosper**.

_B_ *Prosper* means   A. to believe.   B. to do well.   C. to take back.

6 strive
(strīv)
- *verb*

- Many people **strive** to become movie stars, but few succeed.
- Every year, many mountain climbers **strive** to reach the top of Mount Everest.

_C_ *Strive* means   A. to make a mistake.   B. to make a discovery.   C. to make an effort.

7 substance
(sŭb′stəns)
- *noun*

- Gold is such a soft **substance** that it can be pounded into a very thin sheet.
- Cat litter does a good job of soaking up spilled **substances** such as gasoline or motor oil.

A *Substance* means   A. material.   B. light.   C. force.

8 tolerance
(tŏl′ər-əns)
- *noun*

- That teacher is known for her **tolerance**. She encourages students to speak freely in her classroom, even when their ideas differ from hers.
- Because of the Johnsons' **tolerance**, their son-in-law's different religion is not a problem for the family.

B *Tolerance* means   A. planning.   B. respect for others.   C. financial success.

9 trait
(trāt)
- *noun*

- My best friend's nicest **trait** is her ability to laugh at herself.
- My worst **trait** is always worrying about what people think of me.

A *Trait* means   A. personal quality.   B. goal.   C. preparation.

10 withdraw
(wĭth-drô′)
- *verb*

- When Warren realized he was working Thursday, he had to **withdraw** his offer to baby-sit for his sister's kids.
- When I saw a large spider in my desk drawer, I **withdrew** my hand and decided to find a pen somewhere else.

C *Withdraw* means   A. give.   B. find.   C. take back.

Matching Words with Definitions

Following are definitions of the ten words. **Print** each word next to its definition. If you look closely at each word in context, you will be able to figure out its meaning.

1. _____trait_____   A quality or feature, as of personality, for which a person is known

2. _____tolerance_____   Respect for the differing views, practices, and characteristics of others; lack of prejudice

3. _____energetic_____   Lively; spirited; full of energy

4. _____withdraw_____   To take back (something or a statement); remove

5. _____agonizing_____   Causing great physical or mental pain

6. _____foresight_____   Care in planning or preparing for the future

7. _____interval_____   The period of time between two events

8. _____strive_____   To try hard

9. _____prosper_____   To succeed, especially financially

10. _____substance_____   A physical material; matter of a particular type

CAUTION: Do not go any further until you are sure the above answers are correct. Then you can use the definitions to help you in the following practices. Your goal is eventually to know the words well enough so that you don't need to check the definitions at all.

Check 1

Using the answer lines, complete each item below with the correct word from the box.

A. **agonizing**	B. **energetic**	C. **foresight**	D. **interval**	E. **prosper**
F. **strive**	G. **substance**	H. **tolerance**	I. **trait**	J. **withdraw**

withdraw   1. I wished I could ___ my angry words, but it was too late.

energetic   2. Don't worry when Paul and Linda raise their voices to each other. "We both like an ___ argument; we aren't really mad," Linda says.

strive   3. Shelby ___s to do well in all her classes.

trait   4. Patience is an important ___ for a preschool teacher.

foresight   5. Budgeting requires the ___ to think of future expenses.

tolerance   6. Martin Luther King taught that all people should be viewed with ___, no matter what their race or religious beliefs.

agonizing   7. Dad went to the emergency room because of ___ pain in his lower back.

interval   8. There's an ___ of an hour between my last class and the track meet.

substance   9. The silver-colored ___ inside an old-fashioned thermometer is called mercury.

prosper   10. At first, the Savings Mart didn't do well, but after it lowered its prices and increased its advertising, the store began to ___.

NOTE: Now check your answers to these items by turning to page 240. Going over the answers carefully will help you prepare for the remaining practices, for which answers are not given.

Check 2

Using the answer lines, complete each item below with **two** words from the box. Use each word once.

trait
tolerance   1–2. One of Paul's unpleasant ___s is that he has very little ___ for anyone who disagrees with his opinions.

prosper
strive   3–4. People who ___ tend to be individuals who ___ to do their jobs well, spend less than they earn, and save for the future.

energetic
interval   5–6. Lisa loves her ___ workout at the gym, but she also loves the quiet ___ after exercising and before leaving. That's when she sits and talks with friends.

agonizing
foresight   7–8. The unfortunate man fell asleep on the beach and woke up with an ___ sunburn. He hadn't had the ___ to put on sunblock lotion.

substance
withdraw   9–10. One of the sad things about addiction to any ___, such as drugs or alcohol, is that the addiction makes the person ___ from normal life and friendships. The addiction becomes his or her whole life.

Word Work

A. In the space provided, write the letter of the choice that best completes each item.

____B____ 1. If a person has an **agonizing** injury, he or she would probably
A. laugh it off.
B. scream in pain.
C. limp slightly.

____A____ 2. A sign of Rob's **tolerance** is that
A. he has friends of many different races and religions.
B. he studies very hard.
C. he wears expensive clothes.

____C____ 3. An especially **energetic** activity is
A. reading.
B. resting.
C. running.

____B____ 4. If you and a friend have an argument and you **strive** to understand her point of view, you
A. don't care what she thinks.
B. really want to understand why she thinks the way she does.
C. know that she is right and you are wrong.

____B____ 5. The candidate for student council president **withdrew** her name from the race when she realized
A. she was sure to win.
B. she didn't have time to serve as president.
C. being president would give her experience in managing people.

B. In the space provided, write the letter of the word that most closely relates to the situation in each item.

____A____ 6. Just in case she needs them, my mother keeps one pair of reading glasses in her purse and another in her car.

A. foresight   B. agonizing   C. tolerance

____A____ 7. People who were in on the "ground floor" of the personal computer industry became extremely wealthy.

A. prosper   B. withdraw   C. energetic

____C____ 8. Of the children in our family, my sister is known as the funny one, my brother is the hard-working one, and I am the athletic one.

A. substance   B. interval   C. trait

____C____ 9. Kaylin spent a lot of time worrying during the five days between her job interview and the day she learned she was hired.

A. withdraw   B. substance   C. interval

____B____ 10. What is that blob of glowing green stuff on the kitchen table?

A. tolerance   B. substance   C. trait

Word Parts

A. The suffix *-ous* means "full of" or "having much."

Examples: *fury* — violent anger   *prosper* — to succeed financially
furious — full of violent anger   *prosperous* — having much financial success

On each answer line, write the word from the box that best completes the item.

| A. **envious** | B. **famous** | C. **furious** |
| D. **joyous** | E. **prosperous** | |

famous _____ 1. Elvis Presley is still very well known; in fact, he may be more ___ today than he was when he was alive.

furious _____ 2. After her latest fight with her boyfriend, Jill was so ___ that she wrote him a long, angry letter—and then burned it.

prosperous _____ 3. Not many people "get rich quick" by winning the lottery; most of us have to work long and hard to become ___.

joyous _____ 4. The wedding of my eighty-year-old grandmother was a ___ occasion for the family.

envious _____ 5. It is hard not to feel ___ of Phan, who seems to have everything good in life: a great marriage, a wonderful job, terrific kids, and lots of friends.

B. The suffix *-al* often means "the act of."

Examples: *deny* — to say that something is not true
denial — the act of saying that something is not true

refuse — to say "no" to doing, or giving, or accepting something
refusal — the act of saying "no" to something

On each answer line, write the word from the box that best completes the item.

| F. **approval** | G. **betrayal°** | H. **denial** |
| I. **survival** | J. **withdrawal** | |

withdrawal _____ 6. The ___ of one thousand dollars from the man's bank account was unusual. He usually took out only fifty dollars or so.

betrayal _____ 7. Giving secret information to an enemy is a ___ of one's country.

survival _____ 8. My mother strongly believes in the soul's ___ after death, but my father believes there is nothing after death.

denial _____ 9. Mark's ___ that he had eaten the cookies surprised me because I noticed Oreo crumbs all over his bed.

approval _____ 10. We can't leave work early without our boss's ___.

Final Check

Read the passages carefully. Then fill in each blank with the word that best fits the context.

A. What's Your Type?

A. **agonizing**	B. **prosper**	C. **strive**	D. **tolerance**	E. **trait**

If you find it (1)____agonizing____ to be stuck behind a slow-moving car, or if you are often impatient with a friend's progress in completing a task, you may be what researchers classify° as a Type A personality. A (2)____trait____ shared by Type A people is the desire to make effective use of time. They (3)____strive____ to accomplish more in an hour than other people do in a day. A typical example of Type A behavior is the man who built a desk onto the front of his exercise bike. Sitting in front of the TV set, he could exercise, watch football, and pay bills all at the same time. Type A's often have little (4)____tolerance____ for the calmer Type B people; Type A's feel the Type B's waste a lot of time.

Naturally, Type A people often (5)____prosper____ financially, driven as they are to achieve the maximum° success at whatever they do. However, they also suffer from heart disease more often than the more relaxed Type B's. The Type A's great need for success creates a lot of tension, which raises blood pressure and can aggravate° a heart condition. Sadly, no matter how many Type B's counsel° them to "slow down" and "take it easy," Type A's ignore their advice and continue to pursue° their goals.

B. What a Circus!

F. **energetic**	G. **foresight**	H. **interval**	I. **substance**	J. **withdraw**

I didn't actually volunteer to go to the circus. I was sort of volunteered. My son Tommy was going with his first-grade class, and he told his teacher to sign me up. When I saw how eager° he was for me to accompany° his class, I couldn't (6)____withdraw____ the offer.

So there I was, along with a handful of other parents and ninety (7)____energetic____ six- and seven-year-olds. I don't really recollect° a great deal of the circus. What I do remember is the purple (8)____substance____ that someone spilled on my sneaker, because it never washed off. I remember a lot about the inside of the bathroom, because I took so many children there. I remember washing cotton candy off a lot of faces, since I had the (9)____foresight____ to bring a box of baby wipes along. And I remember the boy who exclaimed°, "Oh, no!" and hid his face in my lap when an acrobat took a scary walk across a high horizontal° wire.

But nothing could spoil the fun those kids had. To them, every act was a wonderful spectacle°. Even when the juggler dropped three of his four bowling pins, the kids thought he was great. Afterward, they were tired. In the brief (10)____interval____ between our boarding the bus to go home and Tommy's falling asleep, he gave me his verdict°: "That was the bestest circus ever. You were really lucky to get to come along." Looking back at it all, I think I was, too.

Scores	Check 2 _____%	Word Work _____%	Word Parts _____%	Final Check _____%

Enter your scores above and in the **Vocabulary Performance Chart** on the inside back cover of the book.

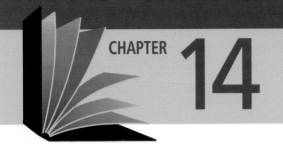

approximately	plea
consistent	practical
cope	random
evaluate	significant
phrase	sole

Ten Words in Context

In the space provided, write the letter of the meaning closest to that of each **boldfaced** word. Use the context of the sentences to help you figure out each word's meaning.

1 approximately
(ə-prŏk′sə-mĭt-lē)
- *adverb*

- A month is **approximately** thirty days long.
- The suspect in the murder case is a dark-haired white woman who is **approximately** forty years old.

<u>C</u> *Approximately* means   A. certainly.   B. never.   C. about.

2 consistent
(kən-sĭs′tənt)
- *adjective*

- To be rated number one in tennis, a player must be a **consistent** winner, not a winner only sometimes.
- I would rather work for someone with a **consistent** manner than someone who is full of praise one day and screaming insults the next.

<u>A</u> *Consistent* means   A. steady.   B. early.   C. surprising.

3 cope
(kōp)
- *verb*

- The death of a beloved pet is hard to **cope** with.
- I read an interesting article on how to **cope** with difficult people.

<u>C</u> *Cope with* means   A. to value.   B. to predict.   C. to handle.

4 evaluate
(ĭ-văl′yoo-āt′)
- *verb*

- Reading movie reviews can help you **evaluate** whether a film is worth seeing.
- Several long-distance phone companies make the same promises, so it is hard to **evaluate** which is best.

<u>B</u> *Evaluate* means   A. to ignore.   B. to judge.   C. to remember.

5 phrase
(frāz)
- *noun*

- The **phrase** "at this point in time" can be reduced to a single word: "now."
- The **phrase** "Tom, Dick, or Harry" means "any member of the general public."

<u>B</u> *Phrase* means   A. puzzle.   B. word group.   C. answer.

6 plea
(plē)
- *noun*

- The parents of the missing baby made this **plea** to the kidnapper: "We beg you to return our baby to us unharmed!"
- "Please don't cut it too short, the way you did last time!" Eileen hoped the hair stylist would listen to her **plea**.

<u>B</u> *Plea* means   A. big joke.   B. urgent request.   C. long story.

7 practical
(prăk′tĭ-kəl)
- *adjective*

- Mom puts old socks to **practical** use as dust rags.
- The two single friends realized it would be **practical** to move in together and split the rent.

C Practical means   A. done for practice.   B. expensive.   C. sensible.

8 random
(răn′dəm)
- *adjective*

- We studied two paintings in art class. One was a clearly organized arrangement of black and white dots; the other seemed to be a **random** collection of spots and streaks of brilliant color.
- The movement of clouds may seem to be **random**, but scientists know that there is a pattern to how they move.

A Random means   A. without order.   B. rare.   C. useful.

9 significant
(sĭg-nĭf′ĭ-kənt)
- *adjective*

- Teron's factory job was hard but worthwhile, because he earned a **significant** part of his college expenses.
- Doctors have found that a good attitude can play a **significant** role in helping people recover from diseases.

B Significant means   A. busy.   B. large.   C. easy.

10 sole
(sōl)
- *adjective*

- After her husband died, Ramona became the **sole** supporter of a large family.
- The **sole** reason my cousin ever calls me is to ask for money.

A Sole means   A. only.   B. friendly.   C. early.

Matching Words with Definitions

Following are definitions of the ten words. **Print** each word next to its definition. If you look closely at each word in context, you will be able to figure out its meaning.

1. _____significant_____   Quite large in amount or number; important

2. _____approximately_____   Almost, but not exactly; more or less

3. _____random_____   Not having a plan, purpose, or pattern; chance

4. _____evaluate_____   To decide on the value of (something)

5. _____cope_____   To deal with difficulties; handle

6. _____sole_____   Only; being the only one

7. _____practical_____   Useful and sensible

8. _____plea_____   A request, especially a deeply felt, emotional one; an appeal°

9. _____consistent_____   Steady; regular

10. _____phrase_____   A group of words with a meaning; an expression

CAUTION: Do not go any further until you are sure the above answers are correct. Then you can use the definitions to help you in the following practices. Your goal is eventually to know the words well enough so that you don't need to check the definitions at all.

Check 1

Using the answer lines, complete each item below with the correct word from the box.

A. **approximately**	B. **consistent**	C. **cope**	D. **evaluate**	E. **phrase**
F. **plea**	G. **practical**	H. **random**	I. **significant**	J. **sole**

consistent   1. Rhonda is a ___ student, bringing home B's regularly.

significant   2. The Murphys have so many pets that they spend a ___ amount of their grocery money to feed them.

evaluate   3. The course on "Smart Shopping" teaches people how to ___ the worth of products and services.

plea   4. Barry begged the waitress to hurry with his meal, but she ignored his ___ and served the other diners first.

random   5. I like to take ___ walks, without any plan in mind.

cope   6. My friends helped me ___ with my father's death.

phrase   7. People just learning English are often puzzled by ___s such as "on the up-and-up" and "You don't say!"

sole   8. I barely know my neighbor. The ___ conversation we ever have is saying "Good morning" to each other.

practical   9. White furniture is not ___ for a family with little kids who wear dirty shoes and spill Kool-Aid.

approximately   10. "I'd like you to cut off this much," Eileen told her hairdresser, indicating° ___ two inches.

NOTE: Now check your answers to these items by turning to page 240. Going over the answers carefully will help you prepare for the remaining practices, for which answers are not given.

Check 2

Using the answer lines, complete each item below with **two** words from the box. Use each word once.

practical
cope   1–2. Dave found an inexpensive, ___ way to ___ with the problem of mice in his house: he got a cat.

approximately
significant   3–4. Pizza is Little Italy's best seller, bringing in ___ 30 percent of the profits, a very ___ part of the restaurant's income.

plea
evaluate   5–6. Giving in to her students' ___s, the teacher reluctantly° promised to ___ their projects and tell them their grades before the weekend.

phrase
random   7–8. The ___ "a chance meeting" refers to a ___ meeting—in other words, one that happens accidentally.

sole
consistent   9–10. The ___ exercise I get is walking—nothing else. But I am ___ about it; I do it every day. I prefer solitary° walks so that I don't have to talk to anyone.

Word Work

A. In the space provided, write the letter of the word that most closely relates to the situation in each item.

| A. **consistent** | B. **evaluate** | C. **phrase** |
| D. **random** | E. **significant** | |

_____evaluate_____   1. Our teacher will grade the history projects for originality, neatness, and accuracy—with an emphasis° on accuracy.

_____consistent_____   2. Kyle is never late for work. He walks in that door at 8:50 every morning, just like clockwork.

_____significant_____   3. You may think my earnings from baby-sitting are small, but they are an important part of my budget. They paid for all my books this semester.

_____random_____   4. The visitors to the city just wandered up and down the streets with no plan in mind, stopping to look at anything that caught their interest.

_____phrase_____   5. We've all heard movie lines such as "Go ahead—make my day," "Bond. James Bond," and "Show me the money."

B. Write each word next to the examples that best match it.

| F. **approximately** | G. **cope** | H. **plea** |
| I. **practical** | J. **sole** | |

_____practical_____   6. Buying milk for the family instead of a cola drink
Patching old jeans instead of throwing them out
Getting enough sleep before an important test

_____approximately_____   7. A distance of around two miles between the cousins' houses
About 150 people at the meeting
A cost of close to two dollars a pint for strawberries this summer

_____plea_____   8. "We appeal to you to vote for smoke-free restaurants!"
"Will you buy a box of cookies to support our summer sports program?"
"Please donate your spare change to help a local family whose home has burned down."

_____cope_____   9. Having a flat tire and then putting on a new one
Losing a job and then signing up for a class to learn new job skills
Feeling lonely and then deciding to join a social club

_____sole_____   10. Just one person living on the island
One egg left in the refrigerator
A boy with no brothers or sisters

Synonyms and Antonyms

A. Synonyms. Write the letter of the word or phrase that most nearly means the **same** as each boldfaced word.

_B_   1. **cope**

    A. compete with   C. quarrel

    B. manage   D. agree

_A_   2. **evaluate**

    A. judge   C. see

    B. pay for   D. borrow

_C_   3. **plea**

    A. joke   C. appeal

    B. abuse   D. pretend

_D_   4. **phrase**

    A. a practice   C. a plan

    B. something useful   D. a group of words

_B_   5. **sole**

    A. important   C. sensible

    B. only   D. unplanned

B. Antonyms. Write the letter of the word or phrase that most nearly means the **opposite** of each boldfaced word.

_B_   6. **approximately**

    A. well-known   C. not clear

    B. exactly   D. often

_D_   7. **consistent**

    A. having a plan   C. valuable

    B. not close   D. not regular

_A_   8. **practical**

    A. useless   C. boring

    B. valuable   D. common

_D_   9. **random**

    A. not steady   C. unknown

    B. interesting   D. planned

_D_ 10. **significant**

    A. wrong   C. dull

    B. unclear   D. small in amount

Final Check

Read the passages carefully. Then fill in each blank with the word that best fits the context.

A. Practicing Kindness

A. **consistent**	B. **evaluate**	C. **phrase**	D. **plea**	E. **random**

Maybe you've heard the (1)_____*phrase*_____ or seen the words printed on a bumper sticker. The saying is a (2)_____*plea*_____ for people to do kind things for no particular° reason, with no particular° plan. It goes like this: "Practice (3)_____*random*_____ acts of kindness and senseless beauty." I don't know where it originated° or who said it first. But I have seen people putting the idea into practice. I've noticed people inserting quarters into parking meters so that a stranger wouldn't be penalized° with a parking ticket. I've heard of someone paying a family's bill in a restaurant, then leaving before the family found out. I know a man who is (4)_____*consistent*_____ in not letting a day go by without giving someone a sincere compliment.

Why do these people bother? They probably don't stop to (5)_____*evaluate*_____ their actions. But if they did, I assume° they would say something like this: Kindness can be catching, just as cruelty can be. When we do something unexpected and nice for another person, who knows where that act of kindness might ultimately° end?

B. The Stinking Rose

F. **approximately**	G. **cope**	H. **practical**	I. **significant**	J. **sole**

Centuries ago in Rome, it was called "the stinking rose." It was then used to flavor food and for such (6)_____*practical*_____ purposes as fighting colds. Today we call it garlic, and we, too, find this wonderful substance° delicious and useful. In fact, in one recent year, Americans bought enough garlic to provide every man, woman, and child with (7)_____*approximately*_____ one and a half pounds of the stuff. It is added to a wide variety° of foods, from appetizers to zucchini—even to chocolate peanut butter cups. The unfortunate thing about garlic is that it produces bad breath. One way to (8)_____*cope*_____ with garlic breath is to chew parsley, an excellent natural breath cleaner. Or eat garlic only with others who are also eating it.

Being tasty, though, is not the (9)_____*sole*_____ good thing about garlic. It turns out that the ancient Romans were absolutely right about its having health benefits. A (10)_____*significant*_____ number of studies (about 3,000) have been done of the onionlike plant. They suggest that besides fighting colds, garlic could also be a remedy° for more serious internal° conditions. The studies indicate° that garlic may strengthen the immune system, cause a reduction° in blood pressure, and even help prevent cancer.

Scores	Check 2 _____%	Word Work _____%	Synonyms and Antonyms _____%	Final Check _____%

authentic	eligible
characteristic	harsh
concept	remote
confront	shallow
disrupt	thrive

Ten Words in Context

In the space provided, write the letter of the meaning closest to that of each **boldfaced** word. Use the context of the sentences to help you figure out each word's meaning.

1 authentic
(ô-thĕn′tĭk)
- *adjective*

- Don't be fooled if someone tries to sell you an **authentic** diamond ring for $10.99. The stone in that ring is sure to be fake.
- An **authentic** Van Gogh painting would cost many millions of dollars, but you can buy a copy of the same painting for very little money.

_C_ *Authentic* means   A. old.   B. qualified.   C. real.

2 characteristic
(kăr′ək-tə-rĭs′tĭk)
- *adjective*

- Lorenzo has his father's **characteristic** warm smile.
- Olive oil, garlic, pasta, and cheese are **characteristic** parts of the Italian diet.

_A_ *Characteristic* means   A. usual.   B. convenient.   C. strange.

3 concept
(kŏn′sĕpt′)
- *noun*

- When asked for her **concept** of heaven, the child said, "A room full of toys and chocolate."
- My aunt, who's always in debt, doesn't understand the **concept** of living within a budget.

_A_ *Concept* means   A. idea.   B. worst fear.   C. memory.

4 confront
(kən-frŭnt′)
- *verb*

- The restaurant manager really should **confront** that waiter and tell him directly about his rude behavior.
- The opposing lawyer plans to **confront** the accused man with a surprise piece of evidence.

_B_ *Confront* means   A. to avoid.   B. to face.   C. to prepare.

5 disrupt
(dĭs-rŭpt′)
- *verb*

- Tina thought it would be fun to sneak her tiny dog into the movie theater. But then the dog got loose and **disrupted** the show.
- Parents who are angry about budget cuts plan to **disrupt** tonight's school board meeting with a noisy demonstration.

_C_ *Disrupt* means   A. to manage.   B. to go to.   C. to upset.

6 eligible
(ĕl′ĭ-jə-bəl)
- *adjective*

- Because of his high grades and his parents' low income, my cousin is **eligible** for some good college scholarships.
- It's not true that any American can become president of the United States. To be **eligible**, you have to be at least thirty-five years old.

_A_ *Eligible* means   A. qualified.   B. known.   C. pleased.

7 harsh
(härsh)
- *adjective*

- The **harsh** ruler decided to punish the entire village for one man's crime.
- The scolding that the children received was too **harsh**. They hadn't done anything all that bad.

B *Harsh* means   A. fair.   B. rough.   C. wasteful.

8 remote
(rĭ-mōt′)
- *adjective*

- Humans have explored even the most **remote** parts of the planet, areas deep in forests and beneath the seas.
- Some parts of the park are so **remote** that visitors seldom reach them.

C *Remote* means   A. large.   B. typical.   C. distant.

9 shallow
(shăl′ō)
- *adjective*

- The lifeguard at the pool insists that young children stay at the **shallow** end.
- The cake won't rise very high in that **shallow** pan; you'll need a smaller pan with higher sides.

B *Shallow* means   A. real.   B. not deep.   C. very wide.

10 thrive
(thrīv)
- *verb*

- African violets like light, so they should **thrive** in that sunny window.
- In the past, many premature babies died; but with modern medical care, most of them **thrive** and live normal lives.

A *Thrive* means   A. to do very well.   B. to grow weaker.   C. to need too much care.

Matching Words with Definitions

Following are definitions of the ten words. **Print** each word next to its definition. If you look closely at each word in context, you will be able to figure out its meaning.

1. _____ shallow _____   Not deep

2. _____ confront _____   To face or oppose boldly

3. _____ thrive _____   To grow very well; improve physically

4. _____ disrupt _____   To cause disorder or confusion; upset

5. _____ eligible _____   Qualified to be chosen; desirable as a candidate

6. _____ harsh _____   Unkind or cruel; strict; severe

7. _____ remote _____   Far away; very distant; hidden away

8. _____ characteristic _____   Typical of someone or something

9. _____ concept _____   A general thought; an idea

10. _____ authentic _____   Real; true; actual

CAUTION: Do not go any further until you are sure the above answers are correct. Then you can use the definitions to help you in the following practices. Your goal is eventually to know the words well enough so that you don't need to check the definitions at all.

Check 1

Using the answer lines, complete each item below with the correct word from the box.

A. **authentic**	B. **characteristic**	C. **concept**	D. **confront**	E. **disrupt**
F. **eligible**	G. **harsh**	H. **remote**	I. **shallow**	J. **thrive**

shallow   1. The creek was so ___ that the water came up only to my ankles.

authentic   2. Some imitation pearl necklaces are so beautiful that only a jeweler can tell that the pearls are not ___.

harsh   3. When the new employee forgot to lock up the store one night, his boss gave him a ___ warning: "Another mistake like that, Buddy, and you're out of a job!"

concept   4. The preschool teacher tries to help her little students understand the ___ of sharing.

disrupt   5. The student assembly was ___ed by a fire drill.

thrive   6. The weak, sickly child began to ___ after doctors corrected her heart problem.

remote   7. Professor Liu studies little-known plants in ___ parts of our state forests.

confront   8. After a man dropped a bag of trash on the ground, another man picked it up and ___ed him, saying, "I think this is yours. Find a trash can."

eligible   9. Students must have at least a B average to be ___ for any of the school sports teams.

characteristic   10. Fat, fleshy leaves are ___ of cactus plants.

NOTE: Now check your answers to these items by turning to page 240. Going over the answers carefully will help you prepare for the remaining practices, for which answers are not given.

Check 2

Using the answer lines, complete each item below with **two** words from the box. Use each word once.

characteristic
authentic   1–2. The two rings looked alike to me, but the jeweler said that only one had the colorful sparkle that is ___ of an ___ diamond.

confront
disrupt   3–4. "Tomorrow I'll ___ our neighbors," Alonso said, "and protest° about the way their unleashed dog ___s the children's backyard games."

harsh
thrive   5–6. A child who does poorly in school with a ___, bad-tempered teacher might ___ with a teacher who is gentle and caring.

eligible
remote   7–8. Because she is a biologist, Mia is ___ to be part of a research team that will study turtles on a ___ island.

concept
shallow   9–10. Because babies can drown in very little water, the ___ that they are safe in a ___ pool is false. A reliable° adult must watch them every second.

Word Work

A. Write each word by the examples that best match it.

| A. **authentic** | B. **characteristic** | C. **disrupt** |
| D. **harsh** | E. **thrive** | |

disrupt   1. A baby cries during a religious service.
A cat runs onto a baseball field in the middle of a game.
A fire drill occurs° in the middle of a class.

authentic   2. A red stone that a jeweler says is a ruby
An old desk known to be an antique from the seventeenth century
Cave paintings proven to be the work of Stone Age artists

characteristic   3. The red color of many barns
The sweet smell of roses
The hot summers of Florida

harsh   4. A clerk who insults all the customers in the store
A boss who forces his employees to work through lunch
A drill sergeant screaming orders at a group of new soldiers

thrive   5. Betsy settles into her new school quickly, makes friends, and earns good grades.
An orphaned kitten grows strong and healthy by drinking formula from a bottle.
A fern hanging in the sunny window grows full and beautiful.

B. In the space provided, write the letter of the word that most closely relates to the situation in each item.

_C_   6. I plan to walk up to my neighbor and tell him that the junk car on his lawn is an eyesore.

     A. shallow   B. eligible   C. confront

_A_   7. The idea of infinity—of time and space that have no beginning and no end—is difficult for most people to understand.

     A. concept   B. thrive   C. eligible

_C_   8. Any child between the ages of 5 and 9 who is a resident of Ohio may enter a drawing in the art contest.

     A. confront   B. disrupt   C. eligible

_B_   9. The hermit lived many miles from town, in a part of the hills that was hard to reach. He wasn't able to cope° very well with the demands of society.

     A. confront   B. remote   C. thrive

_A_ 10. That box isn't deep enough—don't you have one that is a better size to hold a salad bowl?

     A. shallow   B. authentic   C. harsh

Analogies

Each item below starts with a pair of words in CAPITAL LETTERS. For each item, figure out the relationship between these two words. Then decide which of the choices (A, B, C, or D) expresses a similar relationship. Write the letter of your choice on the answer line. (All the repeated words in these items are from this unit.)

_B_ 1. AUTHENTIC : REAL ::

    A. lost : found   C. expected : surprising

    B. expensive : high-priced   D. inner : external

_C_ 2. EXTERNAL° : INTERNAL° ::

    A. outside : weather   C. agonizing° : pleasant

    B. sole° : only   D. red : bright

_C_ 3. HARSH : KIND ::

    A. late : tardy   C. permanent : temporary°

    B. helpful : useful   D. incredible° : amazing

_C_ 4. ORANGE : FRUIT ::

    A. cat : dog   C. penicillin : remedy°

    B. triumph° : loss   D. strawberry : cherry

_D_ 5. CONFRONT : AVOID ::

    A. strive° : try   C. tear : rip

    B. eligible : qualified   D. prosper° : fail

_C_ 6. SHALLOW : DEEP ::

    A. brief : short   C. smiling : frowning

    B. disrupt : upset   D. random° : unplanned

_D_ 7. WINDOW : TRANSPARENT° ::

    A. door : doorknob   C. car : highway

    B. window : curtain   D. grass : green

_A_ 8. THRIVE : WEAKEN ::

    A. protest° : approve   C. protect : guard

    B. smile : grin   D. spectacle° : watch

_B_ 9. TRAIT° : PATIENCE ::

    A. promise : withdraw°   C. banker : money

    B. substance° : clay   D. kindness : intelligence

_B_ 10. GIVE : GIFT ::

    A. run : walk   C. concept : idea

    B. detect° : clue   D. verdict° : opinion

Final Check

Read the passages carefully. Then fill in each blank with the word that best fits the context.

A. A Modern Fairy Tale

A. **concept**	B. **confront**	C. **disrupt**	D. **eligible**	E. **harsh**

Many fairy tales are versions° of the same story: A prince has his pick of all the (1)___eligible___ women in the kingdom. But the girl he likes best is in big trouble, so the prince bravely rescues her. The girl doesn't do much of anything. She just looks pretty. The stories all end with more or less the same phrase°: "They lived happily ever after."

But one fairy tale, "The Paper Bag Princess," gets rid of the (2)___concept___ of the brave prince and the helpless girl who is dependent° on him. In it, Princess Elizabeth is engaged to Prince Ronald. But a dragon (3)___disrupt___s their plans by burning the castle and capturing Ronald. Elizabeth decides to rescue him. Since all her pretty clothes have been burned up, she puts on a paper bag. She bravely (4)___confront___s the dragon and tricks him into using up all his strength on silly tasks. Then she goes into the dragon's cave and finds Ronald.

Instead of being grateful, however, Ronald gives Elizabeth a (5)___harsh___ scolding for being covered with dirt and smoke and for wearing a bag. He tells her to come back when she looks like "a real princess." Elizabeth tells Ronald that though he looks like a real prince, with his fancy clothes and neat hair, he is, in fact, "a bum." The last picture in the book shows Elizabeth dancing happily off into the sunset, with the final line, "They didn't get married after all."

B. Wolf Children

F. **authentic**	G. **characteristic**	H. **remote**	I. **shallow**	J. **thrive**

A tale of children being raised by wolves sounds incredible°. However, though hard to believe, one story about wolf children appears to be (6)___authentic___. In Singapore during the early 1920s, Reverend J.A.L. Singh heard stories of "man-beasts" that were frightening the people of a (7)___remote___ jungle village. Along with a group of other men, Singh went in search of that hidden village and the strange creatures.

In the village, Singh was taken to a large hill. When he dug a (8)___shallow___ hole in the hill, he quickly discovered a family of wolves. From within the wolves' den, two pale creatures peeked out. Singh's party killed the adult wolves and dug further into the den. There they found two human children curled up with the cubs. The children were captured and brought to the village in bamboo cages.

The children did not speak like other humans; instead, they howled and growled like animals. Their diet was equally wolflike; they preferred raw meat, mice, and cockroaches. And they had the wolf's (9)___characteristic___ desire to be active at night, as well as a dislike of the indoors. Sadly, the children did not (10)___thrive___. Within an interval° of a few years, both grew weak and died.

Scores	Check 2 _____%	Word Work _____%	Analogies _____%	Final Check _____%

The box at the right lists twenty-five words from Unit Three. Using the clues at the bottom of the page, fill in these words to complete the puzzle that follows.

Word box:
- artificial
- complicate
- concept
- cope
- counsel
- detect
- energetic
- external
- foresight
- harsh
- internal
- phrase
- protest
- random
- remedy
- remote
- shallow
- significant
- sole
- strive
- thrive
- tolerance
- trait
- triumph
- verdict

ACROSS

3. Quite large in amount or number

6. Far away; very distant

7. A cure; something that heals

9. Only; being the only one

10. A group of words with a meaning; an expression

12. To give advice or guidance

13. Not deep

16. Outer; located outside

18. Inner; located inside

19. To make difficult by adding or involving many parts or details; make complex

21. Not having a plan, purpose, or pattern; chance

22. Unkind or cruel; strict; severe

23. Made to imitate something natural

24. An opinion or judgment

DOWN

1. Lively; spirited; full of energy

2. To deal with difficulties

3. To try hard

4. To grow very well; improve physically

5. Care in planning or preparing for the future

8. To notice; discover that something exists or is present

11. To complain

14. Respect for the differing views, practices, and characteristics of others

15. An outstanding or very satisfying success; victory

17. A general thought; an idea

20. A quality or feature, as of personality, for which a person is known

PART A

Choose the word that best completes each item and write it in the space provided.

_____triumph_____ 1. Since my math class was very difficult for me, I consider the B I got for the course to be a great ___.

    A. foresight   B. triumph   C. tolerance   D. trait

_____verdict_____ 2. The veterinarian's ___ was that our dog was limping because the dog had cracked a bone in her ankle.

    A. verdict   B. conscience   C. tolerance   D. substance

_____counsels_____ 3. It's hard to believe in a doctor who ___ his patients not to smoke, but who smokes himself.

    A. counsels   B. copes with   C. withdraws   D. prospers

_____frequency_____ 4. The ___ of Lonnell's ear infections when he was a little boy was great, but he hasn't had one for years now.

    A. phrase   B. spectacle   C. frequency   D. conscience

_____represent_____ 5. "Remember that you ___ all of the people of our city," one man yelled to the mayor, "not just the rich ones."

    A. represent   B. detect   C. protest   D. thrive

_____temporary_____ 6. It turned out that Peter's interest in collecting stamps was only ___. He forgot about it after a couple of months.

    A. temporary   B. agonizing   C. external   D. transparent

_____detect_____ 7. If I ___ a hair in my food, then I can't eat another bite of that food, even after I remove the hair.

    A. strive   B. evaluate   C. assume   D. detect

_____conscience_____ 8. As much as I would love to skip my chores and go the baseball game, my ___ won't let me.

    A. substance   B. conscience   C. phrase   D. interval

_____assume_____ 9. Just because Donald is quiet in class, don't ___ that he is stupid.

    A. assume   B. protest   C. disrupt   D. withdraw

_____conscious_____ 10. As she read in the living room, Vanessa became ___ of loud voices coming from her parents' room.

    A. appropriate   B. shallow   C. authentic   D. conscious

(Continues on next page)

complicated   11. My daughter invited some friends over for dinner and then ___ my planning by telling me that one is allergic to eggs, another is allergic to milk, and the third is a vegetarian.

    A. prospered   B. complicated   C. thrived   D. detected

transparent   12. When they visited the coast, the Martins enjoyed a trip in a glass-bottomed boat. They looked through its ___ bottom and saw many fish and other sea creatures.

    A. transparent   B. random   C. remote   D. harsh

artificial   13. The hardware store sells ___ stones made of plastic that you can open and hide a house key in. Then you can hide the key by leaving the "stone" somewhere near your door.

    A. eligible   B. authentic   C. artificial   D. spectacle

PART B

Write **C** if the italicized word is used **correctly**. Write **I** if the word is used **incorrectly**.

_I_   14. After using the _external_ part of onions and potatoes in a meal, I use the peels to make broth.

_C_   15. As _incredible_ as it seems, the Nile River in Africa has frozen over at least twice.

_I_   16. The house's _internal_ appearance is neat, but inside, it's a real mess.

_C_   17. The _maximum_ legal driving speed in our state is sixty miles an hour.

_I_   18. We put away the rollers and paint cans and sat down to enjoy the _spectacle_ of watching the paint dry.

_C_   19. The play was so bad that we slipped out of the theater during the _interval_ between the first and second acts.

_I_   20. Joan's sickness seemed to be getting better, but over the weekend she had a _remedy_ and is now seriously ill.

_I_   21. Instead of looking for a job, my _energetic_ brother is spending his summer lying on the couch watching TV.

_C_   22. Knowing that his children often bring home friends after a baseball game, Mr. Hendricks had the _foresight_ to make extra hamburgers for dinner.

_C_   23. The chickens _protest_ loudly whenever someone takes their eggs out from under them.

_I_   24. I couldn't wait to tell my father the _agonizing_ news: I had made the basketball team!

_I_   25. That boss is so _harsh_ that he gives every employee an extra day off on his or her birthday.

Score   (Number correct) _____ x 4 = _____ %

Enter your score above and in the **Vocabulary Performance Chart** on the inside back cover of the book.

PART A

On the answer line, write the word from the box that completes each item below. Use each word once.

A. approximately	B. authentic	C. consistent	D. cope	E. disrupt
F. eligible	G. phrase	H. prosper	I. remote	J. shallow
K. substance	L. trait	M. withdraw		

_____disrupt_____ 1. A swarm of bees ___ed the picnic, sending people running and yelling in every direction.

_____cope_____ 2. One way to ___ with winter weather is to stay indoors, turn the heat up, play old Beach Boys records, and watch videotapes of Hawaiian hula dancers.

_____trait_____ 3. When asked what ___ is most important in a boyfriend or girlfriend, many people answer, "A sense of humor."

_____remote_____ 4. In order to have the peace and quiet he needed to finish his book, the writer moved to a ___ cabin where there were no other people nearby, no Internet connection, and not even a telephone.

_____prosper_____ 5. A lemonade stand would ___ on this corner. Hundreds of hot, thirsty people walk by every day.

_____substance_____ 6. The librarian complained that someone had returned a book with a strange green ___ all over its cover.

_____authentic_____ 7. If someone tells you he can sell you an ___ diamond bracelet for twenty dollars, don't believe him.

_____eligible_____ 8. Do you have to be a high-school graduate to be ___ to join the Army?

_____approximately_____ 9. The car sells for ___ fifteen thousand dollars; the exact price depends on what "extras" you order, such as power windows or a CD player.

_____consistent_____ 10. I don't think I'd like to live in a place where the weather is so ___ that there is never any change from day to day.

_____shallow_____ 11. Don't bury those carrot seeds too deep. Just dig a ___ hole for each one and cover it with a small amount of soil.

_____withdraw_____ 12. I had to ___ my offer to buy my friend's old car when I realized I couldn't afford automobile insurance.

_____phrase_____ 13. My grandfather usually spoke English, but he always greeted friends with the Spanish __ "Qué pasa?" which means "What's happening?"

(Continues on next page)

PART B

Write **C** if the italicized word is used **correctly**. Write **I** if the word is used **incorrectly**.

_C_ 14. Manuel is a hard-working person who always *strives* to do his best.

_C_ 15. Amanda was the *sole* person at the table who ate meat. Everyone else was a vegetarian.

_C_ 16. After being put in the sun and watered regularly, the sickly plant soon *thrived*.

_I_ 17. When I asked the traffic cop for directions to the post office, he *evaluated* that it was just down the block.

_I_ 18. Reading a funny story on the bus, Jeremy suddenly burst out laughing. The people around him were surprised by his *plea*.

_I_ 19. My father's blood pressure is so high that he has scheduled a *random* appointment with his doctor.

_C_ 20. The little girl taught herself the *concept* of "right" and "left" by remembering, "I **write** with my **right** hand."

_I_ 21. The families decided it would be too *practical* to eat in an expensive restaurant.

_I_ 22. I keep a couple of quarters in my pocket for *significant* purchases, such as a pack of gum.

_C_ 23. The letters "ski" are a *characteristic* part of many Polish names, such as Kwilinski and Paderewski.

_I_ 24. Because Linda is so shy, she usually *confronts* people rather than daring to face them and actually talk to them.

_I_ 25. It's plain to see from the way Diane quarrels so often with her friends that she has lots of *tolerance* for other people's opinions.

Score   (Number correct) _____ x 4 = _____%

Enter your scores above and in the **Vocabulary Performance Chart** on the inside back cover of the book.

PART A: Synonyms

In the space provided, write the letter of the choice that is most nearly the **same** in meaning as the **boldfaced** word.

__D__ 1. **assume**   A. improve   B. tire   C. manage   D. take for granted

__A__ 2. **characteristic**   A. typical   B. strong   C. important   D. amazing

__A__ 3. **concept**   A. idea   B. goal   C. period   D. knowledge of right and wrong

__C__ 4. **confront**   A. interrupt   B. take away from   C. face boldly   D. succeed

__B__ 5. **conscience**   A. respect for others   B. sense of right and wrong   C. feature
   D. how often something happens

__D__ 6. **cope with**   A. judge   B. remove   C. believe   D. manage

__A__ 7. **counsel**   A. give advice to   B. bring together   C. send away   D. search for

__D__ 8. **detect**   A. take from   B. speak for   C. stop briefly   D. discover

__A__ 9. **disrupt**   A. upset   B. watch   C. tire   D. complain

__C__ 10. **eligible**   A. important   B. chosen   C. qualified   D. amazing

__A__ 11. **evaluate**   A. judge   B. try   C. grow   D. take back

__B__ 12. **foresight**   A. purpose   B. care in planning   C. cure   D. attention

__D__ 13. **frequency**   A. material   B. goal   C. word group
   D. how often something happens

__A__ 14. **interval**   A. time in between   B. thought   C. system   D. word group

__C__ 15. **phrase**   A. period of time   B. shape   C. group of words   D. amount

__C__ 16. **plea**   A. absence   B. reason   C. request   D. mistake

__B__ 17. **remote**   A. not usual   B. far away   C. believable
   D. able to be seen through

__A__ 18. **represent**   A. speak for   B. feel anger against   C. make smaller   D. send again

__D__ 19. **sole**   A. outer   B. best   C. large   D. only

__B__ 20. **spectacle**   A. angry conversation   B. unusual sight   C. loud noise
   D. embarrassing accident

__C__ 21. **substance**   A. care   B. general thought   C. material   D. knowledge

__D__ 22. **tolerance**   A. win   B. possibility   C. confusion   D. lack of prejudice

__D__ 23. **trait**   A. meeting   B. story   C. plan   D. feature

__D__ 24. **transparent**   A. fake   B. amazing   C. proud   D. able to be seen through

__B__ 25. **verdict**   A. excuse   B. judgment   C. reason   D. fright

(Continues on next page)

PART B: Antonyms

In the space provided, write the letter of the choice that is most nearly **opposite** in meaning to the **boldfaced** word.

B	26.	**agonizing**	A. careless	B. painless	C. hopeless	D. useless
C	27.	**approximately**	A. always	B. useful	C. exactly	D. properly
D	28.	**artificial**	A. perfect	B. likeable	C. suitable	D. natural
D	29.	**authentic**	A. demanding	B. believable	C. sharp	D. fake
A	30.	**complicate**	A. make easy	B. speed up	C. pass over	D. take advice
D	31.	**conscious**	A. unqualified	B. unusual	C. unexpected	D. unaware
B	32.	**consistent**	A. gentle	B. changing	C. rude	D. weak
A	33.	**energetic**	A. not active	B. necessary	C. lengthy	D. new
C	34.	**external**	A. useless	B. harmful	C. inner	D. close
D	35.	**harsh**	A. planned	B. nearby	C. useful	D. kind
C	36.	**incredible**	A. regular	B. not possible	C. easy to believe	
			D. disagreeable			
D	37.	**internal**	A. real	B. deep	C. honest	D. outer
A	38.	**maximum**	A. lowest possible	B. legal	C. exact	D. able
A	39.	**practical**	A. not useful	B. not inside	C. not easy	D. not possible
C	40.	**prosper**	A. make easy	B. face	C. grow poor	D. help
B	41.	**protest**	A. put an end to	B. approve	C. give	D. grow stronger
C	42.	**random**	A. believable	B. not wanted	C. planned	D. pleasant
D	43.	**remedy**	A. thought	B. distance	C. purpose	D. disease
A	44.	**shallow**	A. deep	B. crowded	C. weak	D. least
C	45.	**significant**	A. not real	B. done on purpose	C. not important	
			D. not steady			
D	46.	**strive**	A. give advice	B. put in	C. ask for	D. give up
A	47.	**temporary**	A. long-lasting	B. not qualified	C. weak	D. not typical
D	48.	**thrive**	A. know	B. argue	C. change	D. grow weak
D	49.	**triumph**	A. suggestion	B. patience	C. distance	D. loss
B	50.	**withdraw**	A. erase	B. put back	C. give up	D. forget

Score   (Number correct) _____ x 2 = _____%

Enter your score above and in the **Vocabulary Performance Chart** on the inside back cover of the book.

Unit Four

Chapter 16

apparent	fulfill
automatic	influence
burden	security
economical	sympathize
extravagant	transfer

Chapter 17

bewilder	fiction
communicate	investigate
deceive	legible
earnest	outspoken
emotion	theory

Chapter 18

assure	hostile
crucial	humiliate
divert	impulse
extraordinary	perceive
frantic	revive

Chapter 19

abandon	function
alert	idle
circumstances	overcome
devote	primary
dominate	theme

Chapter 20

disregard	monotonous
excerpt	obtain
exclude	prey
hinder	seize
misleading	severe

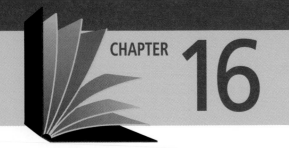

apparent	fulfill
automatic	influence
burden	security
economical	sympathize
extravagant	transfer

Ten Words in Context

In the space provided, write the letter of the meaning closest to that of each **boldfaced** word. Use the context of the sentences to help you figure out each word's meaning.

1 apparent
(ə-păr′ənt)
- *adjective*

● Marcie's smile made it **apparent** that she had done well on the test.

● It's **apparent** that Will and Bess have settled their quarrel, since they are dating steadily again.

_B_ *Apparent* means   A. helpful.   B. clear.   C. secret.

2 automatic
(ô′tə-măt′ĭk)
- *adjective*

● Our new coffeemaker is **automatic**. We set it at night, and it turns on by itself in the morning.

● Before the **automatic** washing machine, laundering clothes was not so easy.

_A_ *Automatic* means   A. self-operating.   B. unusual.   C. low in cost.

3 burden
(bûr′dn)
- *noun*

● Although others think raising a special-needs child must be a **burden**, my neighbor says she has found joy, not hardship, in caring for her son.

● At first the lie he had told didn't bother the boy, but after a few days it became a great **burden** to him. He wished he could go back in time and undo what he had done.

_C_ *Burden* means   A. freedom.   B. protection.   C. heavy load.

4 economical
(ĕk′ə-nŏm′ĭ-kəl)
- *adjective*

● It's usually more **economical** to buy food and soap in large packages. Smaller packages cost more per ounce.

● To decide which car is most **economical**, compare prices, gas mileage, and repair costs.

_B_ *Economical* means   A. difficult.   B. money-saving.   C. easy to see.

5 extravagant
(ĭk-străv′ə-gənt)
- *adjective*

● I think it's **extravagant** to buy a prom dress that will be worn only once, so I'm borrowing one from a friend.

● Rhoda's budget is so tight that she feels it would be **extravagant** to buy herself a ten-dollar pair of earrings.

_C_ *Extravagant* means   A. not effective.   B. obvious.   C. spending too much.

6 fulfill
(fŏol-fĭl′)
- *verb*

● One day, Chen hopes to **fulfill** his dream of visiting China again and renewing ties with his family there.

● Jill doesn't like her job, but she promised to stay with it at least one year, and she plans to **fulfill** that promise.

_B_ *Fulfill* means   A. repeat.   B. carry out.   C. have an effect on.

7 influence
(ĭn′floō-əns)
- *verb*

● My father thinks my friends **influence** me too much. He says they are the reason that I study so little and waste so much time.

● Do advertisements **influence** what you buy, or do you ignore them and make your own choices?

C *Influence* means   A. delay.   B. protect.   C. affect.

8 security
(sĭ-kyoŏr′ĭ-tē)
- *noun*

● For nighttime **security**, the owner of the jewelry shop turns on a burglar alarm.

● People with homes near the river like having the **security** of flood insurance.

C *Security* means   A. hardship.   B. expense.   C. safety.

9 sympathize
(sĭm′pə-thīz′)
- *verb*

● The whole town **sympathized** with the family whose house burned down.

● To show he **sympathized** with Mrs. Jackson when her husband died, Scott sent her flowers and a card.

A *Sympathized with* means   A. felt sorry for.   B. sent for.   C. talked to.

10 transfer
(trăns′fər)
- *verb*

● Before I can paint the bookcase, I have to **transfer** all the books into boxes.

● In April, the Army will **transfer** Jamal from a base in South Carolina to one in Virginia.

B *Transfer* means   A. reach.   B. move.   C. see.

Matching Words with Definitions

Following are definitions of the ten words. **Print** each word next to its definition. If you look closely at each word in context, you will be able to figure out its meaning.

1. _____economical_____   Costing or spending little; thrifty

2. _____transfer_____   To move or send from one place to another

3. _____automatic_____   Moving or operating by itself

4. _____influence_____   To have an effect on

5. _____sympathize_____   To feel or express sorrow or pity for

6. _____fulfill_____   To carry out; achieve; do

7. _____burden_____   A hardship; something difficult to bear

8. _____apparent_____   Obvious; easy to see

9. _____security_____   Protection; freedom from danger, fear, or worry

10. _____extravagant_____   Spending much more than is necessary or wise; wasteful

CAUTION: Do not go any further until you are sure the above answers are correct. Then you can use the definitions to help you in the following practices. Your goal is eventually to know the words well enough so that you don't need to check the definitions at all.

Check 1

Using the answer lines, complete each item below with the correct word from the box.

A. **apparent**	B. **automatic**	C. **burden**	D. **economical**	E. **extravagant**
F. **fulfill**	G. **influence**	H. **security**	I. **sympathize**	J. **transfer**

_____transfer_____ 1. Sian's boss intends to assign her to another office for two weeks. In other words, he wants to ___ her there temporarily°.

_____burden_____ 2. A ___ may be a physical or a mental hardship, or both.

_____influence_____ 3. Political candidates try to ___ elections with numerous ads.

_____extravagant_____ 4. An ___ person enjoys spending a lot of money.

_____sympathize_____ 5. When we've had the same difficult experience as someone else, it's easier for us to ___ with him or her.

_____apparent_____ 6. Because Kira was smiling, it was ___ that she was happy about something.

_____fulfill_____ 7. When you make an agreement with people, they expect you to ___ your part of the deal.

_____security_____ 8. After people are robbed, they often feel a greater need for ___.

_____economical_____ 9. An ___ person doesn't like to waste money.

_____automatic_____ 10. Do you think there will ever be a fully ___ car, one that needs no driver?

NOTE: Now check your answers to these items by turning to page 240. Going over the answers carefully will help you prepare for the remaining practices, for which answers are not given.

Check 2

Using the answer lines, complete each item below with **two** words from the box. Use each word once.

_____transfer_____
_____sympathize_____
1–2. "Because we are moving," Gina said, "our children will have to ___ to different schools. I can ___ with them because I went through the same experience as a child."

_____Automatic_____
_____security_____
3–4. ___ yard lights, which go on by themselves° at dark, can add to the ___ of a home.

_____economical_____
_____fulfill_____
5–6. Clark had to think of an ___ way to ___ his promise to give each of his twelve nieces and nephews a gift, so he baked them each a pie.

_____apparent_____
_____burden_____
7–8. From the young hiker's slowed walk, it was ___ that his large backpack had become a ___.

_____influence_____
_____extravagant_____
9–10. Having a credit card has ___d Barry in a sad way. He has become so ___ that he now has a closet full of more clothes than he can wear—and a huge credit-card bill.

Word Work

A. Write each word next to the examples that best match it.

A. **automatic**	B. **economical**	C. **extravagant**
D. **security**	E. **sympathize**	

_____extravagant_____ 1. Eating in fancy restaurants every night
Buying two dresses for the same party because you can't decide between them
Purchasing a sterling silver collar for your dog

_____automatic_____ 2. Automobile headlights that turn off when the motor stops running
A door that slides open when a person approaches it
An oven that cleans itself

_____security_____ 3. A burglar alarm
Fire insurance
Armed guards

_____sympathize_____ 4. Sending a card when a friend's mother dies
Hugging a crying child
Taking a friend who is depressed out to dinner

_____economical_____ 5. Figure out the best grocery buys
Turn off lights when you leave a room
Use old envelopes for shopping lists

B. In the space provided, write the letter of the choice that most closely relates to the situation in each item.

_C_ 6. The outside porch light comes on at the same time every evening.

  A. extravagant   B. unfulfilled   c. automatic

_B_ 7. To make up for being sick last semester, the student is taking a full load plus two extra classes.

  A. apparent   B. burden   c. transfer

_A_ 8. When I saw an ad for chocolate-chip cookies, I decided to go to the kitchen and bake some.

  A. influence   B. automatic   c. burden

_C_ 9. I made a New Year's resolution to lose ten pounds, and I'm sticking to it. So I'm not eating any of those chocolate-chip cookies.

  A. transfer   B. burden   c. fulfill

_B_ 10. When Jen moved into the attic bedroom, she spent hours carrying her belongings up there.

  A. automatic   B. transfer   c. influence

Word Parts

A. The suffix *-ment* often means "the result, state, act, or process of ___."

Examples: *fulfillment* — the result of fulfilling   *argument* — the act of arguing
            enjoyment — the state of enjoying   *placement* — the process of placing

On each answer line, write the word from the box that means the same as the *italicized* words.

> A. **astonishment°**   B. **fulfillment**   C. **management**
> D. **replacement**   E. **statement**

astonishment   1. The magician's surprising act filled us with a *state of being astonished°*.

replacement   2. The *act of replacing* of our old kitchen floor was not easy. We had to tear the old floor out before the new one could be put in.

management   3. It is obvious that the *process of managing* of this company is excellent. The company is very successful, and the workers are very happy.

fulfillment   4. For me, a small home in the country would be the *result of fulfilling* of a dream.

statement   5. Kareem likes to study for tests with another person. He says that the *act of stating* of an idea out loud to someone else helps him remember it better.

B. The suffix *-ly* means "in a certain way."

Examples: *economical* — thrifty   *secure* — safe
            economically — in a thrifty way   *securely* — in a safe way

On each answer line, write the word from the box that best completes the item.

> F. **consistently°**   G. **economically**   H. **exactly**
> I. **extravagantly**   J. **securely**

consistently   6. Ralph may not be the perfect worker, but at least he is steady about one thing: he is ___ late for work each day.

securely   7. Here's some practical° advice: Before leaving for a vacation, make sure all doors and windows are closed ___. Then lock them.

extravagantly   8. Wanting to impress his date, Dan spent money ___ on lobster, champagne, and a hired limousine.

exactly   9. If a math answer is not ___ right, you may not get full credit for it.

economically   10. The three families got a new lawn mower ___ by buying it together, then sharing it.

Final Check

Read the passages carefully. Then fill in each blank with the word that best fits the context.

A. A Mismatched Couple

| A. **burden** | B. **economical** | C. **extravagant** | D. **security** | E. **sympathize** |

Stacy and Ken have completely different attitudes° toward money. For example, Stacy is (1)_____ economical _____ to an extreme, always trying to get the best price on even the smallest purchase. Ken, on the other hand, is very (2)_____ extravagant _____. He's accustomed° to spending money on anything that catches his eye. If there's a dime in his pocket, he feels that it's a (3)_____ burden _____, as hard to carry around as a heavy load. He'll find something to spend it on just to be rid of it. Knowing she has money in case of accident or illness gives Stacy a feeling of (4)_____ security _____, but Ken doesn't worry about the future—it's too remote° to think about. Each is puzzled by the other's "strange" behavior. Stacy sees Ken as wasteful and irresponsible, and Ken calls Stacy "cheap." Because he doesn't understand the concept° of "saving for a rainy day," he can't (5)_____ sympathize _____ with her when she's worried about an empty bank account. Since they have very little tolerance° for each other's views on money, no one was surprised when these two got divorced.

B. A Campaign to Become Class President

| F. **apparent** | G. **automatic** | H. **fulfill** | I. **influence** | J. **transfer** |

In her senior year, Holly wanted very much to be elected class president. But she knew that the other girl who was competing for the office was much better known and had more experience in student government. As a result, Holly began to do all she could to (6)_____ influence _____ her classmates so that they would vote for her. She listened to every plea° and promised her classmates anything they asked for. "If I'm elected," she told one student, "I will see that the school puts in (7)_____ automatic _____ doors to make it easy to enter when our arms are full of books." To another, she said that a hot tub would be installed in the school gym. She promised a third student that he would be eligible° to (8)_____ transfer _____ to the school across town that his girlfriend attended. As the election drew near, it became (9)_____ apparent _____ that Holly had a good chance of winning. This scared her because she realized that she could not (10)_____ fulfill _____ all her promises. Finally, she had the foresight° to quit the race, saying she couldn't maintain° her grades and serve as class president, too. She felt foolish for having let her desire to win run away with her good sense.

| Scores | Check 2 _____% | Word Work _____% | Word Parts _____% | Final Check _____% |

Enter your scores above and in the **Vocabulary Performance Chart** on the inside back cover of the book.

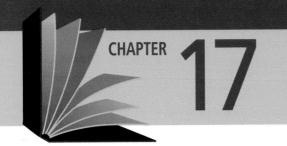

bewilder	fiction
communicate	investigate
deceive	legible
earnest	outspoken
emotion	theory

Ten Words in Context

In the space provided, write the letter of the meaning closest to that of each **boldfaced** word. Use the context of the sentences to help you figure out each word's meaning.

1 bewilder
(bǐ-wǐl′dər)
- *verb*

● The large new school at first **bewildered** Anton, but after a day or two, getting around was no longer confusing to him.

● My grandmother's poor health **bewildered** her doctor until he found out she wasn't taking her medicines.

B *Bewilder* means   A. to calm.   B. to puzzle.   C. to attract.

2 communicate
(kə-myōō′nǐ-kāt′)
- *verb*

● Ruby and I rarely see each other, but we **communicate** often by sending text messages.

● Even today, many people still **communicate** by telephone.

B *Communicate* means   A. to call.   B. to exchange information.   C. to visit.

3 deceive
(dǐ-sēv′)
- *verb*

● In order to **deceive** a buyer, a used-car seller sometimes turns back the mileage counter on the car.

● Marcy **deceived** her boyfriend when she went out with Paul behind his back.

C *Deceive* means   A. to help.   B. to find.   C. to fool.

4 earnest
(ûr′nǐst)
- *adjective*

● I like our new babysitter because she is very **earnest**; she clearly takes her job very seriously.

● Jimmy seemed **earnest** when he promised to clean the windows by Friday, so I was surprised to see he hadn't done them.

C *Earnest* means   A. confused.   B. quiet.   C. serious.

5 emotion
(ǐ-mō′shən)
- *noun*

● Stan rarely shows his **emotions**. We have to guess what he is really feeling.

● Many people have trouble talking about their **emotions**, especially anger and fear.

A *Emotion* means   A. feeling.   B. explanation.   C. movement.

6 fiction
(fǐk′shən)
- *noun*

● One of Mark Twain's most amusing pieces of **fiction** is his story about a Connecticut man who travels back to the time of King Arthur.

● Some newspapers print obvious **fiction**, such as, "Nine-year-old girl has triplets who weigh 100 pounds more than she does!"

B *Fiction* means   A. news.   B. made-up writing.   C. facts.

7 investigate
(ĭn-vĕs′tĭ-gāt′)
- *verb*

- The FBI has been called in to **investigate** the disappearance of some important papers from a government laboratory.
- When I heard a noise downstairs at 3 a.m., I lay still in bed, too frightened to get up and **investigate** the situation.

A *Investigate* means   A. to look into.   B. to delay.   C. to exchange.

8 legible
(lĕj′ə-bəl)
- *adjective*

- My father used to make me rewrite my sloppy homework. "I can barely read this," he would say. "Make it **legible**."
- The fancy script on that new restaurant sign isn't very **legible**. Does it say "Peretti's," "Perelli's," or "Pepetti's"?

B *Legible* means   A. easy to believe.   B. easy to read.   C. easy to prove.

9 outspoken
(out-spō′kən)
- *adjective*

- Being **outspoken** doesn't have to mean being rude. It's possible to say what you really think without insulting other people.
- The host of the radio call-in show is extremely **outspoken**. She's not afraid to disagree strongly with her callers.

C *Outspoken* means   A. angry but quiet.   B. secretly pleased.   C. open and truthful.

10 theory
(thē′ə-rē)
- *noun*

- According to the **theory** of evolution, plants and animals have developed in ways that help them do well in their environment.
- The detective's **theory** was that the killer was a short man with dark hair, but the murderer turned out to be a blonde woman wearing a dark wig.

B *Theory* means   A. action.   B. explanation.   C. question.

Matching Words with Definitions

Following are definitions of the ten words. **Print** each word next to its definition. If you look closely at each word in context, you will be able to figure out its meaning.

1. _____communicate_____   To exchange or give information

2. _____bewilder_____   To confuse; puzzle

3. _____earnest_____   Serious and sincere

4. _____emotion_____   A strong feeling

5. _____theory_____   An explanation based on facts; a statement believed to be true

6. _____legible_____   Clear enough to be read

7. _____fiction_____   Literature consisting of imaginary stories; anything made up

8. _____outspoken_____   Direct and open; not shy about stating one's opinion

9. _____deceive_____   To make (someone) believe something that is not true

10. _____investigate_____   To explore or examine carefully in order to learn the facts

CAUTION: Do not go any further until you are sure the above answers are correct. Then you can use the definitions to help you in the following practices. Your goal is eventually to know the words well enough so that you don't need to check the definitions at all.

Check 1

Using the answer lines, complete each item below with the correct word from the box.

A. **bewilder**	B. **communicate**	C. **deceive**	D. **earnest**	E. **emotion**
F. **fiction**	G. **investigate**	H. **legible**	I. **outspoken**	J. **theory**

___outspoken___   1. Every class is made up of a mix of ___ students, very quiet students, and students who are somewhere in between.

___deceive___   2. Charlotte's sweet smiles don't ___ me. I know that she really dislikes me.

___communicate___   3. Dolphins ___ with one another through a language of squeaks and grunts.

___bewilder___   4. The many noises, flashing lights, and whirling rides at the fair ___ed the children. They didn't know where to go first.

___theory___   5. Murphy has a ___ about life. He believes that everything that can possibly go wrong, will go wrong.

___investigate___   6. When we go on our walks, my dog ___s every bush and tree we come across.

___legible___   7. Ten years ago, I carved my initials in a tree. Recently I was surprised to see that they were still ___.

___earnest___   8. When Gordon begged his boss for another chance, he seemed so ___ that his employer decided to give him his job back.

___fiction___   9. When I want to relax, I read romances, mysteries, and other kinds of ___.

___emotion___   10. Which do you think is the more powerful ___, love or hate?

NOTE: Now check your answers to these items by turning to page 240. Going over the answers carefully will help you prepare for the remaining practices, for which answers are not given.

Check 2

Using the answer lines, complete each item below with **two** words from the box. Use each word once.

___fiction___
___investigate___   1–2. Agatha Christie wrote wonderful works of ___ about Miss Marple, a woman who loved to ___ crimes the police could not solve.

___theory___
___legible___   3–4. Some people believe the ___ that you can teach yourself to write well with either hand, but when I use my left hand, what I write is not ___.

___communicate___
___bewilder___   5–6. The lost little girl spoke no English, so the police officer's attempts to ___ with her only ___ed her more.

___earnest___
___deceive___   7–8. The man claiming to have lost his wallet seemed so ___ that I believed him and gave him money, but when I saw him doing the same thing a week later, I knew he had ___d me.

___emotion___
___outspoken___   9–10. When her boss tried to fire her, strong ___s made my usually quiet sister quite ___. She stood up to him, told him what she thought of his leadership, and finally said, "I quit."

Word Work

A. Write each word next to the examples that best match it.

| A. **communicate** | B. **deceive** | C. **fiction** |
| D. **outspoken** | E. **theory** | |

outspoken 1. A parent who stands up and complains at a school board meeting
A newspaper editorial that states the police chief should be fired
A neighbor who calls and says, "Your grass is too high. You ought to cut it!"

deceive 2. Pretending to be collecting money for a charity and then keeping the money yourself
Faking an accident in order to collect insurance money
Saying your dog ate your homework when you really didn't do the work

communicate 3. Talking on the phone about a problem
Writing notes about a date to friends
Discussing an assignment with a teacher

fiction 4. "Goldilocks and the Three Bears"
A movie about a talking donkey
An imagined meeting between Abraham Lincoln and Oprah Winfrey

theory 5. Maybe dinosaurs were wiped out by a meteor that hit the Earth.
The Egyptian pyramids may have been built by aliens from outer space.
Police think the person who stole the jewels may have once worked in the store.

B. In the space provided, write the letter of the choice that best completes each item.

_C_ 6. An **earnest** person is likely to tell you

    A. a lie.   B. what he or she thinks you want to hear.   C. the truth.

_A_ 7. If math **bewilders** you, that probably means

    A. you are having trouble with math.
    B. you find math easy to do.
    C. the math class was too full and you had to take another class instead.

_C_ 8. **Emotions** are likely to be strong during

    A. a nap.   B. an elevator ride.   C. an argument.

_B_ 9. A person whose job is mainly to **investigate** is a

    A. pet shop owner.   B. private detective.   C. gardener.

_C_ 10. A second-grader whose writing is very **legible** can expect

    A. criticism from the teacher.
    B. to be asked to write smaller.
    C. praise from the teacher.

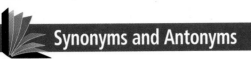

Synonyms and Antonyms

A. Synonyms. Write the letter of the word or phrase that most nearly means the **same** as each boldfaced word.

___D___ 1. **bewilder**

    A. make certain   C. insist

    B. release   D. confuse

___B___ 2. **communicate**

    A. hide   C. remove

    B. make known   D. forget

___A___ 3. **emotion**

    A. feeling   C. excuse

    B. energy   D. movement

___C___ 4. **investigate**

    A. puzzle   C. inspect

    B. write   D. fool

___C___ 5. **theory**

    A. agreement   C. explanation

    B. problem   D. question

B. Antonyms. Write the letter of the word or phrase that most nearly means the **opposite** of each boldfaced word.

___B___ 6. **outspoken**

    A. modern   C. graceful

    B. quiet   D. tiny

___C___ 7. **deceive**

    A. stay away from   C. tell the truth to

    B. argue   D. find

___A___ 8. **earnest**

    A. not sincere   C. not accurate

    B. unusual   D. not perfect

___D___ 9. **fiction**

    A. justice   C. reason

    B. ability   D. fact

___D___ 10. **legible**

    A. not for sale   C. not on purpose

    B. not lasting   D. not readable

Final Check

Read the passages carefully. Then fill in each blank with the word that best fits the context.

A. The Famous Detective

A. **deceive**	B. **emotion**	C. **fiction**	D. **investigate**	E. **theory**

One of the most famous characters from the world of (1)_____ fiction _____ is Sherlock Holmes, created by the writer Arthur Conan Doyle. Holmes first appeared in a book Conan Doyle wrote in 1887. It was called *A Study in Scarlet*. Holmes was a detective—someone whose job is to detect,° or discover, who is really guilty of a crime. No criminal, no matter how clever, could (2)_____ deceive _____ him for long. Rather than being affected by (3)_____ emotion _____s such as fear or hate, Holmes used his great powers of observation and logical thinking to solve crimes. As he (4)_____ investigate _____d crimes, he noticed significant° small details that were not apparent° to others or that had been misinterpreted°. Then he analyzed° these clues and developed a perfect (5)_____ theory _____ to explain the crime.

B. Why So Quiet?

F. **bewilder**	G. **communicate**	H. **earnest**	I. **legible**	J. **outspoken**

I still remember my first day in first grade. My first-grade teacher probably does, too. I had grown up in a very large, very noisy family. Everybody yelled, all the time. It wasn't because we were angry. There were just so many of us that we thought it was the only way to (6)_____ communicate _____. I didn't realize that our characteristic° loudness wasn't typical of all families. So by the time I went to school, I was, to say the least, an energetic° and (7)_____ outspoken _____ kid. I assumed° that when you wanted to be heard, the right thing to do was to say what you meant and say it loudly. My teacher was a very gentle person. She talked slowly and never, ever raised her voice. I remember her writing her name on the board in large, (8)_____ legible _____ letters and saying, "My name is Mrs. Henderson. Can you say 'Mrs. Henderson,' boys and girls?" My shy classmates whispered, "Mrs. Henderson." I shouted, "MRS. HENDERSON!!" at the top of my lungs. (I don't exaggerate°; I was really loud.) Throughout the day, my classmates continued to whisper, and I continued to shout. By the end of the first day, school had totally (9)_____ bewilder _____ed me. I was so confused that I thought I had been assigned to the wrong class. I went home and begged my parents to have me placed in a class with people who "talked right." I wasn't kidding; my plea° was completely (10)_____ earnest _____. It took a couple of weeks for me to figure out how to fit in with my quieter classmates.

Scores	Check 2 _____%	Word Work _____%	Synonyms and Antonyms _____%	Final Check _____%

Enter your scores above and in the **Vocabulary Performance Chart** on the inside back cover of the book.

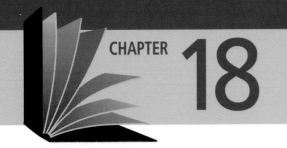

assure	hostile
crucial	humiliate
divert	impulse
extraordinary	perceive
frantic	revive

Ten Words in Context

In the space provided, write the letter of the meaning closest to that of each **boldfaced** word. Use the context of the sentences to help you figure out each word's meaning.

1 assure
(ə-shŏŏr′)
- *verb*

- If you leave jewelry in your hotel room, the hotel cannot **assure** you that it will be safe.
- I asked the salesperson, "Can you **assure** me that this watch is really waterproof?"

C *Assure* means   A. to remind.   B. to agree with.   C. to promise.

2 crucial
(krōō′shəl)
- *adjective*

- The trial had to stop when a **crucial** witness suddenly disappeared.
- Protein is a **crucial** part of a healthy diet.

B *Crucial* means   A. rare.   B. necessary.   C. useless.

3 divert
(dĭ-vûrt′)
- *verb*

- Traffic had to be **diverted** around the accident for several hours.
- I tried to **divert** Mom's attention from the broken window by saying, "Look at all the windows I didn't break!"

B *Divert* means   A. to keep quiet.   B. to move away.   C. to look at.

4 extraordinary
(ĭk-strôr′dn-ĕr′ē)
- *adjective*

- The restaurant made **extraordinary** attempts to attract new customers, even giving away free meals on certain days.
- The cancer patient inspired others with the **extraordinary** courage she showed in dealing with her illness.

C *Extraordinary* means   A. unfriendly.   B. normal.   C. very unusual.

5 frantic
(frăn′tĭk)
- *adjective*

- The mother robin became **frantic** when we came near her nest, so we quietly backed away.
- Because she thought she was going to miss her plane, Cyndi was **frantic** as she raced to the ticket counter.

A *Frantic* means   A. excited and nervous.   B. warm and friendly.   C. tired and hungry.

6 hostile
(hŏs′təl)
- *adjective*

- The **hostile** crowd threw tomatoes and eggs at the speaker.
- The cat acted **hostile** toward the new kitten, snarling and spitting at it.

B *Hostile* means   A. fearful.   B. unfriendly.   C. embarrassed.

7 humiliate
(hyōō-mǐl′ē-āt′)
- *verb*

● Good teachers do not **humiliate** students for making mistakes by calling them names or holding up their work for everyone to see.

● In dreams, people often **humiliate** themselves by doing things like going outdoors without their clothing on.

A *Humiliate* means   A. to shame.   B. to protect.   C. to misunderstand.

8 impulse
(ĭm′pŭls′)
- *noun*

● People who go food shopping when they are hungry often get an **impulse** to buy something they don't really need.

● Carmen had planned on staying home alone, but at the last minute she had an **impulse** to phone her new neighbors and invite them to come over that evening for coffee and cake.

A *Impulse* means   A. unplanned desire.   B. view.   C. fear.

9 perceive
(pər-sēv′)
- *verb*

● I **perceive** from the wonderful smell that someone is barbecuing ribs.

● Hawks have such good eyesight that they can **perceive** a tiny mouse from hundreds of feet in the air.

C *Perceive* means   A. to remember.   B. to include.   C. to notice.

10 revive
(rǐ-vīv′)
- *verb*

● Even if you've lost all desire to learn history, Mr. Berg, who is a wonderful teacher, can **revive** your interest in that subject.

● No matter how tired our dog is, the question "Want to go for a walk?" will **revive** him.

B *Revive* means   A. to show.   B. to bring back to life.   C. to embarrass.

Matching Words with Definitions

Following are definitions of the ten words. **Print** each word next to its definition. If you look closely at each word in context, you will be able to figure out its meaning.

1. _____assure_____   To make (someone) sure about something; tell with certainty

2. _____frantic_____   Very excited and anxious; extremely worried, panicked, or fearful

3. _____humiliate_____   To make ashamed; embarrass

4. _____crucial_____   Extremely important

5. _____hostile_____   Unfriendly; having or showing ill will

6. _____revive_____   To give new energy, spirit, or strength

7. _____impulse_____   A sudden urge to do something

8. _____extraordinary_____   Beyond the ordinary; special

9. _____divert_____   To turn aside from a course or direction; draw away attention

10. _____perceive_____   To be aware of or to become aware of (something) through one's senses; see, hear, feel, taste, or smell

CAUTION: Do not go any further until you are sure the above answers are correct. Then you can use the definitions to help you in the following practices. Your goal is eventually to know the words well enough so that you don't need to check the definitions at all.

Check 1

Using the answer lines, complete each item below with the correct word from the box.

A. assure	B. crucial	C. divert	D. extraordinary	E. frantic
F. hostile	G. humiliate	H. impulse	I. perceive	J. revive

_____humiliate_____ 1. Bullies ___ other people in order to make themselves feel powerful.

_____divert_____ 2. Engineers are trying to ___ the river to the west, so that it will not flood the town when it overflows.

_____assure_____ 3. My boss ___s me that I will definitely get a raise soon.

_____revive_____ 4. The flowers in the garden were beginning to droop in the dry weather, but a heavy rain shower soon ___d them.

_____impulse_____ 5. Grocery-store managers often place candy bars, combs, and other small, inexpensive items near the checkout, hoping that shoppers will have an ___ to buy them.

_____crucial_____ 6. To succeed at a job interview, it is ___ that you arrive on time.

_____perceive_____ 7. Because parents know their children so well, they can often ___ that the children are not feeling well just by looking at them.

_____hostile_____ 8. Two of my coworkers are very ___ toward each other. They glare at each other and argue at staff meetings.

_____frantic_____ 9. "I've lost my purse!" my mother cried. After a ___ ten-minute search, she realized she had left it in our car.

_____extraordinary_____ 10. The newspaper carried a story about an ___ woman who is a terrific tennis player, even though she uses a wheelchair.

NOTE: Now check your answers to these items by turning to page 240. Going over the answers carefully will help you prepare for the remaining practices, for which answers are not given.

Check 2

Using the answer lines, complete each item below with **two** words from the box. Use each word once.

_____humiliate_____
_____impulse_____ 1–2. When his boss ___d him in front of his coworkers, Len felt a sudden ___ to grab the man's necktie and snip it off with scissors.

_____perceive_____
_____divert_____ 3–4. Once I ___d the aroma of fried chicken, I stopped doing my homework because my attention was ___ed by the wonderful smell.

_____crucial_____
_____assure_____ 5–6. The builders know it is ___ that the bathroom be finished before our visitors arrive next week, and they have ___d us the work will be done.

_____extraordinary_____
_____revive_____ 7–8. When Sandra got the chance to work with an ___ coach—one who had coached many champions—it ___d her childhood dream of someday competing in the Olympics.

___hostile___   9–10. The more ___ the angry, impatient bus driver became, the more ___ he

___frantic___   made the little girl who had lost her bus ticket.

Word Work

A. In the space provided, write the letter of the choice that best completes each item.

___B___ 1. A common **hostile** comment is
   A. "Nice to meet you."   B. "Mind your own business."   C. "See you later."

___A___ 2. A little child would probably become **frantic** if
   A. he couldn't find his mother in a store.
   B. someone gave him a kitten.
   C. he had just learned to ride a bicycle.

___B___ 3. Something that might **divert** the attention of a person studying late at night is
   A. a textbook.   B. a dripping faucet.   C. coffee.

___C___ 4. While eating pizza for dinner, Chang **perceived**
   A. the events of his day.
   B. a thought about his girlfriend.
   C. a dash of hot pepper in the sauce.

___A___ 5. The company president **assured** the workers that
   A. there would be no layoffs.
   B. the company might be for sale.
   C. there might be pay cuts at the end of the year.

B. In the space provided, write the letter of the word that most closely relates to the situation in each item.

___C___ 6. These beautiful paintings are the work of a nine-year-old artist with amazing talent.
   A. frantic   B. revive   C. extraordinary

___C___ 7. "I've got an idea!" said Nelson, jumping up from his desk. "Let's take a break and all go get some ice cream."
   A. hostile   B. perceive   C. impulse

___C___ 8. After talking for a while to the prettiest girl at the dance, the boy glanced in a mirror and realized he had a large piece of spinach stuck in his teeth.
   A. assure   B. crucial   C. humiliate

___A___ 9. The first two years of life greatly affect the mental and emotional development of a child.
   A. crucial   B. perceive   C. hostile

___B___ 10. Aisha came home from work feeling tired, but a short nap made her refreshed and energetic.
   A. perceive   B. revive   C. extraordinary

Word Parts

A. The suffix *-ity* means "the quality or state of being ___."

Examples: *brutal* — cruel   *rare* — unusual
            brutality — the quality of being cruel   *rarity* — the state of being unusual

On each answer line, write the word from the box that best completes the item.

A. **brutality°**	B. **generosity**	C. **hostility**
D. **rarity**	E. **security°**	

_____security_____ 1. Mrs. Lee likes the ___ of living in an apartment that's on the tenth floor, where no thieves can enter through the windows.

_____generosity_____ 2. Everyone was amazed by the ___ of the man who won a huge lottery prize and then gave it all away to charity.

_____brutality_____ 3. There are laws to protect animals from ___; it is against the law to beat or otherwise harm them.

_____hostility_____ 4. Ever since Margo asked Rose's boyfriend out on a date, there has been ___ between the two women.

_____rarity_____ 5. There are only a few white tigers known to exist. Because of their ___, thousands of people go to see them every year in zoos.

B. The suffixes *-able* and *-ible* can mean "able to be ___."

Examples: *manage* — to control   *perceive* — to notice through one's senses
            manageable — able to be controlled   *perceptible* — able to be noticed through
                                                                        the senses

On each answer line, write the word from the box that best completes the item.

F. **legible°**	G. **manageable°**	H. **perceptible**
I. **transferable**	J. **usable**	

_____legible_____ 6. Nadia's handwriting is so bad that it is usually not ___.

_____transferable_____ 7. If you decide to leave one college and go to another one, you may lose some credits. Some of your credits may not be ___.

_____manageable_____ 8. I have tons of homework to do this weekend, but it is ___. If I use my time well, I can handle it.

_____perceptible_____ 9. The odor of fried fish is ___ in the house even hours after we've had dinner.

_____usable_____ 10. These bananas are too ripe, but they are still ___ for banana bread. You could also freeze them and utilize° them later in fruit drinks.

Final Check

Read the passages carefully. Then fill in each blank with the word that best fits the context.

A. Fear of Public Speaking

| A. **divert** | B. **frantic** | C. **hostile** | D. **humiliate** | E. **impulse** |

Some people are afraid of spiders. Others fear heights. But for many people, the scariest thing of all is having to speak in front of a group of strangers. Even people who are ordinarily quite outspoken° can become (1)_____*frantic*_____ with fear at the idea of facing an audience. They often imagine that the audience will be (2)_____*hostile*_____, even when it is actually friendly. Because they are so sure that they will (3)_____*humiliate*_____ themselves, they usually manage to do just that. They are so awkward° when they walk to the front of the room that they almost trip over their own feet. When they begin to speak, their hands shake, causing the papers they are holding to rattle loudly. This annoying noise (4)_____*divert*_____s the attention of the audience from what the speakers are trying to say. Embarrassed by their poor performance, the unfortunate speakers have to fight the (5)_____*impulse*_____ to crawl under a chair and vanish°. One of the best things people like this can do for themselves is take a course in public speaking. Even if they never learn to love public speaking, they can learn to face an audience without having to endure° the emotion° of fear.

B. Do You Believe in Magic?

| F. **assure** | G. **crucial** | H. **extraordinary** | I. **perceive** | J. **revive** |

Have you ever wondered how magic tricks work? Magicians work hard to make their tricks look like authentic° magic. But no other magician has done what Horace Goldin did to make a trick look real. Goldin performed the well-known act in which a volunteer from the crowd is placed in a box, cut in half, and then reconnected right in front of the audience. But Goldin's trick was (6)_____*extraordinary*_____ because of a special added twist. After the victim was sawed in half and reconnected, the audience was (7)_____*assure*_____d that the volunteer was fine and could return to his seat. When the man stood up, however, the top half of his body seemed to separate and fall to the floor. Meanwhile, the bottom half also fell, but then it (8)_____*revive*_____d, got up, and ran off the stage! The trick totally bewildered° the audience. No one could detect° how Goldin managed to do it.

How *did* Goldin do it? The secret was the volunteer, a close friend of Goldin's. The volunteer had a twin brother who had no legs. What the audience (9)_____*perceive*_____d as the volunteer's upper half was really the legless twin. The separate walking legs were just a very short person hidden inside full-length pants. In 1921, however, the legless twin brother demanded a higher salary. When Goldin refused to pay, the twin quit the act. With a (10)_____*crucial*_____ part of the act gone, Goldin had to cease° performing the trick.

| Scores | Check 2 _____% | Word Work _____% | Word Parts _____% | Final Check _____% |

Enter your scores above and in the **Vocabulary Performance Chart** on the inside back cover of the book.

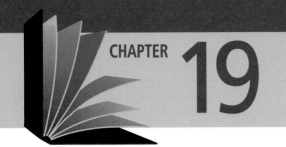

abandon	function
alert	idle
circumstances	overcome
devote	primary
dominate	theme

Ten Words in Context

In the space provided, write the letter of the meaning closest to that of each **boldfaced** word. Use the context of the sentences to help you figure out each word's meaning.

1 abandon
(ə-băn′dən)
- *verb*

- When it got dark outside, the players had to **abandon** their search for the lost softball.
- Because they ran out of money, the scientists had to **abandon** their research project.

_C_ *Abandon* means   A. to begin.   B. to sell.   C. to quit.

2 alert
(ə-lûrt′)
- *adjective*

- If you are riding a bicycle on a busy city street, you need to be **alert** at all times.
- Many people need a cup of coffee in the morning to make them feel really **alert**.

_C_ *Alert* means   A. bad-tempered.   B. well dressed.   C. fully awake.

3 circumstances
(sûr′kəm-stăns′əz)
- *noun*

- My sister and brother-in-law had a big argument about something yesterday, but I do not know the exact **circumstances**.
- Here are the main **circumstances** of the robbery: A man wearing a Santa Claus mask took some money from a toy store.

_A_ *Circumstances* means   A. facts.   B. answers.   C. people.

4 devote
(dĭ-vōt′)
- *verb*

- The kids **devoted** the entire evening to playing video games.
- Professor Morales **devoted** her life to the study of ancient Egypt.

_B_ *Devote* means   A. to look at.   B. to give completely.   C. to win over.

5 dominate
(dŏm′ə-nāt′)
- *verb*

- McDonald's and Burger King seem to **dominate** the country's fast-food market.
- My brother likes to dream about a time when his favorite team will be so good that it will **dominate** football.

_B_ *Dominate* means   A. to take pity on.   B. to be a leader in.   C. to lose interest in.

6 function
(fŭngk′shən)
- *noun*

- A waiter's **function** is to take the diners' orders and then to bring them their food.
- What is the **function** of that red button on the front of your camera?

_A_ *Function* means   A. purpose.   B. subject.   C. length of time.

7 idle
 (īd′l)
 - *adjective*

● After being at home for a week with the flu, I was sick of being **idle**, and I was happy to get back to work.

● When the boss is out of town, many of the workers in this store are **idle** much of the time.

<u>A</u> *Idle* means

  A. not busy.   B. outside.   C. in a group.

8 overcome
 (ō′vər-kŭm′)
 - *verb*

● My brother had to **overcome** a learning disability to become a successful student.

● With the help of swimming lessons, I **overcame** my fear of water.

<u>C</u> *Overcome* means

  A. to know.   B. to write about.   C. to beat.

9 primary
 (prī′měr′ē)
 - *adjective*

● My sister's **primary** interest in life seems to be playing basketball. She practices day and night.

● The **primary** reason for the family reunion is to celebrate Great-Grandma's ninetieth birthday.

<u>C</u> *Primary* means

  A. easiest.   B. forgotten.   C. main.

10 theme
 (thēm)
 - *noun*

● The writing assignment is a five-hundred-word paper on the **theme** "a surprising event."

● *Romeo and Juliet* and *West Side Story* share the same **theme**: young lovers separated by other people's hatred.

<u>C</u> *Theme* means

  A. answer.   B. rule.   C. idea.

Matching Words with Definitions

Following are definitions of the ten words. **Print** each word next to its definition. If you look closely at each word in context, you will be able to figure out its meaning.

1. ____primary____ Most important; major

2. ____overcome____ To win in a struggle over; defeat

3. ____abandon____ To stop trying to continue; discontinue; quit; let go of

4. ____devote____ To give one's time or attention completely to something or someone

5. ____function____ The expected activity of a person or thing; purpose; role

6. ____alert____ Wide-awake and watchful; highly aware

7. ____idle____ Not doing anything; inactive

8. ____dominate____ To have a leading place or position in; be at the head of

9. ____circumstances____ Condition or facts of a particular situation or event

10. ____theme____ The main subject; the topic around which something is organized

CAUTION: Do not go any further until you are sure the above answers are correct. Then you can use the definitions to help you in the following practices. Your goal is eventually to know the words well enough so that you don't need to check the definitions at all.

Check 1

Using the answer lines, complete each item below with the correct word from the box.

A. abandon	B. alert	C. circumstances	D. devote	E. dominate
F. function	G. idle	H. overcome	I. primary	J. theme

alert   1. An ___ person is wide-awake and very much aware of his or her surroundings.

primary   2. It is clear that the ___ reason my aunt's boyfriend likes her is her money.

idle   3. When the boss is just staring out the window, she may look ___, but she is really trying to figure out a problem.

theme   4. Dances often have a special ___, such as "Winter Wonderland."

overcome   5. Before Teresa can visit her grandparents in Italy, she needs to ___ her fear of flying in an airplane.

abandon   6. When a friend called to ask if I wanted to go to the movies, I quickly ___ed my ironing and got ready to go out.

devote   7. The young skater ___s five hours each day to practicing.

circumstances   8. At first I thought Lamar was unfriendly, but when I learned the ___ of his life—he is a single parent who is also caring for his elderly father—I understood that he doesn't have much time to chat.

function   9. A pen and a pencil have the same ___: they are both used to write.

dominate   10. Coca-Cola and Pepsi ___ the cola market.

NOTE: Now check your answers to these items by turning to page 240. Going over the answers carefully will help you prepare for the remaining practices, for which answers are not given.

Check 2

Using the answer lines, complete each item below with **two** words from the box. Use each word once.

circumstances
abandon   1–2. During the Depression of the 1930s, ___ were so bad that many young people had to ___ their education and go to work full-time.

function
idle   3–4. Some bosses get angry when they see workers taking a long break. "Your ___ is to get work done," they snap, "not to sit around ___!"

theme
alert   5–6. "You'll have to read carefully to find the ___ of this story," our teacher said. Then he assured° us, "But if you are ___ and pay attention to every clue, I think you can figure out what the author is actually writing about."

primary
devote   7–8. Some women's ___ interest is their careers, and some ___ themselves entirely to their families; others manage to do both.

overcome
dominate   9–10. There are many true stories of very successful people who have ___ serious physical problems and gone on to ___ a sport.

Word Work

A. In the space provided, write the letter of the choice that best completes each item.

___B___ 1. Today at the store, the other salespeople and I were **idle** most of the day because
    A. there were so many customers to take care of.
    B. there were very few customers.
    C. we didn't have time for a lunch break.

___A___ 2. If someone says that Mindy always tries to **dominate** the conversation, you can guess that Mindy
    A. doesn't let anyone else speak much.   C. is too shy to speak up.
    B. is very funny.

___C___ 3. Your **primary** goal in life is
    A. something that doesn't matter much to you.
    B. the goal you would say is second or third in importance.
    C. your most important goal.

___C___ 4. A student might **abandon** her homework one night if she
    A. really needed a good grade.
    B. had a friend who wanted to study with her.
    C. suddenly felt sick.

___B___ 5. "Look **alert**!" my father sometimes said to us. He meant
    A. "Quiet down and go to sleep this minute!"   C. "Comb your hair!"
    B. "Pay attention!"

B. Write each word next to the examples that best match it.

A. **circumstances**	B. **devote**	C. **function**
D. **overcome**	E. **theme**	

___overcome___ 6. Wheelchair users compete in tennis and basketball.
    Someone gets over a stutter to become a fine public speaker.
    An alcoholic stays sober for many years.

___devote___ 7. People spend many hours with and for their children.
    People put a lot of time and energy into their jobs.
    People contribute much effort to the cause of civil rights.

___theme___ 8. Cheating as the topic of a student paper
    A book about how to survive a divorce
    A circus cake, circus decorations, and a clown at a kid's birthday party

___circumstances___ 9. The details of Anna's financial situation
    Living conditions in Betsy's house
    The realities of life in Cory's neighborhood

___function___ 10. Of a bathroom scale: to measure people's weight
    Of the red light on the dashboard: to let you know the oil is low
    Of a traffic police officer: to control traffic

Synonyms and Antonyms

A. Synonyms. Write the letter of the word or phrase that most nearly means the **same** as each boldfaced word.

_A_ 1. **circumstances**

    A. conditions   C. activities

    B. jobs   D. abilities

_A_ 2. **dominate**

    A. lead   C. be active

    B. follow   D. leave

_D_ 3. **devote**

    A. get rid of   C. hide from

    B. win over   D. give attention to

_C_ 4. **function**

    A. subject   C. purpose

    B. fact   D. rule

_D_ 5. **theme**

    A. fact   C. use

    B. safety   D. subject

B. Antonyms. Write the letter of the word or phrase that most nearly means the **opposite** of each boldfaced word.

_B_ 6. **abandon**

    A. leave   C. lose

    B. continue with   D. work badly

_A_ 7. **alert**

    A. sleepy   C. complete

    B. curious   D. late

_C_ 8. **idle**

    A. new   C. active

    B. stiff   D. grateful

_D_ 9. **overcome**

    A. win   C. continue

    B. follow   D. give in to

_B_ 10. **primary**

    A. least expensive   C. not enough

    B. least important   D. not prepared

Final Check

Read the passages carefully. Then fill in each blank with the word that best fits the context.

A. The Miracle Runner

A. **devote**	B. **dominate**	C. **idle**	D. **primary**	E. **overcome**

Glenn Cunningham was one of the most famous and extraordinary° athletes of the 1930s. To succeed, he had to (1)_____*overcome*_____ challenges° that might have stopped anyone else. When Glenn was eight years old, he and his older brother, Floyd, were trapped in a burning building. Floyd was killed, and Glenn was badly burned. The fire had eaten deep into his legs, and the toes of one foot were gone. In fact, the doctors who evaluated° him advised° his parents to have Glenn's legs taken off and replaced with artificial° ones. Glenn lay in bed for months, his legs thin as sticks. He hated being (2)_____*idle*_____, so he struggled to learn to stand and then to take a few steps. Then he began to run. At first, his (3)_____*primary*_____ goal in running was just to get rid of his limp. Then he discovered that he was a very good runner.

At age 13, Glenn entered a mile race at a local fair and won easily. From then on, he (4)_____*devote*_____d himself to running—and to winning. Nothing diverted° him from his goal. In high school, then in college, and later when he was a member of the United States Olympic team, he (5)_____*dominate*_____d his sport. He set a world-record time for running the mile: 4 minutes, 4.4 seconds. And this was someone who had been told he would never walk again!

B. One of Those Days

F. **abandon**	G. **alert**	H. **circumstances**	I. **function**	J. **theme**

My poor brother! Last Friday, he had one of those days whose (6)_____*theme*_____ seemed to be "things that go wrong." He is taking some college classes, and his class began at 8 a.m. But his alarm clock did not perform its (7)_____*function*_____; it didn't make a sound. When he finally woke up, he had no time to eat. But because he was sleepy, he made a cup of coffee to help him feel more (8)_____*alert*_____. When he poured milk into the coffee, though, he found that the milk was sour. Yuck! So he (9)_____*abandon*_____ed his effort to have a cup of coffee, grabbed his car keys, and ran out. A minute later he remembered that his car was in the shop for repairs. The last I saw of him, he was racing to catch the bus.

Later, he told me the rest of the story. Just as he got to the bus stop, the bus drove off. By then he was so frantic° that he could hardly think. Desperate° to get to school, he began running again. Then along came a car that hit a deep puddle and splashed him with mud from head to foot.

At school, he told his instructor the (10)_____*circumstances*_____ that had made him late, muddy, and out of breath. Looking annoyed that he had disrupted° the class, she told him harshly° to hand in his assignment. At that point, he discovered he had brought the wrong textbook and notebook.

I think the next time my brother oversleeps, he should just stay in bed!

Scores	Check 2 _____%	Word Work _____%	Synonyms and Antonyms _____%	Final Check _____%

Enter your scores above and in the **Vocabulary Performance Chart** on the inside back cover of the book.

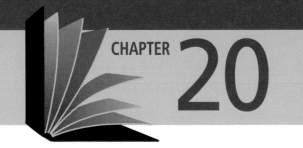

disregard	monotonous
excerpt	obtain
exclude	prey
hinder	seize
misleading	severe

Ten Words in Context

In the space provided, write the letter of the meaning closest to that of each **boldfaced** word. Use the context of the sentences to help you figure out each word's meaning.

1 disregard
(dĭs′rĭ-gärd′)
- *verb*

- I suggested that Patty put some of her money in a savings account, but she **disregarded** my idea and spent it all.
- The drive with Bruno was frightening. Even though the road was icy, he **disregarded** the speed limit and drove seventy miles an hour.

_B_ *Disregard* means   A. to follow.   B. to ignore.   C. to get in the way of.

2 excerpt
(ĕk′sûrpt′)
- *noun*

- *The New York Times* printed all of the President's speech, but most newspapers printed only brief **excerpts** from it.
- Previews advertise films by showing several **excerpts**, short scenes that will make people want to come see the whole movie.

_A_ *Excerpt* means   A. part.   B. price.   C. speech.

3 exclude
(ĭk-sklo̅o̅d′)
- *verb*

- When you preserve pickles, you must be sure to **exclude** air from the jars. Otherwise, the pickles will spoil.
- The little boy ran crying to his teacher after other children **excluded** him from their game.

_C_ *Exclude* means   A. to watch.   B. to invite.   C. to keep out.

4 hinder
(hĭn′dər)
- *verb*

- Not having computer skills **hindered** Jane in her search for an office job.
- Bad weather **hindered** the climbers on their hike up the mountain.

_A_ *Hinder* means   A. to get in the way of.   B. to cheer up.   C. to find.

5 misleading
(mĭs-lē′dĭng)
- *adjective*

- The fact that the two close friends happen to have the same last name is **misleading**. Many people think they are really sisters.
- My cousin may appear rich, but his fancy car and nice clothes are **misleading**. In reality, he owes thousands of dollars on his credit card.

_C_ *Misleading* means   A. hard to find.   B. recent.   C. giving the wrong idea.

6 monotonous
(mə-nŏt′n-əs)
- *adjective*

- The child in the supermarket kept repeating a **monotonous** request: "I want some candy. I want some candy. I want some candy."
- My days had become **monotonous**. I got up, went to school, came home, slept, then did it all over again.

_A_ *Monotonous* means   A. dull.   B. pleasant.   C. messy.

7 obtain
(əb-tān′)
- *verb*

- After completing the driver's education class, Reiko **obtained** a driver's license.
- The soldier **obtained** a three-day pass in order to attend his sister's wedding.

B *Obtain* means   A. to hide.   B. to get.   C. to give away.

8 prey
(prā)
- *noun*

- Because a cat's **prey** includes mice, farmers like to keep cats in their barns.
- Movie stars are the **prey** of thoughtless photographers who will do anything to get a photo.

A *Prey* means   A. those that are hunted.   B. part of a whole.   C. sickness.

9 seize
(sēz)
- *verb*

- The woman screamed when a thief **seized** her pocketbook.
- Before anyone could stop him, the baby **seized** the cat's tail and pulled.

B *Seize* means   A. to laugh at.   B. to grab.   C. to know.

10 severe
(sə-vîr′)
- *adjective*

- A **severe** storm hit our area, causing great damage and several deaths.
- Patients with the most **severe** illnesses are kept in a separate part of the hospital, where they receive special care.

B *Severe* means   A. fair.   B. dangerous.   C. boring.

Matching Words with Definitions

Following are definitions of the ten words. **Print** each word next to its definition. If you look closely at each word in context, you will be able to figure out its meaning.

1. _____prey_____   A creature or creatures that are hunted by another animal; the victim or victims of an attack

2. _____excerpt_____   A part of a whole work (such as a book, speech, or film)

3. _____disregard_____   To pay no attention to

4. _____exclude_____   To refuse to allow in; not include

5. _____obtain_____   To get something through planning or effort

6. _____misleading_____   Leading to a mistake in thought or action

7. _____monotonous_____   Boring because of lack of change or differences; repetitious; always the same

8. _____severe_____   Causing great physical or mental suffering; very serious

9. _____seize_____   To take hold of suddenly or with force

10. _____hinder_____   To stop or slow down (someone or something); block; interfere with

CAUTION: Do not go any further until you are sure the above answers are correct. Then you can use the definitions to help you in the following practices. Your goal is eventually to know the words well enough so that you don't need to check the definitions at all.

Check 1

Using the answer lines, complete each item below with the correct word from the box.

| A. **disregard** | B. **excerpt** | C. **exclude** | D. **hinder** | E. **misleading** |
| F. **monotonous** | G. **obtain** | H. **prey** | I. **seize** | J. **severe** |

_____misleading_____ 1. Cynthia's bright smile is ___; actually, she is feeling quite angry.

_____prey_____ 2. The robbers' usual ___ were newlyweds, whose houses might contain expensive wedding gifts.

_____exclude_____ 3. My aunt is a vegetarian and ___s all meat from her house.

_____hinder_____ 4. A huge snowstorm ___ed Thanksgiving travelers.

_____severe_____ 5. Although the car wasn't damaged much in the crash, the driver—who wasn't wearing a seat belt—had ___ injuries.

_____monotonous_____ 6. No matter how much you like your favorite food, having it at every meal would soon become ___.

_____obtain_____ 7. Members of the Environmental Club went door-to-door to ___ signatures in favor of a new recycling center in town.

_____excerpt_____ 8. Angel and Cristina devoted° the evening to watching brief ___s from their favorite talk shows on YouTube.

_____seize_____ 9. When she realized her train would leave in just an hour, Rita ___d her suitcase from the shelf and quickly began stuffing clothes into it.

_____disregard_____ 10. Minh lost his money when he ___ed the "Out of Order" sign and put five quarters in the soda machine.

NOTE: Now check your answers to these items by turning to page 240. Going over the answers carefully will help you prepare for the remaining practices, for which answers are not given.

Check 2

Using the answer lines, complete each item below with **two** words from the box. Use each word once.

_____seize_____
_____prey_____ 1–2. It is striking to see a hawk drop out of the sky and ___ a field mouse, then fly away with its ___ in its claws.

_____severe_____
_____exclude_____ 3–4. When my uncle had a ___ illness, the doctor ___ed everyone from his hospital room except my aunt.

_____misleading_____
_____excerpt_____ 5–6. The TV ads for the movie were ___. They used an ___ from the film that was funny, even though the movie was not a comedy at all.

_____obtain_____
_____hinder_____ 7–8. Yolanda wanted to ___ tickets by phone for a very special concert, but the large volume of callers ___ed her from placing the order.

_____disregard_____
_____monotonous_____ 9–10. Because Wendy is so shy, she ___s invitations to go out. As a result, she stays home night after night and leads a very ___ life.

Word Work

A. In the space provided, write the letter of the choice that best completes each item.

___B___ 1. If someone **seizes** a book from you, then probably
 A. you gave that person the book.
 B. the person took the book without permission.
 C. the person bought the book from you.

___A___ 2. One way to **hinder** a friend who is housecleaning is to
 A. hide the vacuum cleaner.
 B. hire a cleaning company.
 C. do the dusting for him or her.

___C___ 3. A job that is **monotonous** will involve
 A. danger.   B. no boss.   C. the same duties day after day.

___B___ 4. An animal goes looking for **prey** when the animal is feeling
 A. sleepy.   B. hungry.   C. playful.

___C___ 5. A person who **disregards** a "No Smoking" sign
 A. will wait and smoke somewhere else.
 B. will put the sign in his or her pocket and leave.
 C. will smoke in spite of the sign.

B. Write each word by the examples that best match it.

A. **excerpt**	B. **exclude**	C. **misleading**
D. **obtain**	E. **severe**	

___misleading___ 6. An ad for a broken-down old car that says, "Classic antique; needs just a little work"
A store window sign that says "Reductions up to 80 percent!" when only several items are reduced 80 percent
A letter that says in big type, "You have won the grand prize!" and in tiny type, "if you have the winning number"

___excerpt___ 7. A chapter from a novel
A scene from a movie
A paragraph from a short story

___obtain___ 8. Earning a high-school diploma
Being hired for a job
Getting a license to drive a school bus

___severe___ 9. A hailstorm that breaks car windows and destroys crops
A fever of 104 degrees
A loss of electrical power that lasts for three days

___exclude___ 10. A diet that contains no salt
A club that does not allow everyone to join
A bar that does not let underage people in

Analogies

Each item below starts with a pair of words in CAPITAL LETTERS. For each item, figure out the relationship between these two words. Then decide which of the choices (A, B, C, or D) expresses a similar relationship. Write the letter of your choice on the answer line. (All the repeated words in these items are from this unit.)

___D___ 1. MONOTONOUS : EXCITING ::

    A. healthy : strong   C. five : fifteen

    B. film : camera   D. hinder : help

___B___ 2. PREY : VICTIM ::

    A. artist : painting   C. security° : lock

    B. baby : infant   D. doctor : patient

___A___ 3. SEVERE : MILD ::

    A. painful : pleasant   C. harmful : dangerous

    B. angry : frowning   D. loud : noisy

___C___ 4. COMMUNICATE° : TELEPHONE ::

    A. fiction° : book   C. sweep : broom

    B. divert° : attention   D. screwdriver : nail

___D___ 5. EXTRAORDINARY° : COMMON ::

    A. assure° : promise   C. mask : face

    B. chew : gum   D. hostile° : friendly

___A___ 6. DISREGARD : IGNORE ::

    A. recall : remember   C. protect : reveal

    B. important : silly   D. sing : choir

___D___ 7. ECONOMICAL° : EXTRAVAGANT° ::

    A. country : map   C. pitch : ball

    B. earnest° : sincere   D. calm : worried

___B___ 8. PRETTY : UGLY ::

    A. friendly : nice   C. important : crucial°

    B. frantic° : calm   D. difficult : burden°

___B___ 9. SEIZE : TAKE ::

    A. exclude : include   C. pull : push

    B. humiliate° : embarrass   D. shout : whisper

___D___ 10. PERCEIVE° : SENSES ::

    A. lazy : idle°   C. write : letter

    B. song : music   D. run : legs

Final Check

Read the passages carefully. Then fill in each blank with the word that best fits the context.

A. The All-Too-Common Cold

A. **excerpt**	B. **exclude**	C. **hinder**	D. **misleading**	E. **severe**

Your throat feels a little scratchy. Your nose is a little stuffy. And then—"Ah-CHOO!" You have a cold. It's called the "common" cold, for almost no one is (1)_____exclude_____d from experiencing it. The average child catches a cold 6–8 times a year. For adults, the average frequency° is 2–4 times a year.

What causes the common cold? First, let's talk about what *doesn't* cause it. People catch colds more often in the winter, but it's (2)_____misleading_____ to think that cold weather *causes* colds. It doesn't. This (3)_____excerpt_____ from a website explains the real connection: "More people catch colds when the weather is cold than when it is warm because they tend to be inside more often and longer . . . in closer, prolonged contact with other people who have colds." In addition, the viruses that cause colds thrive° in dry conditions, such as heated buildings, where the air is typically very dry.

There are some things you can do to (4)_____hinder_____ the spread of the common cold. Wash your hands frequently with soap. Avoid being close to people who have colds. When you are around infected people, avoid touching your eyes, nose, or mouth, so you don't introduce the virus into your own body.

Most colds are mild and go away on their own in approximately° one week. If a cold is (5)_____severe_____, however, it can lead to other complications. If you develop a high fever, sinus pain, or a cough that won't go away, see a doctor. Maybe your "common cold" has turned into something less common.

B. A Criminal with a Tail?

F. **disregard**	G. **monotonous**	H. **obtain**	I. **prey**	J. **seize**

Did you hear the incredible° story about the heartless Pennsylvania governor and the Labrador retriever? Here's how the story goes: In 1924, a dog named Pep killed a cat. Unfortunately for Pep, his furry (6)_____prey_____ belonged to Governor Gifford Pinchot. In response, the angry governor had police (7)_____seize_____ the poor dog. He (8)_____disregard_____ed the fact that Pep was a dog and put him on trial for murder. Pep was sent to prison, where he spent the rest of his life. Versions° of this story have been in print for almost 100 years.

However, the story is mostly fiction°. Here's what really happened: Pep was the governor's own dog. The governor's family had (9)_____obtain_____ed him from a cousin. Unfortunately, Pep had a bad habit—he liked to eat sofa cushions. He was making a mess of the governor's house. The governor had an idea: Why not send Pep to live where there were no sofa cushions? That is how Pep became an "inmate" of Eastern State Penitentiary.

In prison, Pep was treated very kindly. Although he had to live in a cell, he could transfer° from one cell to another. His fellow prisoners were very fond of him. His furry face and wagging tail were a welcome change in the otherwise (10)_____monotonous_____ world of the prison, where each day seemed like the one before it.

Pep lived a long and happy life, and when he finally died, he was buried on the prison grounds.

Scores	Check 2 _____%	Word Work _____%	Analogies _____%	Final Check _____%

The box at the right lists twenty-five words from Unit Four. Using the clues at the bottom of the page, fill in these words to complete the puzzle that follows.

abandon
alert
apparent
automatic
bewilder
crucial
deceive
divert
dominate
emotion
exclude
fulfill
function
hinder
hostile
humiliate
idle
impulse
influence
legible
monotonous
prey
security
seize
theory

ACROSS

1. Obvious; easy to see
6. The expected activity of a person or thing; purpose
7. To turn aside from a course or direction
8. To stop or slow down; block
10. To discontinue; quit
12. To have an effect on
14. Boring because of lack of change or differences
17. To refuse to allow in; not include
20. Clear enough to be read
22. Wide-awake and watchful
23. A creature or creatures that are hunted by another animal
24. Unfriendly; having or showing ill will

DOWN

2. A strong feeling
3. Moving or operating by itself
4. Not doing anything; inactive
5. To make (someone) believe something that is not true
6. To carry out; achieve; do
9. To take hold of suddenly or with force
11. To have a leading place or position in; be at the head of
13. To make ashamed; embarrass
15. A statement that explains events or facts
16. Protection; freedom from danger, fear, or worry
18. Extremely important
19. To confuse; puzzle
21. A sudden urge to do something

PART A

Choose the word that best completes each item and write it in the space provided.

outspoken   1. It's not surprising that Lisa does well on the debate team. She is a naturally ___ person, with strong opinions on many issues.

     A. primary   B. legible   C. alert   D. outspoken

bewildered   2. In my dream, my family had suddenly started speaking a foreign language, which I didn't understand at all. Naturally, I was ___.

     A. bewildered   B. obtained   C. communicated   D. revived

communicate   3. Letters are still my favorite way to ___ with faraway friends and family.

     A. fulfill   B. seize   C. communicate   D. humiliate

deceived   4. Mel kept his wife from knowing he had lost his job. He ___ her by leaving the house each morning as if he were going to work.

     A. alerted   B. fulfilled   C. devoted   D. deceived

earnest   5. To show how ___ he was about wanting the job, Ira offered to work for no pay for a week.

     A. automatic   B. primary   C. hostile   D. earnest

emotions   6. A raised voice can mean one of several ___: anger, excitement, happiness, or surprise.

     A. emotions   B. preys   C. burdens   D. fictions

legible   7. It is hard for a right-handed person to write a ___ message using his or her left hand.

     A. severe   B. frantic   C. legible   D. primary

investigate   8. Not satisfied with the way the local police were handling the murder case, the victim's family hired a detective to ___ it.

     A. revive   B. influence   C. investigate   D. exclude

fiction   9. When my daughter said, "There is a monster under my bed," her story was not pure ___: there was a large spider hiding there.

     A. fiction   B. burden   C. function   D. excerpt

theory   10. I used to believe that all dog lovers were nice people. But Doreen proved that my ___ was wrong. She is very nice to dogs, but nasty to human beings.

     A. prey   B. theme   C. function   D. theory

security   11. To increase her feeling of ___ when she walks home from the bus stop at night, Lana learned karate.

     A. security   B. circumstances   C. burden   D. impulse

(Continues on next page)

_____apparent_____ 12. It's ___ that your shoes are muddy—you're leaving dirty footprints on the carpet.

     A. extravagant   B. hostile   C. apparent   D. crucial

_____extraordinary_____ 13. Although many of our neighbors have gardens, Mr. Soo's is really ___. He grows thirty-pound watermelons, tomatoes as big as softballs, and flowers as beautiful as anything in a flower shop.

     A. hostile   B. extraordinary   C. misleading   D. monotonous

PART B

Write **C** if the italicized word is used **correctly**. Write **I** if the word is used **incorrectly**.

_C_ 14. Because my sister skipped assignments and classes, it's hard for me to *sympathize* with her disappointment over failing algebra.

_I_ 15. Mario's boss *fulfilled* his request for a day off, saying, "No, you've had too much time off already."

_C_ 16. Someday I'd like to replace my old-fashioned camera with a new *automatic* one that does everything by itself, even advancing the film.

_I_ 17. Fay is so *extravagant* that she purposely finds fault with waiters so that she can refuse to leave them a tip.

_C_ 18. Some parents worry that Barbie dolls, with their impossibly long legs and tiny waists, can *influence* little girls, making them feel bad about their own bodies.

_C_ 19. Dan is worried about his math test because he knows it is *crucial* to his grade for the course.

_C_ 20. It is more *economical* to buy a six-pack of sodas for $1.99 than to buy six single sodas at 50 cents each.

_C_ 21. Since he was a little boy, Jon has *devoted* himself to becoming a pilot. He reads constantly about airplanes and flying, and he saves all his money for flying lessons.

_I_ 22. I feel so tired that instead of getting up this morning, I would love just to *transfer* in bed.

_C_ 23. Having our grandfather live with us is not a *burden*. He is easy to live with, and he is also very helpful around the house.

_I_ 24. I was really excited when my parents *humiliated* me with a plane ticket to visit my sister in England.

_I_ 25. As Dan studied for his test, his family tried to *divert* his attention by turning off the TV and keeping the house quiet and peaceful.

Score   (Number correct) _____ x 4 = _____ %

PART A

On the answer line, write the word from the box that completes each item below. Use each word once.

A. abandon	B. circumstances	C. disregard	D. function	E. hinder
F. hostile	G. misleading	H. monotonous	I. perceive	J. prey
K. revive	L. seize	M. severe		

_____function_____ 1. It is the ___ of advertising to persuade you that you will be happier and better off if you will buy a certain product.

_____abandon_____ 2. When Della's voice teacher said she had no talent, Della didn't ___ her efforts to become a singer; instead, she got a new teacher.

_____severe_____ 3. When children get chicken pox, the disease is just a minor problem, but for adults, chicken pox can be a ___ illness.

_____circumstances_____ 4. Paula's parents live in unusual ___; although they have been divorced for years, they continue to live in separate parts of the same house.

_____misleading_____ 5. Our Morrisville address is ___. We actually live much closer to the town of Hendrix.

_____monotonous_____ 6. I prefer a job that takes a lot of effort to one that is easy but ___, with little or no change from hour to hour and day to day.

_____disregard_____ 7. Foolishly, Randy ___ed the fact that he is allergic to seafood, ate a lobster, and ended up in the hospital.

_____seize_____ 8. Before I could take a bite of my grilled cheese sandwich, a hungry dog ___d it, pulling it out of my hand and gulping it down.

_____hinder_____ 9. Eduardo does not let his lack of a car ___ him from getting to work; he rides his bicycle.

_____revive_____ 10. Early in the season, the football team's chances of getting to the Super Bowl were not very good. But then the team ___d its hopes by winning six games in a row.

_____perceive_____ 11. Long before I entered the house, I could ___ that Mom was making her famous spaghetti sauce. Its wonderful smell was the clue.

_____prey_____ 12. To catch its ___, the anteater sticks its tongue into an anthill.

_____hostile_____ 13. Never run up to pat a dog you don't know. To avoid getting bitten, move toward it slowly until you are sure it is not ___.

(Continues on next page)

PART B

Write **C** if the italicized word is used **correctly**. Write **I** if the word is used **incorrectly**.

_C_ 14. I will let my cousin move into my apartment only if he *assures* me it will be for no more than a week.

_I_ 15. Mr. Henderson does everything according to *impulse*. For example, when he decided to buy a car, he spent months comparing models and prices, reading articles in car magazines, and visiting car dealers.

_I_ 16. Anitra is the most *idle* one in her family. She does all of the cooking and cleaning by herself.

_I_ 17. Every group of friends seems to have one especially *frantic* member who helps keep the others calm and peaceful.

_C_ 18. In 2008, one film—*Slumdog Millionaire*—*dominated* the Academy Awards, winning eight Oscars.

_I_ 19. The videotapes of the robbery showed that as it was going on, the night watchman was *alert* and snoring in his office.

_C_ 20. Although Marla was abused as a child, she has *overcome* that terrible experience and is a kind, loving parent herself.

_C_ 21. The sweater has bits of blue and green in it, but its *primary* color is red.

_C_ 22. Have you ever really had to write a paper on the *theme* "How I Spent My Summer Vacation"?

_C_ 23. I read *excerpts* from the book but did not take the time to read the entire book.

_C_ 24. "No bacon for me, thank you," said Ahmed. "We Muslims *exclude* pork from our diet."

_I_ 25. Scientists are working on a treatment that will help people *obtain* the virus that causes AIDS.

Score	(Number correct) _____	x 4 = _____ %

PART A: Synonyms

In the space provided, write the letter of the choice that is most nearly the **same** in meaning as the **boldfaced** word.

B   1. **assure**   A. argue with   B. promise   C. run from   D. reach out to

A   2. **automatic**   A. operating by itself   B. money-saving   C. clear   D. ashamed

C   3. **bewilder**   A. discontinue   B. hide   C. confuse   D. examine

B   4. **circumstances**   A. feelings   B. situation   C. hardships   D. enemies

D   5. **communicate**   A. take seriously   B. make strong   C. pay for   D. talk

D   6. **devote**   A. slow down   B. turn away   C. get rid of   D. give one's time

A   7. **divert**   A. turn away   B. point toward   C. get near   D. make better

D   8. **emotion**   A. movement   B. victim   C. hardship   D. feeling

C   9. **excerpt**   A. sudden decision   B. effect   C. part of a work   D. whole

D   10. **fulfill**   A. hurry   B. embarrass   C. search for   D. carry out

D   11. **function**   A. knowledge   B. hardship   C. topic   D. use

A   12. **humiliate**   A. shame   B. give energy to   C. send   D. calm

B   13. **impulse**   A. position   B. sudden desire   C. heartbeat   D. difficulty

D   14. **influence**   A. say   B. activity   C. get   D. have an effect on

A   15. **investigate**   A. examine   B. ignore   C. punish   D. lose

C   16. **misleading**   A. proper   B. aware   C. giving the wrong idea   D. unfriendly

D   17. **obtain**   A. protect   B. explore   C. move   D. get

A   18. **perceive**   A. notice   B. grab   C. ignore   D. lie to

C   19. **prey**   A. hardship   B. subject   C. victim   D. struggle

B   20. **primary**   A. small   B. main   C. moving by itself   D. aware

A   21. **seize**   A. grab   B. tell   C. puzzle   D. convince

D   22. **sympathize**   A. ignore   B. slow down   C. leave out   D. feel pity

C   23. **theme**   A. difficulty   B. condition   C. main topic   D. hardship

A   24. **theory**   A. explanation   B. effect   C. activity   D. choice

D   25. **transfer**   A. puzzle   B. study closely   C. win   D. move

(Continues on next page)

PART B: Antonyms

In the space provided, write the letter of the choice that is most nearly **opposite** in meaning to the **boldfaced** word.

___D___ 26. **abandon**   A. make clear   B. surprise   C. lose   D. continue

___B___ 27. **alert**   A. patient   B. sleepy   C. serious   D. special

___B___ 28. **apparent**   A. not proper   B. hidden   C. difficult   D. unfriendly

___B___ 29. **burden**   A. truth   B. something easy to handle   C. something usual   D. thought

___B___ 30. **crucial**   A. not real   B. not important   C. not clear   D. not wanted

___C___ 31. **deceive**   A. tire   B. give away   C. tell the truth to   D. let go of

___D___ 32. **disregard**   A. know   B. throw away   C. make fun of   D. pay attention to

___D___ 33. **dominate**   A. accept as true   B. lie to   C. argue with   D. have a low position

___B___ 34. **earnest**   A. weak   B. dishonest   C. not fearful   D. not important

___D___ 35. **economical**   A. exciting   B. expected   C. expert   D. expensive

___D___ 36. **exclude**   A. set free   B. support   C. lose to   D. include

___C___ 37. **extraordinary**   A. friendly   B. careless   C. usual   D. important

___B___ 38. **extravagant**   A. troubled   B. money-saving   C. confident   D. not serious

___D___ 39. **fiction**   A. action   B. idea   C. subject   D. truth

___B___ 40. **frantic**   A. unclear   B. relaxed   C. important   D. fast

___B___ 41. **hinder**   A. give away   B. help   C. change   D. lose

___D___ 42. **hostile**   A. not sincere   B. brave   C. not boring   D. friendly

___A___ 43. **idle**   A. busy   B. valuable   C. not proper   D. brave

___B___ 44. **legible**   A. not boring   B. unreadable   C. untruthful   D. not easy

___B___ 45. **monotonous**   A. unusual   B. interesting   C. true   D. easy to understand

___D___ 46. **outspoken**   A. least important   B. friendly   C. exact   D. silent

___B___ 47. **overcome**   A. continue   B. lose to   C. have faith in   D. find fault with

___D___ 48. **revive**   A. make clear   B. pay attention   C. listen carefully   D. make weak

___D___ 49. **security**   A. relief   B. activity   C. anger   D. danger

___D___ 50. **severe**   A. sad   B. fast   C. new   D. mild

Score   (Number correct) _____ x 2 = _____%

Unit Five

Chapter 21

conflict	resources
convert	stress
possess	unanimous
procedure	vary
renew	vicinity

Chapter 22

abolish	precise
corrupt	promote
decay	reform
expand	tendency
nevertheless	vast

Chapter 23

assert	preconception
clarify	resemble
evade	rigid
extend	senseless
precaution	vertical

Chapter 24

anxious	illustrate
comprehend	impression
convince	inferior
dramatic	overwhelm
frank	thorough

Chapter 25

acquire	precede
commitment	resent
formal	solemn
fragment	spite
fundamental	symbolize

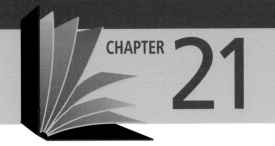

conflict	resources
convert	stress
possess	unanimous
procedure	vary
renew	vicinity

Ten Words in Context

In the space provided, write the letter of the meaning closest to that of each **boldfaced** word. Use the context of the sentences to help you figure out each word's meaning.

1 conflict
(kŏn'flĭkt')
- *noun*

- When the **conflict** between the two diners became noisy, the restaurant manager asked them to settle their quarrel outside.
- Marsha's children often have an angry **conflict** about whose turn it is to put out the trash.

<u>A</u> *Conflict* means   A. fight.   B. joke.   C. duty.

2 convert
(kən-vûrt')
- *verb*

- Cold can turn water into ice, while heat can **convert** it into steam.
- Scientist George Washington Carver was the first to **convert** peanuts into peanut butter. He also used them in more than three hundred other products, including glue, ink, and dyes.

<u>B</u> *Convert* means   A. to buy.   B. to change.   C. to copy.

3 possess
(pə-zĕs')
- *verb*

- I can't understand the desire to **possess** very expensive cars and jewelry. If I had more money, I'd spend it on travel.
- People who spend time with young children need to **possess** plenty of patience.

<u>A</u> *Possess* means   A. to have.   B. to know.   C. to see.

4 procedure
(prə-sē'jər)
- *noun*

- What **procedure** should I follow to become a citizen?
- Even kindergarten students can learn the **procedure** for reporting an emergency: Dial 911, give your name and address, and describe the problem.

<u>B</u> *Procedure* means   A. answer.   B. steps.   C. support.

5 renew
(rĭ-nōō')
- *verb*

- After helping to pay for their children's education, many parents barely have time to **renew** their savings in time for retirement.
- We need a good rain to **renew** the supply of water throughout this area. In the meantime, people are being asked not to water their lawns.

<u>C</u> *Renew* means   A. to change.   B. to upset.   C. to build up again.

6 resources
(rē'sôrs'əs)
- *noun*

- West Virginia's natural **resources** include coal and timber.
- A country's **resources** include its workers—the people who help to keep the economy strong.

<u>C</u> *Resources* means   A. plans.   B. expenses.   C. wealth.

7 stress
(strĕs)
- *noun*

- My doctor said my headaches were caused by **stress**. He suggested that I think of ways to reduce the tension in my life.

- Troy and Angie are experiencing a lot of **stress**. Angie's mother is very sick, Troy lost his job, and they just learned that Angie is going to have twins.

B *Stress* means   A. relief.   B. pressures.   C. details.

8 unanimous
(yōō-năn′ə-məs)
- *adjective*

- The vote electing Wayne president of the book club was **unanimous**. In fact, there was no other candidate to vote for.

- The jury's decision was **unanimous**. Every juror believed that the woman on trial had robbed the beauty parlor after getting her hair cut.

A *Unanimous* means   A. in full agreement.   B. uncertain.   C. hard to understand.

9 vary
(vâr′ē)
- *verb*

- There are often great changes in weather along the coast. In one day, the temperature can **vary** by as much as forty degrees.

- Joan's lunches never **vary**. Every day, she eats a peanut butter and celery sandwich, pretzels, and a banana.

B *Vary* means   A. to begin.   B. to change.   C. to disappear.

10 vicinity
(vĭ-sĭn′ĭ-tē))
- *noun*

- In the **vicinity** of the elementary school, the speed limit is fifteen miles an hour.

- The Johnsons decided not to buy the house when they learned that there was a nuclear power plant in the **vicinity**.

C *Vicinity* means   A. yard.   B. building.   C. neighborhood.

Matching Words with Definitions

Following are definitions of the ten words. **Print** each word next to its definition. If you look closely at each word in context, you will be able to figure out its meaning.

1. _____resources_____ Whatever makes up the present and future wealth of a country, state, etc., including natural supplies and labor force

2. _____renew_____ To fill up again; replace; start up again

3. _____vicinity_____ The area near or around a place

4. _____conflict_____ A quarrel or fight; disagreement

5. _____unanimous_____ Based on complete agreement

6. _____stress_____ Mental or emotional tension; strain

7. _____vary_____ To experience change; become different

8. _____convert_____ To make something change completely; transform

9. _____possess_____ To own; have

10. _____procedure_____ A method; the way in which something is done

CAUTION: Do not go any further until you are sure the above answers are correct. Then you can use the definitions to help you in the following practices. Your goal is eventually to know the words well enough so that you don't need to check the definitions at all.

Check 1

Using the answer lines, complete each item below with the correct word from the box.

A. **conflict**	B. **convert**	C. **possess**	D. **procedure**	E. **renew**
F. **resources**	G. **stress**	H. **unanimous**	I. **vary**	J. **vicinity**

__resources__   1. A country's ___ include all of its minerals, such as coal, gold, and silver.

__unanimous__   2. If there is no disagreement among jurors, we say that their decision is ___.

__conflict__   3. Whether two people or groups are fighting with words or weapons, we can say they are having a ___, in which one is trying to dominate° the other.

__vicinity__   4. If someone lives in the ___ of your home, you would call that person a neighbor.

__possess__   5. If you are always patient, we can say that you ___ lots of patience.

__vary__   6. Roses ___ greatly in color, size, and shape.

__procedure__   7. A ___ is a process that often involves a series of steps.

__convert__   8. The beach artist ___ed a pile of wet sand into a statue of a giant turtle.

__renew__   9. To ___ my supply of clean towels, I'll have to do my laundry tonight.

__stress__   10. Anything that puts pressure on our emotions, bodies, or minds can be called ___.

NOTE: Now check your answers to these items by turning to page 241. Going over the answers carefully will help you prepare for the remaining practices, for which answers are not given.

Check 2

Using the answer lines, complete each item below with **two** words from the box. Use each word once.

__conflict__
__stress__   1–2. The ongoing ___ between the Millers and Smiths—an argument over the Smiths' noisy parties—has caused the Millers so much ___ that they are thinking of moving.

__vicinity__
__procedure__   3–4. My father feels lucky that there is a surgeon in our ___ who has developed a special ___ for doing the type of operation that he needs.

__resources__
__vary__   5–6. The natural ___ of the United States ___, depending upon the part of the country. For example, the Midwest is rich in farmland, and the Northeast has more coal.

__unanimous__
__convert__   7–8. The city council's ___ decision was to ___ the vacant lot into a community softball field.

__possess__
__renew__   9–10. According to one fairy tale, a king ___es a magic box full of gold coins; whenever the box becomes empty, it ___s its supply of coins.

Word Work

A. In the space provided, write the letter of the choice that most closely relates to the situation in each item.

__A__ 1. When you arrive at the doctor's office, tell the receptionist your name and sign the check-in chart.
   A. procedure   B. vary   C. vicinity

__B__ 2. Rita uses her blender to turn old, dry bread into bread crumbs.
   A. stress   B. convert   C. conflict

__C__ 3. A hard day at work and a flat tire on the way home left Lou with a pounding headache.
   A. renew   B. resources   C. stress

__A__ 4. All the judges agreed that Evelyn should be named winner of the talent contest.
   A. unanimous   B. renew   C. possession

__B__ 5. The state has attracted investors because of its mineral rights and its well-trained workers.
   A. conflict   B. resources   C. vicinity

B. In the space provided, write the letter of the word that best completes each item.

__C__ 6. The roommates have a **conflict** over housecleaning. They

   A. agree on how clean the room should be.
   B. plan to hire someone else to clean the room.
   C. disagree over how clean the room should be.

__A__ 7. The boss's mood **varies**, so the boss's employees

   A. never know what kind of mood he will be in.
   B. know that he is always in a good mood.
   C. think that he is usually in a good mood.

__B__ 8. Because our house is in the **vicinity** of many great restaurants, we

   A. have to travel a long way to find a good restaurant.
   B. don't have to travel far to find a good restaurant.
   C. can't find any good restaurants.

__B__ 9. A quality that Tony **possesses** is a good sense of humor. Tony

   A. finds it hard to see the funny side of things.
   B. is easily able to laugh at things.
   C. gets angry when people laugh at him.

__C__ 10. The store's supply of milk was **renewed** today. The store

   A. is out of milk.
   B. no longer sells milk.
   C. has a fresh supply of milk.

Word Parts

A. The suffix *-ful* mean "producing ___" or "full of ___."

> *Examples:*   *stress* — tension   *joy* — great happiness
>   *stressful* — producing tension   *joyful* — full of great happiness

On each answer line, write the word from the box that means the same as the *italicized* words.

> A. **beautiful**   B. **playful**   C. **stressful**
> D. **thankful**   E. **wasteful**

___wasteful___   1. "All you can eat" restaurants encourage people to be *producing waste*, piling far more food on their plates than they really want or need.

___beautiful___   2. Although the outside of an oyster shell is rather ugly, the inside is *full of beauty*, with its pale, milky rainbow of colors.

___thankful___   3. When Glenn's car broke down on a dark road far from his home, he was *full of thanks* that a police officer quickly arrived and offered him a ride to town.

___stressful___   4. Most people find it *producing stress* to have to speak in front of a large group.

___playful___   5. That boss may seem overly serious. But when she's not busy, she can be quite *full of play*, laughing and telling jokes.

B. The prefixes *com-* and *con-* mean "with" or "together."

> *Examples:*   *communicate°* — to exchange information with   *combine* — to join together
>   *conflict* — a quarrel with someone   *compress* — to press together

On each answer line, write the word from the box that best completes the item.

> F. **communicate°**   G. **complicate°**   H. **conflict**
> I. **confront°**   J. **contrast°**

___conflict___   6. Thelma had a ___ with her neighbors over their dogs' getting into her garbage cans.

___complicate___   7. The more people you invite, the more you will ___ our job of preparing for the party.

___contrast___   8. There's a big ___ between the two Williams brothers. One is very outgoing and friendly, and the other is quite shy.

___confront___   9. When the Carveys didn't pay their rent for the third month in a row, the landlord actually came to their door to ___ them.

___communicate___   10. In the 1800s, it must have been very difficult to ___ with people who lived far away. Today, many people stay in touch by using cell phones and e-mail.

Final Check

Read the passages carefully. Then fill in each blank with the word that best fits the context.

A. Traveling with Children

A. **conflict**	B. **stress**	C. **unanimous**	D. **vary**	E. **vicinity**

Whether I'm driving in the (1)_____*vicinity*_____ of home or farther away, the trip seems to last longer if my kids are in the car with me. The minute we're on the road, the baby begins to cry, and the older children start a major (2)_____*conflict*_____. These fights (3)_____*vary*_____ from time to time, but they often have something to do with one of these four primary° themes°:

1. One kid is in the front seat when it's another kid's turn.

2. Someone who had a window seat last time got one again.

3. One of the kids hates the music that another has turned on. (No single radio station has won the (4)_____*unanimous*_____ approval of all the children.)

4. One child thinks another "is looking at me funny."

Now that I think about it, maybe I can preserve° the peace in my family and lower the level of (5)_____*stress*_____ in my life by shifting the burden° elsewhere. Starting tomorrow, I'll make my kids take a bus!

B. Saving Earth's Natural Supplies

F. **convert**	G. **possess**	H. **procedure**	I. **renew**	J. **resources**

Once some of Earth's valuable (6)_____*resources*_____ are used up, it will be impossible to (7)_____*renew*_____ them. For example, coal will someday be used up and gone forever. Coal mines will be abandoned°. Coal miners will be idle°.

We do, however, (8)_____*possess*_____ other important supplies that can be used over and over. We can (9)_____*convert*_____ paper, metal, plastics and glass into new products by means of recycling. If we don't recycle, who knows what severe° shortages and garbage problems will result? It's up to each of us to have the interest and foresight° to learn about the recycling methods in our communities and then to follow those (10)_____*procedure*_____s.

Scores	Check 2 _____%	Word Work _____%	Word Parts _____%	Final Check _____%

Enter your scores above and in the **Vocabulary Performance Chart** on the inside back cover of the book.

abolish	precise
corrupt	promote
decay	reform
expand	tendency
nevertheless	vast

Ten Words in Context

In the space provided, write the letter of the meaning closest to that of each **boldfaced** word. Use the context of the sentences to help you figure out each word's meaning.

1 abolish
(ə-bŏl′ĭsh)
- *verb*

- With our advanced farming methods, why can't we **abolish** hunger?
- One way for a school to raise students' test scores is to **abolish** summer vacation and hold classes all year round.

<u>B</u> *Abolish* means   A. to make longer.   B. to get rid of.   C. to pay for.

2 corrupt
(kə-rŭpt′)
- *adjective*

- A **corrupt** police officer went to prison for selling the drugs he took in a raid.
- The country was run by a **corrupt** ruler, who robbed the rich and poor alike.

<u>A</u> *Corrupt* means   A. not honest.   B. respected.   C. poor.

3 decay
(dĭ-kā′)
- *verb*

- Teeth that are brushed and flossed regularly are not likely to **decay**.
- Leaves fall from the trees, **decay**, and become part of the forest floor.

<u>C</u> *Decay* means   A. to increase.   B. to bend.   C. to rot.

4 expand
(ĭk-spănd′)
- *verb*

- The grocery is buying the shop next door so that it can **expand** enough to double its space.
- During a heavy rain, that little creek **expands** into a fast-moving river.

<u>C</u> *Expand* means   A. to bend.   B. to break down.   C. to grow.

5 nevertheless
(nĕv′ər-thə-lĕs′)
- *adverb*

- Too much sun can cause skin cancer; **nevertheless**, many people still try to get a deep suntan.
- The stuffed tiger is old and tattered, but the little boy loves it **nevertheless**.

<u>C</u> *Nevertheless* means   A. rarely.   B. because of that.   C. in spite of that.

6 precise
(prĭ-sīs′)
- *adjective*

- When you bake a cake, it is very important to be **precise** when measuring ingredients.
- We found the house easily, thanks to our host's **precise** directions.

<u>A</u> *Precise* means   A. exact.   B. busy.   C. strong.

7 promote
(prə-mōt′)
- *verb*

● The dentist visited the classroom to **promote** good dental care at home.
● Mr. Sanchez won't let his kids watch movies that seem to **promote** violent behavior.

_A_ *Promote* means   A. to support.   B. to attack.   C. to prevent.

8 reform
(rĭ-fôrm′)
- *verb*

● Does serving time in prison **reform** people, or does it only keep them off the streets?
● Training classes can **reform** dogs so that they don't pull on their leashes and jump on people.

_B_ *Reform* means   A. to annoy.   B. to make better.   C. to confuse.

9 tendency
(tĕn′dən-sē)
- *noun*

● Fishermen have a **tendency** to tell big stories about the fish they almost caught.
● I have a bad **tendency** to put off doing work until the last minute.

_C_ *Tendency* means   A. hard work.   B. limit.   C. habit.

10 vast
(văst)
- *adjective*

● Lake Superior is so **vast** that you could easily mistake it for an ocean.
● The library has a **vast** collection of books for adults, but not so many for children.

_C_ *Vast* means   A. well-known.   B. gradual.   C. very big.

Matching Words with Definitions

Following are definitions of the ten words. **Print** each word next to its definition. If you look closely at each word in context, you will be able to figure out its meaning.

1. _expand_   To spread out; get larger

2. _decay_   To break down gradually; rot

3. _nevertheless_   In spite of that; even so; despite that

4. _corrupt_   Dishonest; crooked

5. _reform_   To cause or persuade to behave better

6. _abolish_   To put an end to

7. _precise_   Exact; correct; accurate

8. _tendency_   A leaning toward thinking or behaving in a certain way

9. _vast_   Very large in size, amount, or area

10. _promote_   To speak for or work toward something; encourage; help make happen

CAUTION: Do not go any further until you are sure the above answers are correct. Then you can use the definitions to help you in the following practices. Your goal is eventually to know the words well enough so that you don't need to check the definitions at all.

Check 1

Using the answer lines, complete each item below with the correct word from the box.

| A. **abolish** | B. **corrupt** | C. **decay** | D. **expand** | E. **nevertheless** |
| F. **precise** | G. **promote** | H. **reform** | I. **tendency** | J. **vast** |

precise 1. I don't know Uncle Hank's ___ age, but I guess he's in his mid-fifties.

nevertheless 2. The sun is shining brightly; ___, it is quite chilly outside.

decay 3. The house is beginning to ___. Its windows are broken, and its paint is peeling off.

expand 4. The high school is going to ___ by adding more classrooms.

promote 5. To ___ reading in the community, the banks have started a "Bucks for Books" program. The bank managers actually pay kids to read.

vast 6. Scholars, writers, and researchers from all over the world visit the Library of Congress in Washington, D.C., to make use of its ___ collection of books and papers on every topic imaginable.

corrupt 7. Former employees told reporters about ___ practices in the supermarket, such as soaking spoiling hams in bleach to get rid of the bad smell.

reform 8. Anton used to answer the phone by yelling, "Who is this?" But a few lessons in phone manners ___ed him so that he now politely says, "Hello?"

tendency 9. I have a ___ to talk loudly and quickly when I am nervous.

abolish 10. The restaurant's owner decided to ___ the smoking section and make the entire restaurant smoke-free.

NOTE: Now check your answers to these items by turning to page 241. Going over the answers carefully will help you prepare for the remaining practices, for which answers are not given.

Check 2

Using the answer lines, complete each item below with **two** words from the box. Use each word once.

tendency
nevertheless 1–2. Joanne has a ___ to be careless and messy at home; ___, she is always neat and careful at work.

reform
abolish 3–4. Many people feel that to ___ politicians and improve politics, it is necessary to ___ all gifts of money from groups that wish to influence° lawmakers.

vast
decay 5–6. The housing project is so ___ that you can get lost walking around in it, and it's so poorly cared for that the buildings are starting to ___.

corrupt
expand 7–8. At his trial, it was revealed that the ___ mayor had used city funds to ___ his automobile collection. While in office, he bought two Rolls-Royces and a Ferrari.

promote
precise 9–10. The new principal promised to ___ better teacher-parent communication. But he didn't explain the ___ ways that he would do that.

Word Work

A. In the space provided, write the letter of the word that most closely relates to the situation in each item.

___A___ 1. The world's largest desert, the Sahara, covers 3½ million square miles of North Africa.

    A. vast   B. corrupt   C. promote

___C___ 2. Some people put their food scraps in a compost heap, where the food slowly rots and turns into rich fertilizer for the garden.

    A. precise   B. expand   C. decay

___C___ 3. Although the earthquake victims were starving, the government officials kept most of the food donations for themselves.

    A. tendency   B. vast   C. corrupt

___B___ 4. Randy, who believes in the benefits of health foods, is trying to persuade his brother and sister to eat tofu and raw vegetables.

    A. corrupt   B. promote   C. expand

___A___ 5. I usually wait until the last minute before beginning a project.

    A. tendency   B. reform   C. expand

B. In the space provided, write the letter of the choice that best completes each item.

___A___ 6. If a school **abolishes** its football team, the football players will probably

    A. be upset.   B. be more popular.   C. win more games.

___C___ 7. A business is likely to **expand** when it is

    A. not honest.   B. closing.   C. doing very well.

___A___ 8. I love chocolate ice cream; **nevertheless**,

    A. I am not going to have any.
    B. I am going to take a large helping.
    C. it is my favorite flavor.

___C___ 9. An example of a **precise** measurement of time is

    A. a few minutes.   B. several hours.   C. forty-three seconds.

___B___ 10. A thief who **reforms** himself

    A. commits more thefts.
    B. stops stealing.
    C. begins hurting people as well as stealing.

Synonyms and Antonyms

A. Synonyms. Write the letter of the word or phrase that most nearly means the **same** as each boldfaced word.

___A___ 1. **reform**

    A. make better   C. make sure

    B. make more difficult   D. get bigger

___B___ 2. **tendency**

    A. thought   C. fear

    B. habit of acting in a certain way   D. making something larger

___D___ 3. **decay**

    A. build   C. leave

    B. continue   D. spoil

___D___ 4. **precise**

    A. helpful   C. dishonest

    B. unclear   D. exact

___C___ 5. **nevertheless**

    A. because   C. despite that

    B. perhaps   D. sometimes

B. Antonyms. Write the letter of the word or phrase that most nearly means the **opposite** of each boldfaced word.

___C___ 6. **corrupt**

    A. small   C. honest

    B. helpless   D. stiff

___A___ 7. **promote**

    A. discourage   C. pay

    B. anger   D. hide

___D___ 8. **vast**

    A. many   C. incorrect

    B. broken   D. tiny

___B___ 9. **expand**

    A. grow stronger   C. break

    B. get smaller   D. build

___D___ 10. **abolish**

    A. end   C. like

    B. become used to   D. create

Final Check

Read the passages carefully. Then fill in each blank with the word that best fits the context.

A. More Fat, Anyone?

A. **decay**	B. **expand**	C. **nevertheless**	D. **precise**	E. **vast**

We know that fatty and sugary foods are bad for us. (1)_____*Nevertheless*_____, we love to eat them. There's a high demand for food with (2)_____*vast*_____ amounts of fat and sugar.

To meet the demand for fat, many fast-food giants offer more and bigger high-fat menu items. Pizza Hut sells its Triple Decker Pizza, a health nightmare with as much fat as a stick and a half of butter! McDonald's offers a super-fat triple cheeseburger. And Taco Bell sells a variety° of fatty bacon products. To make matters worse, the fast-food chains offer sugar-filled ice cream, shakes, sodas, pies, cakes, and cookies that make us fatter. These foods also cause our teeth to (3)_____*decay*_____ and get cavities. Although fat and sugar are not wholesome° for the customer, they are certainly good for the financial health of the fast-food chains, which have no plans to withdraw° them from their menus.

Why do we disregard° what science teaches us about a good diet? Researchers cannot explain the (4)_____*precise*_____ reasons why we ignore what we know about healthy eating, but one thing is certain. As long as our appetite for fat and sugar continues to increase, our waistlines will also continue to (5)_____*expand*_____.

B. Is Prison Effective?

F. **abolish**	G. **corrupt**	H. **promote**	I. **reform**	J. **tendency**

There's a lot of disagreement about how to (6)_____*reform*_____ criminals and make them good citizens. Today, most criminals are sent to prison. But many people believe that serving time in prison does not really make a person less likely to commit another crime. They point out that in prison, a person may spend months or years in the company of more hardened criminals whose sentences coincide° with theirs. Will a prisoner in such company develop a conscience°—or come out of jail with a (7)_____*tendency*_____ to be honest? Not likely, they say. Instead, the prisoner will probably learn only how to be more (8)_____*corrupt*_____.

In addition, many people want to (9)_____*abolish*_____ the death penalty. They believe it is just as wrong to kill a killer as it was for him or her to commit murder in the first place.

Even if you agree with these points, the question remains of how to deal with people who harm others. Some people want to convert° prisons from places where people are just locked up to places where prisoners can obtain° an education, job training, and counseling. They want to see the system adjust to a prisoner's needs, rather than treat everyone the same. They want prisons to be places that (10)_____*promote*_____ positive values, instead of places whose sole° function° is to punish criminals.

Scores	Check 2 _____%	Word Work _____%	Synonyms and Antonyms _____%	Final Check _____%

Enter your scores above and in the **Vocabulary Performance Chart** on the inside back cover of the book.

assert	preconception
clarify	resemble
evade	rigid
extend	senseless
precaution	vertical

Ten Words in Context

In the space provided, write the letter of the meaning closest to that of each **boldfaced** word. Use the context of the sentences to help you figure out each word's meaning.

1 assert
(ə-sûrt′)
- *verb*

- The mayor **asserted** in court that he never took bribes, but the jury did not believe him.
- Every once in a while, the newspapers sold in supermarkets **assert** that Elvis Presley is alive and hiding somewhere.

<u>C</u> *Assert* means   A. to doubt.   B. to fear.   C. to state strongly.

2 clarify
(klăr′ə-fī′)
- *verb*

- Mr. Patel is a great math teacher. He can **clarify** even the hardest problems so that everyone can understand.
- Todd didn't understand his health insurance plan, so he asked someone at the insurance company to **clarify** it for him.

<u>A</u> *Clarify* means   A. to explain.   B. to create.   C. to stop.

3 evade
(ĭ-vād′)
- *verb*

- Our dog will do anything to **evade** a bath. Once we get him near the tub, we have to shut the bathroom door, or he will escape.
- In my favorite cops-and-robbers movie, the robbers tried to **evade** the police by leaving through a hole in the roof. However, their plan failed; the police were waiting on the roof!

<u>B</u> *Evade* means   A. to break down.   B. to get away from.   C. to find.

4 extend
(ĭk-stĕnd′)
- *verb*

- We had so much fun camping that we **extended** our vacation one more day.
- "Because many students are having trouble finishing this project on time," said the instructor, "I will **extend** the deadline by one more week."

<u>A</u> *Extend* means   A. to make longer or later.   B. to make clear.   C. to escape.

5 precaution
(prĭ-kô′shən)
- *noun*

- We took the **precaution** of having the car tuned up before we began our long trip.
- If you walk in the woods, wear long pants as a **precaution** against poison ivy.

<u>C</u> *Precaution* means   A. cure for a problem.   B. something stated.   C. step taken to be safe.

6 preconception
(prē′kən-sĕp′shən)
- *adjective*

- From her voice on the phone, I had a **preconception** of my brother's girlfriend as being rather unfriendly.
- Our **preconception** that the party would be boring was completely wrong. Once we got there, we had a great time.

<u>B</u> *Preconception* means   A. wish.   B. judgment made without experience.   C. statement of fact.

7 resemble
(rĭ-zĕm′bəl)
- *verb*

● A certain worthless mineral is known as "fool's gold" because it **resembles** real gold. Both minerals are shiny yellow.

● Eating wild mushrooms can be dangerous because a poisonous mushroom sometimes **resembles** one that is safe.

B *Resemble* means   A. to be better than.   B. to look the same as.   C. to be easier to find than.

8 rigid
(rĭj′ĭd)
- *adjective*

● Modeling clay is **rigid** when it is cold, but once it warms in your hands, it becomes softer and easier to work with.

● The guards outside the palace stood stiffly—they looked as **rigid** as poles.

C *Rigid* means   A. not heavy.   B. hard to beat.   C. not bending.

9 senseless
(sĕns′lĭs)
- *adjective*

● Building a new high school seems **senseless** to me. I think the school we have is perfectly fine.

● Leo loves desserts. In his opinion, it's **senseless** to fill up on vegetables.

A *Senseless* means   A. silly.   B. possible.   C. smart.

10 vertical
(vûr′tĭ-kəl)
- *adjective*

● Clothes with **vertical** stripes generally make the wearer look taller and thinner.

● The dark **vertical** lines of the telephone poles looked striking against the background of the snowy field.

C *Vertical* means   A. very clear.   B. curving.   C. up-and-down.

Matching Words with Definitions

Following are definitions of the ten words. **Print** each word next to its definition. If you look closely at each word in context, you will be able to figure out its meaning.

1. preconception   An opinion formed before having enough information or experience
2. resemble   To look like or be similar to; be like
3. clarify   To make clear or easy to understand
4. precaution   Something done in advance to avoid a problem
5. senseless   Foolish; not making good sense
6. assert   To state positively, often without proof
7. evade   To escape or avoid through clever action
8. vertical   In a straight, up-and-down line; upright
9. rigid   Stiff; not bending
10. extend   To make longer in time or later in time; continue

CAUTION: Do not go any further until you are sure the above answers are correct. Then you can use the definitions to help you in the following practices. Your goal is eventually to know the words well enough so that you don't need to check the definitions at all.

Check 1

Using the answer lines, complete each item below with the correct word from the box.

A. **assert**	B. **clarify**	C. **evade**	D. **extend**	E. **precaution**
F. **preconception**	G. **resemble**	H. **rigid**	I. **senseless**	J. **vertical**

clarify   1. A good math teacher can ___ a difficult problem.

assert   2. The people who want to build the mall ___ that it will mean more business for local stores, but the local store owners do not believe them.

rigid   3. The children found a ___ board to use as a bridge over the creek.

evade   4. The new employee ___s responsibility whenever possible. "That's not my job!" she says.

extend   5. The teacher ___ed the test so everyone had time to finish.

preconception   6. Before tasting spinach, many kids have the ___ they will not like it.

resemble   7. Expensive silk roses ___ real roses. However, unlike real roses, they do not dry up and decay° if they are deprived° of water.

senseless   8. "Everyone is doing it" is a ___ reason to do anything.

precaution   9. Remember to put on sunblock lotion as a ___ against sunburn.

vertical   10. As we got closer to New York City, we saw the ___ shape of the tall Empire State Building against the bright summer sky.

NOTE: Now check your answers to these items by turning to page 241. Going over the answers carefully will help you prepare for the remaining practices, for which answers are not given.

Check 2

Using the answer lines, complete each item below with **two** words from the box. Use each word once.

senseless
precaution   1–2. It was ___ of the town to open a swimming pool without taking the ___ of hiring a lifeguard first.

resemble
preconception   3–4. Because Krista ___s her sister physically, I had the ___ that she would have a similar personality, but the two girls actually have very different traits°. For example, Krista is economical°, while her sister has a tendency° to be extravagant.°

clarify
evade   5–6. A reporter said the mayor's views on taxes were unclear, and he asked the mayor to ___ her ideas. However, the mayor ___d the question by saying, "Who can think about taxes when our basketball team is striving° to win the state championship?"

assert
extend   7–8. The new advertisements for the motor oil ___ that using the oil is guaranteed to ___ the life of your car.

_____rigid_____   9–10. To build a playhouse, Mac began with four thick, ___ pieces of wood. He
_____vertical_____   stuck one end of each deep in the ground, so that each piece of wood was
                            in a ___ position.

Word Work

A. In the space provided, write the letter of the choice that best completes each item.

__B__ 1. After someone **clarifies** a problem, it should be
   A. a mystery.
   B. easier to understand.
   C. even more troubling.

__A__ 2. Because a snowstorm arrived during the furniture sale, the sale was **extended**, so people
   A. had more time to shop during the sale.
   B. could not buy furniture.
   C. had to pay full price for the furniture.

__C__ 3. A **precaution** against slipping on your icy sidewalk is
   A. an injury, such as a broken bone.
   B. an ice storm.
   C. spreading plenty of sand or salt over the ice.

__C__ 4. Two people who are likely to **resemble** one another physically are
   A. best friends.
   B. members of the same soccer team.
   C. brothers.

__C__ 5. People **evade** questions that they
   A. are happy to answer truthfully.
   B. did not hear.
   C. do not want to answer.

B. In the space provided, write the letter of the word that most closely relates to the situation in each item.

__A__ 6. A hotel clerk claims that she has been offered a part in a Hollywood movie.
   A. assert   B. extend   C. clarify

__C__ 7. Before it is cooked, spaghetti is hard and breaks instead of bending.
   A. evade   B. senseless   C. rigid

__C__ 8. When the phone rang, the mother ran into the house to answer it, leaving her two-year-old alone outside.
   A. vertical   B. clarify   C. senseless

__B__ 9. In the middle of his fifth-grade year, Ben began to think that he was going to have a terrible time in sixth grade.
   A. precaution   B. preconception   C. resemble

__B__ 10. The sunflower grew six feet tall, straight up into the air.
   A. evade   B. vertical   C. clarify

Word Parts

A. The prefix *ex-* can mean "beyond" or "out."

Examples: *extraordinary°* — beyond the ordinary
excerpt° — a part that is taken out of a whole work

On each answer line, write the word from the box that best completes the item.

A. **excerpt°**	B. **exclude°**	C. **extend**
D. **external°**	E. **extraordinary°**	

_____*extend*_____   1. Since so many people had something to say, the committee made a unanimous° decision to ___ the meeting another thirty minutes.

_____*excerpt*_____   2. A TV show titled *That's Entertainment* included ___s from many wonderful musical films.

_____*exclude*_____   3. When the children play, they prefer to ___ Hank because he is such a bully.

_____*external*_____   4. You are supposed to cut off the ___ layer of the kiwi fruit before eating it.

_____*extraordinary*_____   5. Mrs. Martin is an ___ woman. She has brought up four wonderful children by herself and also built a fine career at a bank, where she is now a vice president.

B. The prefix *pre-* often means "before."

Examples: *precaution* — something done beforehand to avoid a problem
preserve° — to protect or keep in good condition, before there's a problem

On each answer line, write the word from the box that best completes the item.

F. **preconception**	G. **preheat**	H. **prepare**
I. **preserve**	J. **pretest**	

_____*prepare*_____   6. To ___ for the trip, I have to wash and pack a lot of clothes.

_____*pretest*_____   7. Sometimes teachers give students a ___ to help them see if they are ready for the real test.

_____*preheat*_____   8. The brownie recipe says to ___ the oven to 350 degrees.

_____*preserve*_____   9. To ___ her wedding dress for her daughter, Mrs. Henry keeps it covered in plastic and in a box.

_____*preconception*_____ 10. New college students often have the ___ that instructors will remind them about assignments and tests. But in college, students must keep track of such things themselves.

Final Check

Read the passages carefully. Then fill in each blank with the word that best fits the context.

A. She Changed My Mind

A. clarify	B. extend	C. preconception	D. resemble	E. rigid

When I entered a Catholic school as a third-grader, I was very scared. The teachers were nuns, and although I had never known any nuns myself, I had a (1)__preconception__ of what a nun would be like. I pictured a hostile° woman dressed in a strange robe and sitting stiffly, as (2)__rigid__ as the ruler in her hand, and frowning when I forgot the answers to her questions. I imagined her deciding to (3)__extend__ my school day by several hours after everyone else went home.

By the time I actually arrived in the classroom, I would not have been surprised if the teacher had had fire coming out of her nostrils. Imagine my surprise, then, when I saw an attractive young woman standing at the front of the classroom. "Good morning!" she said cheerily. "My name is Sister Mary Elizabeth." I stared at her in surprise. She (4)__resemble__d my favorite aunt. Her face was not cold as I had expected, but warm and smiling. When she stopped by my desk later that morning to (5)__clarify__ an arithmetic problem, she knelt beside me and gave my ponytail a gentle, playful tug. One day in class was adequate° for me to fall in love with Sister Mary Elizabeth and to realize how little I had really known about nuns.

B. So Sue Me

F. assert	G. evade	H. precaution	I. senseless	J. vertical

"I'll sue!" This threat is all too often carried out. Americans have a strong tendency° to bring one another to court.

Take the case of the teenager who walked down the street, listening to music through the headphones of his personal stereo. He came to a curb and stepped into the street. A car running through a red light nearly hit him. Because he was listening to music, he was not alert° and had not heard the car coming. Did he sue the driver? No; he sued the maker of the stereo. He claimed the stereo should have come with a note telling him to take the (6)__precaution__ of removing the headphones when he crossed a street. Such a ridiculous legal procedure° is a (7)__senseless__ waste of court time.

Another well-known case involved similar circumstances°. A woman sued a fast-food chain for serving her coffee that was too hot. She spilled the coffee in her own lap, burned herself, and (8)__assert__ed that the restaurant was to blame.

What is next? Should ice-cream cones carry warning labels saying, "Keep the cone in a (9)__vertical__ position or else the ice cream might fall off"? It seems that suing someone else has become yet another way for people to (10)__evade__ responsibility for their own actions.

Scores	Check 2 _____%	Word Work _____%	Word Parts _____%	Final Check _____%

Enter your scores above and in the **Vocabulary Performance Chart** on the inside back cover of the book.

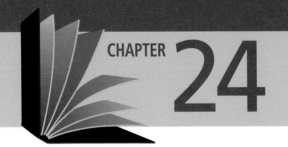

Ten Words in Context

In the space provided, write the letter of the meaning closest to that of each **boldfaced** word. Use the context of the sentences to help you figure out each word's meaning.

1 anxious
(ăngk′shəs)
- *adjective*

- Dean was **anxious** about his new job. He worried about doing well and whether he would like his supervisor.
- You seemed **anxious** before the test, but you look more relaxed now.

_B_ *Anxious* means   A. sure.   B. troubled.   C. late.

2 comprehend
(kŏm′prĭ-hĕnd′)
- *verb*

- Although my Japanese friend knew English pretty well when she came to this country, she did not **comprehend** such slang terms as "cool" and "gross."
- I cannot **comprehend** how a computer works, but at least I understand how to use one for writing papers and e-mail.

_C_ *Comprehend* means   A. to believe.   B. to remember.   C. to understand.

3 convince
(kən-vĭns′)
- *verb*

- The lawyer is sure she can **convince** the jury that her client is innocent.
- Cindy tried to **convince** her roommate that she had not stolen her necklace, but her roommate still did not believe her.

_B_ *Convince* means   A. to learn from.   B. to cause to believe.   C. to keep from.

4 dramatic
(drə-măt′ĭk)
- *adjective*

- To hold our interest, our gym teacher used **dramatic** movements, such as waving her arms or jumping.
- Mr. Johnson prefers not to be noticed when he enters a room, but Mrs. Johnson enjoys making **dramatic** entrances, such as by swirling a bright purple cape around her shoulders.

_C_ *Dramatic* means   A. distant.   B. usual.   C. attracting attention.

5 frank
(frăngk)
- *adjective*

- Mrs. Robins told her doctor, "Please be **frank**. If you know what is wrong with me, please tell me the truth."
- "To be **frank**," my sister said to me, "your new hairdo looks as if you just stuck your finger into an electrical socket."

_B_ *Frank* means   A. careful.   B. honest.   C. worried.

6 illustrate
(ĭl′ə-strāt′)
- *verb*

- Whenever Mrs. Fine wanted to teach us a new word, she **illustrated** its use in a sentence.
- Pastor Gibson **illustrated** his point about forgiving by telling a story about one victim who learned to forgive his attacker.

_A_ *Illustrate* means   A. explain with an example.   B. to change.   C. to make difficult.

7 impression
(ĭm-prĕsh′ən)
- *noun*

- My first **impression** of Leroy was that he was loud and rude, but spending time with him showed me that under all the noise was a warm, friendly person.
- I had the **impression** that Vicky was coming on the ski trip, but at the last minute I learned that she had never really planned to come.

_C_ *Impression* means   A. argument.   B. rule.   C. opinion.

8 inferior
(ĭn-fîr′ē-ər)
- *adjective*

- Silver is considered to be **inferior** to gold, but I still prefer silver jewelry.
- Tara's basketball skills are **inferior** to those of the other team members, but the coach believes that Tara will improve quickly.

_B_ *Inferior to* means   A. just like.   B. worse than.   C. new to.

9 overwhelm
(ō′vər-hwĕlm′)
- *verb*

- You will **overwhelm** children if you give too many instructions at one time.
- A group of bystanders **overwhelmed** the purse-snatcher, holding him down until the police could arrive.

_B_ *Overwhelm* means   A. to encourage.   B. to overpower.   C. to watch.

10 thorough
(thûr′ō)
- *adjective*

- After a **thorough** search of every corner of my apartment, I finally found my glasses—in my pocket.
- Before signing up their children at a day-care center, parents should do a **thorough** check of how kind and well-trained the staff are.

_B_ *Thorough* means   A. quick.   B. careful.   C. exciting.

Matching Words with Definitions

Following are definitions of the ten words. **Print** each word next to its definition. If you look closely at each word in context, you will be able to figure out its meaning.

1. _____frank_____   Honest and open; sincere

2. _____inferior_____   Lower in value or quality

3. _____thorough_____   Complete; very carefully done

4. _____comprehend_____   To understand completely

5. _____illustrate_____   To make clear by using an example, picture, or demonstration°

6. _____anxious_____   Worried; troubled; fearful about what might happen

7. _____dramatic_____   Having very exciting, interesting qualities; striking; very noticeable

8. _____impression_____   A belief, opinion, or feeling—often based on little information

9. _____convince_____   To persuade by argument or proof

10. _____overwhelm_____   To make mentally, emotionally, or physically helpless with too much of something; overpower

CAUTION: Do not go any further until you are sure the above answers are correct. Then you can use the definitions to help you in the following practices. Your goal is eventually to know the words well enough so that you don't need to check the definitions at all.

Check 1

Using the answer lines, complete each item below with the correct word from the box.

A. **anxious**	B. **comprehend**	C. **convince**	D. **dramatic**	E. **frank**
F. **illustrate**	G. **impression**	H. **inferior**	I. **overwhelm**	J. **thorough**

comprehend   1. If you say that you ___ a math problem, it means you understand it well.

inferior   2. A grade of C is ___ to a B.

impression   3. Your first ___ of people may change as you get to know them better.

overwhelm   4. Too much confusing work would ___ anyone.

thorough   5. It usually takes more time to do a ___ job than an incomplete one.

anxious   6. A news report that is frightening or troubling makes people ___.

dramatic   7. A ___ outfit is unusual and will attract attention.

frank   8. A ___ person is likely to tell you just what he or she thinks of your new hairdo, instead of giving you false compliments.

convince   9. It should take a great deal of proof to ___ a jury that someone is guilty.

illustrate   10. A good way to make an idea more clear is to ___ it in some way. To do so, you might use an example or a picture.

NOTE: Now check your answers to these items by turning to page 241. Going over the answers carefully will help you prepare for the remaining practices, for which answers are not given.

Check 2

Using the answer lines, complete each item below with **two** words from the box. Use each word once.

dramatic
impression   1–2. Karla's bright lipstick, false eyelashes, and ___ red dress gave me the ___ that she wanted everyone to notice her.

anxious
comprehend   3–4. Many people would feel ___ about moving to a foreign country, especially if they did not ___ the language.

frank
illustrate   5–6. That boss is so ___ that she will often tell stories about her own mistakes to ___ which procedure° might work best for a new project.

convince
inferior   7–8. A mother in the shoe store was trying to ___ her child not to choose a certain pair of shoes. "You like them because they have your favorite cartoon character on them," she explained. "But they are so ___ to this other pair that they will fall apart in a month."

overwhelm
thorough   9–10. "Don't let this big exam ___ you," said the instructor. "We've done a ___ job of reviewing the material, and I'm sure you will all do well."

Word Work

A. In the space provided, write the letter of the word that most closely relates to the situation in each item.

A. **anxious**	B. **dramatic**	C. **frank**
D. **illustrate**	E. **inferior**	

__D__ 1. As Tri Lee described how North and South Vietnam were once divided, he drew a map of the country on the board.

__A__ 2. Sara chewed her nails and tapped her foot as she waited to learn if she had passed the test.

__E__ 3. I bought these two shirts on the same day. One still looks like new, but the other has faded and is tearing at the seams.

__C__ 4. "I think I should tell you that I've been in prison," said Tom. "I hope you will still consider me for the job."

__B__ 5. In the movie *Aladdin*, Prince Ali makes a grand entrance into the city, surrounded by soldiers, elephants, dancers, and musicians.

B. In the space provided, write the letter of the choice that best completes each item.

__B__ 6. Hana did a **thorough** job of cleaning her room. Hana

A. dusted the room a little.   B. spent a long time carefully cleaning.   C. cleaned the room once a month.

__A__ 7. The magician **convinced** the audience that he could read minds. The audience

A. believed the magician.   B. laughed at the magician.   C. paid no attention to the magician.

__B__ 8. On the first day of school, all the new faces and instructions **overwhelmed** Emmy. Emmy

A. was pleased with the new experience.
B. was confused by being faced with so much that was new.
C. gained a better view of herself.

__C__ 9. Paul quickly **comprehended** the instructions for building the model. When it comes to building models, it seems that Paul is

A. not interested.   B. not experienced.   C. skillful.

__B__ 10. Ivan's main **impression** of his girlfriend's father was that he had a pleasant smile. Ivan and his girlfriend's father

A. were close friends.   B. had seen each other only briefly.   C. had never met face to face.

Synonyms and Antonyms

A. Synonyms. Write the letter of the word or phrase that most nearly means the **same** as each boldfaced word.

C 1. **convince**

    A. point out   C. persuade

    B. study   D. fear

B 2. **dramatic**

    A. helpful   C. confusing

    B. striking   D. not well-known

C 3. **illustrate**

    A. have faith   C. give examples

    B. work hard   D. argue

A 4. **impression**

    A. belief   C. news

    B. proof   D. honesty

C 5. **overwhelm**

    A. delay   C. overpower

    B. make clear   D. overwork

B. Antonyms. Write the letter of the word or phrase that most nearly means the **opposite** of each boldfaced word.

A 6. **anxious**

    A. calm   C. busy

    B. forgetful   D. lonely

D 7. **comprehend**

    A. pretend   C. find

    B. know   D. misunderstand

D 8. **frank**

    A. certain   C. humorous

    B. expert   D. dishonest

C 9. **inferior**

    A. far away   C. better

    B. well-known   D. simple

D 10. **thorough**

    A. truthful   C. sensible

    B. risky   D. incomplete

Final Check

Read the passages carefully. Then fill in each blank with the word that best fits the context.

A. My History Report

A. **anxious**	B. **convince**	C. **inferior**	D. **overwhelm**	E. **thorough**

   I get (1)_____anxious_____ even thinking about getting up in front of the whole class to give my history report. I don't know why I'm so worried. I guess I'm afraid that I will humiliate° myself. I have done a (2)_____thorough_____ job of preparing my report; I don't think I've left out anything important. I guess I compare myself with others and worry about whether my work is (3)_____inferior_____ to theirs. Another thing I worry about is whether my talk will be so monotonous° it puts the whole class and the teacher to sleep. I hope that my fears won't be so strong that they (4)_____overwhelm_____ me and hinder° my ability to do a good job. I'll just have to (5)_____convince_____ myself that as long as I have made an effort, my report will be OK. Once I do that, I'll overcome° the stress° I'm feeling.

B. Mrs. Thornton's Condition

F. **comprehend**	G. **dramatic**	H. **frank**	I. **illustrate**	J. **impression**

   Adults should be honest with children. I can (6)_____illustrate_____ this point by telling how I and my fellow first-graders suffered when our teacher had a baby. It wasn't that we didn't like babies or that we didn't like Mrs. Thornton. Most of us loved them both. The problem was that we did not realize she was pregnant, so her (7)_____dramatic_____ growth frightened us. Could that happen to us some day? Would we suddenly expand° in size for no reason? Also, we were worried about her. But even when we made our concern evident° by asking what was happening to her, she gave us only senseless° and misleading° answers, like "I guess I ate too much breakfast!"

   Finally, one day, she didn't appear at school. Our principal simply announced, "Mrs. Thornton will not be your teacher anymore." We were left with the (8)_____impression_____ that something awful had happened to her. We were fearful and sad. Fortunately, the substitute teacher who took Mrs. Thornton's place sympathized° with us. When she saw our tearful faces, she perceived° we did not (9)_____comprehend_____ the situation. She explained that Mrs. Thornton had just had a baby and that she was fine and very happy. But we could have been saved a great deal of worry and fear if the adults in our lives had just been more (10)_____frank_____ with us and had clarified° the situation—instead of deceiving° us by hiding the truth.

Scores Check 2 _____ %	Word Work _____ %	Synonyms and Antonyms _____ %	Final Check _____ %

Enter your scores above and in the **Vocabulary Performance Chart** on the inside back cover of the book.

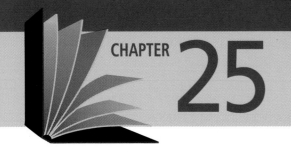

acquire	precede
commitment	resent
formal	solemn
fragment	spite
fundamental	symbolize

Ten Words in Context

In the space provided, write the letter of the meaning closest to that of each **boldfaced** word. Use the context of the sentences to help you figure out each word's meaning.

1 acquire
(ə-kwīr′)
- *verb*

● While living in England, Brad **acquired** a little bit of an English accent.

● Before going on the trip, I **acquired** a good pair of hiking boots.

B *Acquire* means   A. to appreciate.   B. to get.   C. to do without.

2 commitment
(kə-mĭt′mənt)
- *noun*

● Juanita has made a **commitment** to stop smoking this year.

● The Greens made a **commitment** to give 5 percent of their income to charity.

A *Commitment* means   A. promise.   B. piece.   C. symbol.

3 formal
(fôr′məl)
- *adjective*

● Because the boss is a rather **formal** person, people in the office never call him by his first name or try to joke with him.

● A **formal** wedding can be very expensive, so Julie and Ed have decided on a casual wedding in the park.

B *Formal* means   A. interesting.   B. traditional and proper.   C. full of hope.

4 fragment
(frăg′mənt)
- *noun*

● Don't go into the kitchen barefoot. I broke a glass, and there may still be a **fragment** on the floor.

● Scientists digging up an ancient city found a piece of pottery that they think is a tiny **fragment** of a bowl.

C *Fragment* means   A. whole.   B. copy.   C. small part.

5 fundamental
(fŭn′də-mĕn′tl)
- *adjective*

● A **fundamental** rule of water safety is this: Don't go swimming alone.

● One must learn the **fundamental** operations of arithmetic before going on to algebra.

C *Fundamental* means   A. based on fun.   B. unusual.   C. needing to be learned first.

6 precede
(prĭ-sēd′)
- *verb*

● Do you think that friendship **precedes** love in a relationship? Or does love come first?

● On the East Coast, the 11 o'clock news **precedes** the *Tonight Show*, which begins at 11:35 p.m.

A *Precede* means   A. to come before.   B. to be part of.   C. to stand for.

7 resent
(rĭ-zĕnt′)
- *verb*

- The voters **resent** the fact that the mayor made promises he did not keep after his election.
- People often **resent** being given advice they did not ask for.

A *Resent* means   A. to feel bitter about.   B. to feel good about.   C. to feel frightened by.

8 solemn
(sŏl′əm)
- *adjective*

- The fire chief told some jokes to get the children's attention. But when he began to speak about not playing with matches, he became **solemn**.
- The group of laughing children became **solemn** when they heard that their friend had been injured.

C *Solemn* means   A. hard to understand.   B. silly.   C. serious.

9 spite
(spīt)
- *noun*

- Turning against her former friend, the girl said with **spite** in her voice, "Everyone thinks you're a real loser."
- The disk jockeys' **spite** toward each other was obvious. Each of them said nasty things about the other on the air.

B *Spite* means   A. puzzlement.   B. hate.   C. sense of humor.

10 symbolize
(sĭm′bə-līz′)
- *verb*

- In ancient Egypt, a picture of a small circle with a dot in the middle **symbolized** the sun.
- During World War II, holding two fingers up in a V stood for victory; during the 1960s, it **symbolized** peace.

B *Symbolize* means   A. to be like.   B. to stand for.   C. to point toward.

Matching Words with Definitions

Following are definitions of the ten words. **Print** each word next to its definition. If you look closely at each word in context, you will be able to figure out its meaning.

1. _____*formal*_____   Proper; not casual; according to custom or tradition

2. _____*commitment*_____   A promise to do something; pledge

3. _____*acquire*_____   To get through one's own actions; gain something as one's own

4. _____*fundamental*_____   Basic; forming a foundation; essential

5. _____*fragment*_____   A small piece broken off something whole

6. _____*resent*_____   To feel angered and injured by

7. _____*spite*_____   An unfriendly feeling that causes one to want to hurt or shame another

8. _____*symbolize*_____   To stand for; be a symbol of; represent°

9. _____*solemn*_____   Serious and respectful

10. _____*precede*_____   To come before

CAUTION: Do not go any further until you are sure the above answers are correct. Then you can use the definitions to help you in the following practices. Your goal is eventually to know the words well enough so that you don't need to check the definitions at all.

Check 1

Using the answer lines, complete each item below with the correct word from the box.

A. **acquire**	B. **commitment**	C. **formal**	D. **fragment**	E. **fundmental**
F. **precede**	G. **resent**	H. **solemn**	I. **spite**	J. **symbolize**

fragment   1. When I dropped the blue china vase, it broke into ___s.

commitment   2. The neighbors' earnest° ___ to keep their street beautiful shows in their neat lawns and lovely flower gardens.

formal   3. It's fine to wear shorts and a tank top to McDonald's, but at a fancy restaurant, customers are expected to wear something more ___.

acquire   4. Every year, the library ___s about two hundred new books.

spite   5. The soap-opera character is famous for her ___. In almost every episode, she is planning to do something nasty to someone she dislikes.

resent   6. Crystal ___s the way her roommate cooks late-night snacks and then leaves dirty dishes for her to clean up.

precede   7. When I go to a movie theater, I try to get there early enough so that I can see the previews of coming attractions that ___ the film.

solemn   8. Jerome is usually lighthearted, but he becomes ___ when he talks about his brother's struggle with mental illness.

fundamental   9. There are lots of rules about good manners, but the ___ idea behind them all is this: Treat people the way you wish they would treat you.

symbolize   10. After the attacks on the World Trade Center and the Pentagon, many people wore small American flags to ___ their sympathy and patriotism.

NOTE: Now check your answers to these items by turning to page 241. Going over the answers carefully will help you prepare for the remaining practices, for which answers are not given.

Check 2

Using the answer lines, complete each item below with **two** words from the box. Use each word once.

acquire
symbolize   1–2. To remind themselves of why they are saving money, Sam and Chris ___d a dollhouse to ___ the real house they hope to buy someday.

solemn
commitment   3–4. Everyone was very ___ at the much-loved doctor's funeral. Many people expressed their ___ to carrying on his good works and keeping his memory alive.

precede
formal   5–6. Graduation day begins with the principal's speech, which ___s the handing out of diplomas. His speech is always very ___. But afterward, one of the teachers gives a casual, funny talk.

spite
fragment   7–8. When Ray was ordered to share his toy with his sister, he showed his ___ by breaking the toy into pieces and handing the ___s to the girl.

_____resent_____   9–10. Maya ___s the fact that Will told her secret to other people. By doing that,

___fundamental___   he broke a ___ rule of friendship.

Word Work

A. In the space provided, write the letter of the choice that best completes each item.

__C__ 1. The cosmetic company has made a **commitment** never to test its products on animals. The company
    A. never used to test its products on animals, but now does.
    B. is looking into the idea of testing its products on animals.
    C. has promised not to test its products on animals.

__B__ 2. The mood in the courtroom was **solemn**. People in the courtroom had heard something very
    A. exciting.   B. serious.   C. funny.

__C__ 3. Somehow or other, the reporter **acquired** a copy of the secret memo. The reporter had
    A. lost a copy of the memo.   B. sold a copy of the memo.   C. gotten a copy of the memo.

__A__ 4. Since their discussion, Ana has **resented** Mark. Ana
    A. is angry about what Mark said.
    B. agrees with what Mark had to say.
    C. forgot what Mark said.

__B__ 5. Devon's voice was full of **spite** as he spoke to his teammate. Devon
    A. admired his teammate.   B. was angry with his teammate.   C. was entertained by his teammate.

B. Write each word next to the examples that best match it.

A. **formal**	B. **fragment**	C. **fundamental**
D. **precede**	E. **symbolize**	

___formal___   6. A dance at which the men wear tuxedos and the women wear long dresses
    Bowing to the queen
    Standing up when an older person enters the room

___fragment___   7. A bit of broken glass
    A piece of an old dish
    A scrap of torn-up paper

___precede___   8. A before B
    January before February
    President George Washington before President Abraham Lincoln

___symbolize___   9. The color red means anger.
    In a letter, a row of *XXX*'s means kisses.
    The bald eagle stands for the United States.

___fundamental___   10. Spanish I
    The ABCs
    Food, shelter, clothing

Analogies

Each item below starts with a pair of words in CAPITAL LETTERS. For each item, figure out the relationship between these two words. Then decide which of the choices (A, B, C, or D) expresses a similar relationship. Write the letter of your choice on the answer line. (All the repeated words in these items are from this unit.)

B   1. PRECEDE : FOLLOW ::

    A. hurry : rush   C. speak : talk

    B. earlier : later   D. bother : annoy

D   2. SPITE : BITTERNESS ::

    A. insult : compliment   C. love : hate

    B. abolish° : keep   D. friendship : affection

A   3. ACQUIRE : OWN ::

    A. get : possess°   C. locate : lose

    B. clarify° : confuse   D. buy : sell

D   4. SOLEMN : PLAYFUL ::

    A. funny : laughter   C. ugly : talented

    B. fun : party   D. boring : exciting

D   5. FRAGMENT : WHOLE ::

    A. law school : lawyer   C. dog : German shepherd

    B. fixed : broken   D. page : book

A   6. HONEST : CORRUPT° ::

    A. early : late   C. start : begin

    B. fundamental : basic   D. symbolize : flag

C   7. OIL : RESOURCES° ::

    A. hate : love   C. uncle : relatives

    B. give : gift   D. coal : mine

D   8. SENSELESS° : MEANINGFUL ::

    A. old : ancient   C. food : grapes

    B. ball : bat   D. peace : war

B   9 VERTICAL° : FLAGPOLE ::

    A. convert° : change   C. cold : summer

    B. flat : table   D. gray : black

B   10. EXTEND° : SHORTEN ::

    A. frank° : honest   C. precise° : exact

    B. easy : difficult   D. wear : necklace

Final Check

Read the passages carefully. Then fill in each blank with the word that best fits the context.

A. Wacky Weddings

A. **commitment**	B. **formal**	C. **fundamental**	D. **precede**	E. **symbolize**

The basic ingredients needed for a wedding were established° long ago. They include two people who have decided to get married and someone qualified to marry them. But from the same (1)_____*fundamental*_____ ingredients, people create an amazing variety° of ceremonies. Some weddings are very (2)_____*formal*_____. In those, the bride and groom wear traditional outfits—a fancy white dress for her, a tuxedo for him—and have bridesmaids and groomsmen. During such customary° weddings, the groom (3)_____*precede*_____s the bride down the aisle; and afterward, they leave hand in hand. But some people like their weddings to be playful rather than traditional. One man and woman got married while dressed as clowns. Another couple was married while riding a roller coaster. Others have said "I do" while they were doing something energetic°, like skydiving or ice skating. Still others revise° the wedding vows, changing the words to "for richer, for poorer, when the Jets are winning, and when they are losing."

Is an offbeat wedding any less meaningful than a traditional one? The couples that choose unusual weddings say "no." They say the most important thing is the (4)_____*commitment*_____ that they are making to one another. In the case of the two clowns, they said that their unusual wedding (5)_____*symbolize*_____d their desire to keep fun in their marriage.

B. The Cost of Hatred

F. **acquire**	G. **fragment**	H. **resent**	I. **solemn**	J. **spite**

An old story illustrates° the nature of (6)_____*spite*_____ and the terrible effects such meanness can have on people. There were two merchants in a village. They had grown up together, and each always (7)_____*resent*_____ed what the other did. No one could remember how their conflict° began. But by the time they were middle-aged, their hatred of one another influenced° their lives greatly. Neither could endure° seeing the other happy or successful. If one of them (8)_____*acquire*_____d a new house, the other had to get a bigger, better one. If one man's shop prospered°, the other was furious until his shop did better.

One day, one of the men dropped an old jar that had been sitting on a shelf for years. It broke into (9)_____*fragment*_____s. Immediately, a mighty genie appeared. "Oh, lucky man!" said the genie. "You have a great opportunity, for I will fulfill° any request you make. But first I must give you one small warning. Whatever you wish for yourself, your enemy will receive twice as much of it. If you wish for a million dollars, he will receive two million. If you ask for a golden castle, he will possess° two."

The man became (10)_____*solemn*_____ and thought deeply. There were many wonderful things he could ask for, but he could not bear to think of his lifelong enemy receiving twice as much as he did. Finally he thought of an answer to his problem. An evil smile spread over his face as he made his wish. "I wish, Genie," he said, "that you would beat me half to death."

Scores	Check 2 _____%	Word Work _____%	Analogies _____%	Final Check _____%

The box at the right lists twenty-five words from Unit Five. Using the clues at the bottom of the page, fill in these words to complete the puzzle that follows.

abolish
anxious
clarify
commitment
conflict
convince
corrupt
decay
dramatic
evade
formal
fragment
frank
possess
precede
precise
promote
resemble
rigid
senseless
solemn
stress
thorough
vary
vast

ACROSS

1. Foolish; not making good sense

3. A quarrel or fight; disagreement

5. Stiff; not bending

8. To own; have

10. Worried; troubled; fearful about what might happen

12. To come before

14. A promise to do something

15. Having very exciting, interesting qualities; striking; very noticeable

18. Proper; not casual; according to custom or tradition

19. To experience change; become different

20. Exact; correct; accurate

21. Complete; very carefully done

DOWN

1. Mental or emotional strain

2. Serious and respectful

3. Dishonest; crooked

4. Honest and open; sincere

6. To speak for or work toward something; encourage

7. To look like or be similar to

9. To escape or avoid through clever action

11. A small piece broken off something whole

13. To gradually break down; rot

14. To make clear or easy to understand

16. To put an end to

17. To persuade by argument or proof

19. Very large in size, amount, or area

PART A

Choose the word that best completes each item and write it in the space provided.

_____procedures_____ 1. Some of the new ___ for treating cancer are quicker and less unpleasant than older ones.

    A. vicinities   B. fragments   C. conflicts   D. procedures

_____unanimous_____ 2. In court, the decision of the jury must be ___. If even one juror has a different opinion, the decision doesn't count.

    A. senseless   B. vertical   C. solemn   D. unanimous

_____vicinity_____ 3. When we lived in the ___ of a railroad, we got so used to the noise of trains that we stopped noticing it.

    A. resources   B. vicinity   C. precaution   D. tendency

_____vary_____ 4. Marie's moods ___ with the weather. She's cheerful when the sun shines and gloomy when it's cloudy.

    A. decay   B. precede   C. abolish   D. vary

_____stress_____ 5. Even good events can create ___ in people's lives. For example, researchers have found that there's even more strain in getting married than in being fired from one's job.

    A. fragment   B. stress   C. resource   D. precaution

_____illustrate_____ 6. To ___ how much smell affects taste, our teacher had us eat a banana while smelling an onion.

    A. evade   B. illustrate   C. resent   D. overwhelm

_____inferior_____ 7. Emily went through life feeling ___ to her brother, who she believed was more intelligent and talented than she could ever be.

    A. inferior   B. senseless   C. thorough   D. formal

_____abolish_____ 8. The new principal wants to ___ report cards. The kids love the idea of having no report cards, but the teachers do not.

    A. abolish   B. corrupt   C. overwhelm   D. expand

_____evade_____ 9. When Jared's father asked, "What time did you come in last night?" Jared tried to ___ the question by answering, "I wasn't wearing a watch."

    A. comprehend   B. resent   C. evade   D. symbolize

_____rigid_____ 10. When I take jeans off the clothesline, they often feel ___, so I shake them or put them in the clothes dryer for a few minutes to make them soft again.

    A. anxious   B. dramatic   C. fundamental   D. rigid

_____dramatic_____ 11. Myrna's purple and black living room is certainly ___, but I prefer something a little less showy.

    A. corrupt   B. fundamental   C. precise   D. dramatic

(Continues on next page)

_____*impression*_____ 12. From the smile on Rico's face, you might have the ___ that he has no problems. The truth is, however, that his parents are both quite ill, and he lost his job two weeks ago.

          A. commitment   B. precaution   C. impression   D. fragment

_____*acquired*_____ 13. The Masons were not very happy when their daughter ___ a nose-ring.

          A. extended   B. reformed   C. acquired   D. preceded

PART B

Write **C** if the italicized word is used **correctly**. Write **I** if the word is used **incorrectly**.

_C_ 14. I used to be *anxious* about going to the dentist, but then I started going to Dr. Craine. He's so funny and nice that I just can't feel afraid of him.

_I_ 15. Ms. Acosta is respected for being a *corrupt* teacher. She'll make you work hard, but you'll gain a lot from her course.

_I_ 16. The former friends are certainly not nice to each other now. At the party, they *promoted* each other all evening.

_C_ 17. Because I missed the first fifteen minutes of the movie, I didn't really *comprehend* the rest of the story.

_C_ 18. Soaking cucumbers in vinegar will *convert* them into pickles.

_I_ 19. Parties at the Schroeders' house are rather *formal*, with guests taking off their shoes, helping themselves to food from the refrigerator, and generally acting at home.

_I_ 20. I was *frank* enough to tell Edna that she looked lovely in her new purple dress, even though I really thought it made her look like an eggplant.

_C_ 21. After angrily tearing up her boyfriend's letter, Tracy wanted to read it again, so she glued the *fragments* back together.

_I_ 22. Whenever Mr. Fletcher goes for a walk, he *precedes* his dog. The dog runs ahead, pulling Mr. Fletcher by the leash.

_C_ 23. Len did a *thorough* job of cleaning our windows; they seem almost invisible.

_C_ 24. The natural *resources* of South Africa include gold and diamonds.

_I_ 25. The teacher wanted to *overwhelm* his new students, so he gave them just a little homework at first.

Score   (Number correct) _____ x 4 = _____%

Enter your score above and in the **Vocabulary Performance Chart** on the inside back cover of the book.

PART A

On the answer line, write the word from the box that completes each item below. Use each word once.

A. assert	B. conflict	C. convince	D. decay	E. expand
F. fundamental	G. precaution	H. precise	I. renew	J. resemble
K. solemn	L. symbolize	M. tendency		

___conflict___ 1. Two robins in the yard were having a noisy ___ over a worm that they both wanted to eat.

___decay___ 2. In a forest, fallen trees ___ until they become part of the earth on the forest floor.

___precise___ 3. If you're making a pair of pants, you have to be ___ in your measurements if you want the pants to fit well.

___tendency___ 4. Small dogs are quick and lively; large dogs have a ___ to be quiet and slow-moving.

___assert___ 5. The TV ad ___s that this little eight-pound vacuum cleaner does a better job than many full-size vacuums.

___expand___ 6. When Buck plans to eat a big dinner, he wears a pair of pants with a waist that ___s.

___precaution___ 7. Ella is so worried about a house fire that every time she leaves home, she takes the ___ of unplugging all the lamps, the toaster, and the TV.

___resemble___ 8. In my opinion, the smell of blue cheese ___s the smell of an old running shoe.

___convince___ 9. Even though I had homework to do, Raoul ___d me that I should go skating with him instead. He said, "The exercise will wake up your brain."

___fundamental___ 10. My parents were not strict about housekeeping, but they did have two ___ rules: we had to make our beds every morning, and we were never allowed to leave unwashed dishes overnight.

___renew___ 11. Some paper companies are taking steps to ___ the forests they are cutting down, so that in the future, the forests will still be there.

___solemn___ 12. Although everyone was ___ at my grandfather's funeral, there was laughter at the luncheon afterward, when people began telling loving, funny stories about him.

___symbolize___ 13. In many stories and pictures, the dove is used to ___ peace.

(Continues on next page)

PART B

Write **C** if the italicized word is used **correctly**. Write **I** if the word is used **incorrectly**.

___I___ 14. The thing that prisoners *possess* most is freedom.

___C___ 15. In some companies, workers can *extend* their workday by two hours and then enjoy three-day weekends.

___C___ 16. The day was hot and sunny; *nevertheless*, almost no one showed up to use the city swimming pool.

___I___ 17. It is a shame how spending time with the wrong people has *reformed* Nathan. He used to be a nice guy, but now he's rude and not exactly honest.

___C___ 18. Most department stores have a few computer games for sale, but you have to go to a computer store or online for a really *vast* selection of games.

___I___ 19. When Thomas tried to explain how the accident happened, he was so excited and confused that he only *clarified* the story.

___I___ 20. Mr. Lee feels that serving high-quality food at reasonable prices is the most *senseless* way of gaining loyal customers.

___C___ 21. Although I had the *preconception* that Mrs. Arnold would be a difficult person to work for, I soon came to like her very much.

___I___ 22. I painted a line from the left edge of the wall all the way over to the right edge, and then I covered that *vertical* line with a colorful border design.

___I___ 23. The police arrested a man who wrote a *commitment* describing how he had robbed the video store.

___C___ 24. I *resent* what my brother did. After I told him what I was going to buy for our mother's birthday, he rushed out and bought it first, so I had to come up with a new idea.

___I___ 25. Judging from the way Tina and Frank keep smiling and winking at one another, there seems to be a good deal of *spite* between them.

Score   (Number correct) _____ x 4 = _____ %

PART A: Synonyms

In the space provided, write the letter of the choice that is most nearly the **same** in meaning as the **boldfaced** word.

___A___ 1. **assert** A. state as true B. put limits on C. give one's time D. make more difficult

___B___ 2. **commitment** A. location B. promise C. opinion D. difficulty

___A___ 3. **convince** A. persuade B. differ C. listen carefully D. own

___C___ 4. **decay** A. own B. look for C. break down D. replace

___D___ 5. **evade** A. stand for B. struggle C. make clear D. avoid

___C___ 6. **fragment** A. unfriendly feeling B. a snack C. piece of a whole D. true statement

___D___ 7. **fundamental** A. careless B. bored C. stiff D. basic

___C___ 8. **illustrate** A. replace B. stand for C. show through example D. get

___D___ 9. **impression** A. argument B. piece C. effort D. belief

___A___ 10. **nevertheless** A. even so B. afterward C. because D. even better

___B___ 11. **overwhelm** A. receive B. overpower C. understand D. come before

___B___ 12. **possess** A. lie about B. own C. differ D. show

___A___ 13. **precaution** A. something done to prevent a problem C. a problem B. something done to fix a a problem D. a result

___C___ 14. **preconception** A. truth C. opinion formed before knowing about something B. decision D. area nearby

___B___ 15. **procedure** A. part of a whole B. way of doing something C. reason D. goal

___A___ 16. **reform** A. make better B. replace C. learn about D. prevent

___B___ 17. **renew** A. mention again B. start up again C. ignore D. make clear

___B___ 18. **resemble** A. be ahead B. be similar to C. worry about D. improve

___C___ 19. **resent** A. replace B. rot C. feel angry at D. differ

___D___ 20. **resources** A. something missing B. period of time C. enough D. wealth of a country

___A___ 21. **solemn** A. serious B. noticeable C. complete D. careless

___D___ 22. **symbolize** A. show B. make use of C. get larger D. stand for

___B___ 23. **tendency** A. anger B. leaning C. tension D. belief

___A___ 24. **unanimous** A. in full agreement B. quarreling C. carefully done D. basic

___A___ 25. **vicinity** A. neighborhood B. wealth C. promise D. opinion

(Continues on next page)

PART B: Antonyms

In the space provided, write the letter of the choice that is most nearly **opposite** in meaning to the **boldfaced** word.

__B__ 26. **abolish**   A. differ   B. create   C. give away   D. ignore

__C__ 27. **acquire**   A. make worse   B. escape   C. lose   D. see

__D__ 28. **anxious**   A. dishonest   B. tired   C. careless   D. relaxed

__C__ 29. **clarify**   A. include   B. correct   C. confuse   D. grow strong

__C__ 30. **comprehend**   A. enjoy   B. give away   C. misunderstand   D. remain the same

__D__ 31. **conflict**   A. anger   B. loss   C. profit   D. agreement

__A__ 32. **convert**   A. keep the same   B. make more expensive   C. hide from sight
                  D. reduce in size

__B__ 33. **corrupt**   A. useful   B. honest   C. loose   D. careless

__A__ 34. **dramatic**   A. not noticeable   B. brightly colored   C. careful   D. careless

__D__ 35. **expand**   A. agree   B. confuse   C. begin   D. become smaller

__C__ 36. **extend**   A. begin   B. give away   C. shorten   D. make worse

__C__ 37. **formal**   A. attractive   B. not sincere   C. casual   D. troubled

__B__ 38. **frank**   A. careless   B. dishonest   C. loose   D. not enough

__B__ 39. **inferior**   A. recent   B. better   C. far away   D. serious

__D__ 40. **precede**   A. get smaller   B. grow   C. happen again   D. come after

__C__ 41. **precise**   A. not serious   B. not complete   C. not exact   D. not common

__D__ 42. **promote**   A. remember   B. anger   C. increase   D. discourage

__C__ 43. **rigid**   A. dull   B. rude   C. bending   D. correct

__D__ 44. **senseless**   A. depressing   B. dirty   C. active   D. reasonable

__D__ 45. **spite**   A. reaction   B. action   C. growth   D. friendly feeling

__A__ 46. **stress**   A. relaxation   B. argument   C. question   D. idea

__D__ 47. **thorough**   A. not proper   B. harmful   C. boring   D. not complete

__B__ 48. **vary**   A. confuse   B. stay the same   C. disappear   D. make worse

__A__ 49. **vast**   A. small   B. changing   C. unpleasant   D. better

__D__ 50. **vertical**   A. small   B. better   C. not interested   D. horizontal

Score   (Number correct) _____   x   2   = _____%

Enter your score above and in the **Vocabulary Performance Chart** on the inside back cover of the book.

Unit Six

Chapter 26

associate	hospitality
barrier	justify
estimate	mistrust
fatigue	persecute
flimsy	soothe

Chapter 27

debate	identical
discredit	singular
displace	sprawl
enforce	spurt
enumerate	stern

Chapter 28

discard	mature
duration	miniature
essential	peer
exhibit	sanitary
juvenile	tragic

Chapter 29

capability	magnify
content	postpone
duplicate	presentable
immense	realistic
industrious	stun

Chapter 30

accurate	latter
bluff	modify
consist	toxic
discomfort	trifle
elementary	vanity

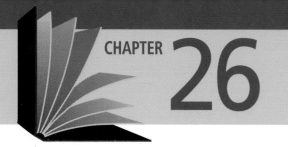

associate	hospitality
barrier	justify
estimate	mistrust
fatigue	persecute
flimsy	soothe

Ten Words in Context

In the space provided, write the letter of the meaning closest to that of each **boldfaced** word. Use the context of the sentences to help you figure out each word's meaning.

1 associate
(ə-sō′shē-āt′)
- *verb*

- My sister's house is always full of African American, Asian, Hispanic, and white kids. "I want my kids to **associate** with all kinds of children, not just children who look like them," she says.
- The people next door don't **associate** with anyone in the neighborhood. They don't even attend the annual Fourth of July block party.

B *Associate* means   A. to study.   B. to get together.   C. to work.

2 barrier
(băr′ē-ər)
- *noun*

- To keep his little brother out of his room, Tim built a **barrier** of toys and clothing.
- Not being able to read is a great **barrier** to success in today's world.

C *Barrier* means   A. something that helps.   B. something that explains.   C. something that gets in the way.

3 estimate
(ĕs′tə-māt′)
- *verb*

- I don't know how old my doctor is, but I **estimate** that she's about 60.
- "I know you haven't figured out our final grades yet, but can you **estimate** what I might get?" Frieda asked her teacher.

A *Estimate* means   A. to make a judgment.   B. to have hope.   C. to fear.

4 fatigue
(fə-tēg′)
- *noun*

- After Mike's first day of factory work, his **fatigue** was so great that he fell asleep during dinner.
- You shouldn't drive when you are very sleepy. **Fatigue** can cause an accident.

A *Fatigue* means   A. tiredness.   B. mood.   C. energy.

5 flimsy
(flĭm′zē)
- *adjective*

- The next time a hard wind blows, that **flimsy** shed in our back yard is likely to fall down.
- That old chair is so **flimsy** that the only family member allowed to sit on it is the cat.

C *Flimsy* means   A. dark.   B. expensive.   C. weak.

6 hospitality
(hŏs′pĭ-tăl′ĭ-tē)
- *noun*

- The family we visited in Mexico showed us true **hospitality**. "Our house is your house," they told us.
- After their cousin had stayed for three weeks, eating their groceries and tying up the phone, the Petersons decided their **hospitality** had to end.

C *Hospitality* means   A. curing the sick.   B. traveling.   C. welcoming visitors.

7 justify
(jŭs′tə-fī′)
- *verb*

- Nothing can **justify** the cruel way that our neighbor speaks to her children.
- Josie tried to **justify** eating her little sister's cookie by saying, "I was afraid she might choke on it."

<u>B</u> *Justify* means A. to bother. B. to excuse. C. to repeat.

8 mistrust
(mĭs-trŭst′)
- *verb*

- The way Donna's latest boyfriend won't give a straight answer to any question makes me **mistrust** him.
- You should **mistrust** any e-mail that says you've won some wonderful prize. Chances are it isn't true.

<u>A</u> *Mistrust* means A. to doubt. B. to believe. C. to harm.

9 persecute
(pûr′sĭ-kyoōt)
- *verb*

- Hitler and his Nazis **persecuted** not only Jewish people; they also killed and imprisoned Gypsies, gay people, and people with disabilities.
- "Hate crimes" occur when attackers **persecute** victims because of the victims' race, color, religion, nationality, or sexual orientation.

<u>B</u> *Persecute* means A. to support. B. to cause to suffer. C. to try to avoid.

10 soothe
(soōth)
- *verb*

- Sometimes the sound of a vacuum cleaner will **soothe** fussy babies and help them go to sleep.
- What **soothes** you when you're feeling tired and cranky? For me, a cup of hot tea and a warm bath usually help.

<u>A</u> *Soothe* means A. to comfort. B. to excite. C. to annoy.

Matching Words with Definitions

Following are definitions of the ten words. **Print** each word next to its definition. If you look closely at each word in context, you will be able to figure out its meaning.

1. _justify_ — To give a good reason for; show to be right
2. _mistrust_ — To have no trust in; doubt
3. _estimate_ — To make a guess at the size, amount, value, etc. of something
4. _flimsy_ — Light, thin, and lacking strength
5. _hospitality_ — Generous, friendly treatment of guests
6. _barrier_ — Something that blocks the way
7. _soothe_ — To calm or comfort someone or something
8. _fatigue_ — The state of being very tired
9. _associate_ — To spend time; join
10. _persecute_ — To harm again and again; treat cruelly, especially because of dislike of a person's ideas, race, religion, etc.

CAUTION: Do not go any further until you are sure the above answers are correct. Then you can use the definitions to help you in the following practices. Your goal is eventually to know the words well enough so that you don't need to check the definitions at all.

Check 1

Using the answer lines, complete each item below with the correct word from the box.

A. **associate**	B. **barrier**	C. **estimate**	D. **fatigue**	E. **flimsy**
F. **hospitality**	G. **justify**	H. **mistrust**	I. **persecute**	J. **soothe**

__associate__ 1. "If you lie down with dogs, you'll get up with fleas." This old saying means that if you ___ with bad people, you'll become more like them.

__estimate__ 2. The saleswoman who sold the dress to me ___d that it needed to be shortened by two inches or so.

__justify__ 3. I'd like to go to that fancy new beauty salon in town, but I can't ___ paying so much for a haircut.

__flimsy__ 4. The little girl shivered. Her ___ dress did not protect her from the cold.

__barrier__ 5. Esperanza wants to learn English quickly. She knows that her poor English is a ___ to getting a good job.

__persecute__ 6. Lee says that his boss ___s him because he has long hair, but I don't think he's right. I think his boss is always yelling at him because he's lazy.

__fatigue__ 7. I think I'm getting sick. I haven't worked hard, but I still feel great ___.

__soothe__ 8. To ___ his crying daughter, Roberto hugged her gently and sang to her.

__mistrust__ 9. It's not fair to ___ Mr. Anderson just because he resembles° your dishonest Uncle Sal. Mr. Anderson's coworkers trust him completely.

__hospitality__ 10. The Thompsons are well-known for their ___. They often have guests staying with them, and people are constantly dropping in for meals.

NOTE: Now check your answers to these items by turning to page 241. Going over the answers carefully will help you prepare for the remaining practices, for which answers are not given.

Check 2

Using the answer lines, complete each item below with **two** words from the box. Use each word once.

__flimsy__
__fatigue__ 1–2. Bernie had to walk for several miles in the snowstorm, wearing only a ___ jacket. By the time he got home, he felt sick with cold and ___.

__hospitality__
__soothe__ 3–4. Sonia arrived at her aunt's house feeling angry and tired after a bad day at work. But her aunt's warm ___ helped to ___ her, and soon she had revived° and was feeling much better.

__justify__
__mistrust__ 5–6. Lamont tries to ___ his ___ of people by saying, "I have no faith in people. They're all just waiting for a chance to stab you in the back."

__barrier__
__estimate__ 7–8. Because the bridge is unsafe to drive on, the mayor has ordered workers to put up ___s at both ends of it. He ___s that the bridge will be closed for about six weeks.

__associate__
__persecute__ 9–10. How can you ___ with people who promote° "white power"? Doesn't it bother you that they ___ people of other races?

Word Work

A. Write each word next to the examples that best match it.

> **A. barrier**   **B. estimate**   **C. flimsy**
> **D. justify**   **E. persecute**

persecute 1. Selling African Americans as slaves
Forcing Jews into Nazi concentration camps
Chasing Gypsies out of European towns

justify 2. "The reason property taxes must be raised is that the money is needed for important school repairs."
"My alarm clock didn't go off, so I was late to work."
"I didn't return your call yesterday because I didn't get home until midnight."

estimate 3. I think our houses are about a mile apart.
The little girl looks about six years old.
It should take an hour or so to finish the job.

flimsy 4. The cheap tennis shoes fell apart quickly.
That lightweight blanket won't keep you warm.
The walls between our apartments are so thin that we hear every word our neighbors say.

barrier 5. A two-foot pile of snow at the end of the driveway
A fence surrounding an open manhole
No high-school diploma

B. In the space provided, write the letter of the choice that best completes each item.

_A_ 6. You are most likely to **mistrust** someone who
A. has lied to you before.
B. offers to lend you money.
C. has a good sense of humor.

_C_ 7. Parents generally want their children to **associate** with other kids who
A. cheat and steal.   B. do poorly in school.   C. are helpful and polite.

_B_ 8. People who are well-known for their **hospitality** probably
A. are fearful of guests.   B. enjoy having guests.   C. are wealthy.

_B_ 9. Some people avoid **fatigue** by
A. wearing warmer clothing.   B. taking a brief nap.   C. being kind to everyone.

_C_ 10. In order to **soothe** her crying daughter, Serena
A. spanked the child.   B. laughed at her.   C. read her a story.

Word Parts

A. The prefix *mis-* means "bad," "badly," "wrong," "incorrectly," or "lack of."

Examples: *misfortune* — bad luck   *misleading*° — giving the wrong idea
mispronounce — to pronounce incorrectly   *mistrust*° — lack of trust

On each answer line, write the word from the box that means the same as the *italicized* word.

A. **misbehave**	B. **misinterpret**°	C. **misplace**
D. **misspell**	E. **misunderstanding**	

_____misbehave_____ 1. Those children often *behave badly*. Yesterday, they finger-painted on the walls with peanut butter and put chewing gum in the cat's fur.

_____misplace_____ 2. I always *put* my glasses *in the wrong place*. I'm going to get a chain and hang them around my neck. Then I'll always know where they are.

_____misunderstanding_____ 3. Because of a *lack of understanding* about the class schedule, we thought our final exam was on May 21 instead of May 25.

_____misinterpret_____ 4. "Don't *interpret incorrectly* what I said," the coach told the player. "I'm not trying to get rid of you; I'm simply trying to get you to play better."

_____misspell_____ 5. The teacher handed out a list of words that people often *spell incorrectly*, such as "weird," "separate," "friend," and "embarrass."

B. The suffix *-fy* means "cause to become," "cause to have," or "make."

Examples: *pure* — clean   *solid* — firm
purify — cause to become clean   *solidify* — make firm

On each answer line, write the word from the box that best completes the item.

F. **beautify**	G. **clarify**	H. **falsify**
I. **satisfy**	J. **terrify**	

_____terrify_____ 6. Some people enjoy Stephen King's horror stories, but they ___ me so badly I can't sleep.

_____falsify_____ 7. The bank employee used his computer to ___ company records and hide the extra checks he wrote to himself.

_____satisfy_____ 8. If people eat only enough to ___ their hunger, they are unlikely to become overweight.

_____clarify_____ 9. "I'm not sure I understand the directions for the project," one student said to the teacher. "Could you ___ them, please?"

_____beautify_____ 10. People try all kinds of things in order to ___ themselves, from dyeing their hair and using makeup to having cosmetic surgery.

Final Check

Read the passages carefully. Then fill in each blank with the word that best fits the context.

A. My Parents' Problem

A. associate	B. hospitality	C. justify	D. mistrust	E. persecute

I feel sorry for parents. It must be hard to know what to do when your child is old enough to make his own choices, and you see him making improper° ones. For instance, last year my brother Jason started hanging around with a kid named Allan. When Allan first came to our house, my parents welcomed him with their usual (1)_____*hospitality*_____. But Allan was rude, as if he resented° them. Worse yet, Jason began to act that way too. There were other things that made me (2)____*mistrust*____ Allan. I knew some of the people he (3)_____*associate*____d with. Most of them had been in trouble at school and even with the police. My parents finally said that Allan could not come to our house, and if they answered the phone when he called, they were cold to him. When they tried to talk to Jason about his new friend, Jason got angry. He said they (4)_____*persecute*_____d Allan for no good reason—just out of spite°. It was an agonizing° time for my family. Finally, though, Jason started pulling away from Allan. And soon after, Allan was arrested for breaking into a drugstore. For Jason, that was enough to (5)_____*justify*_____ our parents' concern. He actually apologized for not listening to them earlier and for causing them stress°.

B. The Hike That Hurt

F. barrier	G. estimate	H. fatigue	I. flimsy	J. soothe

"Want to go for a hike on Saturday?" Bert's words were music to my ears. I'd been hoping for the longest time that Bert would ask me out.

City girl that I am, I thought of a "hike" as being a stroll around the park. My impression° couldn't have been more wrong. To begin with, we started with an hour-long drive into what looked to me like the jungle. The hike, which I had (6)_____*estimate*_____d would take approximately° forty-five minutes, lasted six weeks. Well, not really. But it must have dragged on for at least four hours. I was tired at the end of an hour. After another two hours, I wondered if anyone had ever actually died of (7)_____*fatigue*_____. And then there were my feet. My tennis shoes were very cute, but they were also cheap and (8)_____*flimsy*_____, and soon I had blisters the size of Montana. But we kept on going . . . and going . . . and going. We climbed over large (9)_____*barrier*_____s, including a huge tree that had fallen across the trail. "Isn't this great?" Bert kept saying, in his usual energetic° way. I just smiled weakly, not wanting to give him a frank° answer.

Later, as I (10)_____*soothe*_____d my aching feet in hot water, Bert called. "Today was so much fun," he said. "Let's go for a *really* long hike next weekend!"

"I have another idea," I said. "Let's do something even *more* fun—like scrub the kitchen floor with a toothbrush."

Scores	Check 2 _____%	Word Work _____%	Word Parts _____%	Final Check _____%

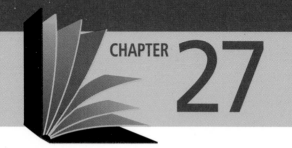

CHAPTER 27

debate	identical
discredit	singular
displace	sprawl
enforce	spurt
enumerate	stern

Ten Words in Context

In the space provided, write the letter of the meaning closest to that of each **boldfaced** word. Use the context of the sentences to help you figure out each word's meaning.

1 debate
(dĭ-bāt′)
- *verb*

- Brad will **debate** anything. If you say it's a nice day, he'll say, "I don't know about that. Wasn't it a little too warm this morning?"
- Over dessert, we were **debating** which was better—chocolate ice cream or vanilla ice cream.

C *Debate* means   A. to agree.   B. to pay attention to.   C. to argue.

2 discredit
(dĭs-krĕd′ĭt)
- *verb*

- When his son was arrested, Mr. Kaufman sadly said, "You've **discredited** our family name."
- The writer had stolen someone else's work and claimed it was his. When this was proved, it **discredited** him forever.

A *Discredit* means   A. to shame.   B. to honor.   C. to know.

3 displace
(dĭs-plās′)
- *verb*

- Why did the bathtub overflow when you sat down in it? The reason is that your body **displaced** the water.
- The endless wars in Afghanistan have **displaced** millions of families, who have been forced to seek safety away from their homes.

C *Displace* means   A. to help.   B. to stop.   C. to cause to move.

4 enforce
(ĕn-fôrs′)
- *verb*

- You're not really supposed to take dogs in the park, but nobody **enforces** the rule.
- The rule in our house is "one hour of TV a day," and our parents **enforce** it. If we're caught breaking the rule, we can't watch TV for a week.

A *Enforce* means   A. to insist on.   B. to break.   C. to build.

5 enumerate
(ĭ-nōō′mə-rāt′)
- *verb*

- On her list for Santa Claus, Emily **enumerated** all the books and toys she wanted.
- As we argued, Jill began to **enumerate** all my faults. "All right, that's enough!" I finally said.

B *Enumerate* means   A. to forget.   B. to list.   C. to get rid of.

6 identical
(ī-dĕn′tĭ-kəl)
- *adjective*

- A famous story called "The Necklace" is about two necklaces that appear to be **identical**: one made of diamonds and another made of fake jewels.
- To me, all stars look **identical**. How can anyone tell them apart?

A *Identical* means   A. the same.   B. beautiful.   C. very different.

206

7 singular
(sĭng′gyə-lər)
- *adjective*

- The word "sheep" can be **singular,** referring to just one animal, or plural, referring to a whole flock.
- Why do we say a "pair" of jeans? It's just a **singular** piece of clothing.

<u>B</u> *Singular* means   A. large.   B. only one.   C. difficult.

8 sprawl
(sprôl)
- *verb*

- Hot and panting from his long run, the dog **sprawled** on the cool kitchen floor.
- When I was a little girl, I thought my brother's high-school friends looked like giants as they **sprawled** all over our living-room chairs and sofa.

<u>A</u> *Sprawl* means   A. to stretch out.   B. to fall.   C. to sit up straight.

9 spurt
(spûrt)
- *verb*

- Amy's brother made her laugh so hard at breakfast that orange juice **spurted** out of her mouth.
- When I turned on the drinking fountain, the water **spurted** out higher and more powerfully than I expected and splashed me in the face.

<u>B</u> *Spurt* means   A. to leak slowly.   B. to shoot out.   C. to hold in.

10 stern
(stûrn)
- *adjective*

- On the job, our principal seems like a **stern** man; but at home, he's quite relaxed and friendly.
- "John, come here *this minute*!" As soon as I heard my father's **stern** voice, I knew I was in trouble.

<u>C</u> *Stern* means   A. not dangerous.   B. warm and friendly.   C. firm and demanding.

Matching Words with Definitions

Following are definitions of the ten words. **Print** each word next to its definition. If you look closely at each word in context, you will be able to figure out its meaning.

1. _____enumerate_____   To name one by one; list
2. _____discredit_____   To damage a good name or reputation
3. _____spurt_____   To flow out suddenly and with force
4. _____enforce_____   To make sure that a rule or law is obeyed
5. _____stern_____   Serious and strict
6. _____identical_____   Exactly alike
7. _____debate_____   To discuss a question by looking at different points of view; argue
8. _____singular_____   Being only one; not plural
9. _____sprawl_____   To sit or lie with the arms and legs thrown outward
10. _____displace_____   To move from the usual or proper place; shift the location of

CAUTION: Do not go any further until you are sure the above answers are correct. Then you can use the definitions to help you in the following practices. Your goal is eventually to know the words well enough so that you don't need to check the definitions at all.

Check 1

Using the answer lines, complete each item below with the correct word from the box.

A. **debate**	B. **discredit**	C. **displace**	D. **enforce**	E. **enumerate**
F. **identical**	G. **singular**	H. **sprawl**	I. **spurt**	J. **stern**

debate   1. "This afternoon," Ms. Reynolds announced, "we will ___ this question: Should classes be pass/fail, or should they have letter grades?"

discredit   2. My new friend's cruel teasing of her brother ___ed her in my eyes.

spurt   3. I got soaked when I began to disconnect the pipe under our sink, and water ___ed out at me. I had forgotten to turn off the supply valve.

enforce   4. The babysitter ___d the twins' 8:30 bedtime. "We don't have to go to bed that early!" they said. "Tonight you do," she answered.

stern   5. Dad was ___ when we whined about having to walk the dog. "You made a commitment° to take care of him. Now stop complaining," he said.

identical   6. Patti and Renee laughed when they showed up at the party wearing ___ dresses. "I guess it just shows we both have good taste," Patti said.

enumerate   7. Mr. Nelson said, "My wife has too many good qualities to ___ here."

singular   8. Some human organs, like the heart and the liver, are ___. Others, such as the kidneys and lungs, come in pairs.

sprawl   9. Mario's mother told him, "Don't ___ on the floor like that when you're studying. You're more likely to fall asleep than to learn something."

displace   10. The tornado destroyed many homes and ___d nearly one hundred people.

NOTE: Now check your answers to these items by turning to page 241. Going over the answers carefully will help you prepare for the remaining practices, for which answers are not given.

Check 2

Using the answer lines, complete each item below with **two** words from the box. Use each word once.

enforce
discredit   1–2. "Parents should ___ their rules," said the counselor. "If they don't, they may ___ themselves in their kids' eyes. Kids respect parents who aren't afraid to be tough sometimes."

debate
singular   3–4. Let's ___ the question of whether the English language makes sense. For example, we say "goose" for a ___ bird and "geese" for more than one. So if it's "moose" for one animal, why isn't it "meese" for two?

displace
sprawl   5–6. As the man tripped and fell in the supermarket, he ___ed a stack of boxes of cereal; then he ___ed on the floor.

spurt
stern   7–8. When George hit Cliff so hard that blood ___ed from Cliff's nose, our usually smiling gym teacher suddenly became very ___.

identical

enumerate

9–10. Libby and Sibby look ___ to me, but my sister knows the twins so well that she can ___ several differences between them.

Word Work

A. In the space provided, write the letter of the choice that best completes each item.

_C_ 1. People often **discredit** themselves by
   A. changing to a better job.
   B. mailing a letter.
   C. doing something dishonest.

_A_ 2. I can **enumerate** the dwarfs in Disney's *Snow White and the Seven Dwarfs.*
   A. They are Bashful, Doc, Dopey, Grumpy, Happy, Sleepy, and Sneezy.
   B. However, I can't list them.
   C. I think the shy one is named Bashful.

_A_ 3. The **singular** form of that insect's name is
   A. butterfly.   B. butterflies.

_A_ 4. A person is likely to **sprawl** in a chair when
   A. chatting on the phone with a friend.
   B. speaking to a large group.
   C. trying to make a good impression at a job interview.

_B_ 5. The water **spurted**
   A. gently down a windowpane.
   B. when the fire fighter turned on his hose.
   C. so still I could see the reflection of the clouds in the puddle.

B. In the space provided, write the letter of the word that most closely relates to the situation in each item.

_B_ 6. In class, we argued about whether there should be stricter handgun laws.
   A. displace   B. debate   C. discredit

_C_ 7. When our cousins moved in with us, my brother and I had to give up our bedroom and start sleeping in the living room.
   A. enumerate   B. spurt   C. displace

_A_ 8. During the test, several teachers stood watching us, to make sure that no one cheated.
   A. enforce   B. enumerate   C. debate

_C_ 9. All the apartments on this side of the building are exactly alike.
   A. singular   B. stern   C. identical

_B_ 10. My father glared at me and said, "Sit down. It's time we had a serious talk."
   A. singular   B. stern   C. enumerate

Synonyms and Antonyms

A. Synonyms. Write the letter of the word or phrase that most nearly means the **same** as each boldfaced word.

_C_ 1. **debate**

    A. undo   C. argue

    B. return   D. agree

_B_ 2. **enumerate**

    A. pronounce   C. explain

    B. name each one   D. expand

_A_ 3. **spurt**

    A. burst   C. drip

    B. divide   D. enlarge

_D_ 4. **enforce**

    A. permit   C. create

    B. push out   D. insist on

_A_ 5. **sprawl**

    A. spread out   C. reach

    B. gather in   D. shelter

B. Antonyms. Write the letter of the word or phrase that most nearly means the **opposite** of each boldfaced word.

_B_ 6. **discredit**

    A. damage   C. pay back

    B. praise   D. help

_D_ 7. **identical**

    A. nasty   C. personal

    B. alike   D. different

_A_ 8. **displace**

    A. keep in place   C. remove

    B. fill   D. borrow

_C_ 9. **singular**

    A. unusual   C. many

    B. old   D. outstanding

_D_ 10. **stern**

    A. strict   C. young

    B. difficult   D. easygoing

Final Check

Read the passages carefully. Then fill in each blank with the word that best fits the context.

A. A Teacher's Lesson

A. **discredit**	B. **enforce**	C. **enumerate**	D. **singular**	E. **stern**

When Gino got his first paper back from the new English teacher, there seemed to be red ink everywhere. At the end of the paper, Ms. Robbins had (1)_____*enumerate*_____d some of his mistakes. Below the list, she wrote, "You'll need to revise° this paper. See me after class."

As he walked up to her desk, Gino felt angry and embarrassed. Why did this teacher have to (2)_____*enforce*_____ the stupid rules of grammar and spelling? Was she going to persecute° him for a few little mistakes?

But the meeting wasn't as bad as Gino expected. Instead of being (3)_____*stern*_____, Ms. Robbins was friendly and helpful. She began showing him how to correct his mistakes. She said, "You wrote 'A pile of bodys was lying in the middle of the football field.' But when the (4)_____*singular*_____ form of a word ends in *y*, you must change the *y* to *ies* when writing about more than one. 'Bodys' should have been 'bodies.'"

"What's the difference?" Gino asked. "People can still figure out what I mean."

"Sometimes they can comprehend° your meaning, and sometimes they can't," the teacher said. "But working without care (5)_____*discredit*_____s you as a writer. Readers take your ideas less seriously if they aren't written well, and poor spelling can be a barrier° to achieving your goals."

Years later, in college, Gino wrote about Ms. Robbins, calling her the most important teacher he ever had. "She made me work hard," he wrote, "but I realize now that she didn't just teach me to write clearly. She taught me to think clearly, too."

B. My Sports Heroes

A. **debate**	B. **displace**	C. **identical**	D. **sprawl**	E. **spurt**

It all happened so fast—it's hard to for me to describe. But I'll try. While having a snack in the kitchen, my brothers Todd and Roger began to (6)_____*debate*_____ whether football or baseball was the more difficult sport to play well. As they argued, each trying to justify° his theory°, they jumped around and waved their arms in a dramatic° way. Then Todd's hand smashed against a table. The action (7)_____*displace*_____d a can of soda that was sitting there. Crash! The soda hit the floor, and foam (8)_____*spurt*_____ed at least three feet into the air. As Todd jumped away from the foam, he stumbled and (9)_____*sprawl*_____ed on the kitchen floor. He yelped in pain, and Roger ran toward him, hoping to soothe° his pain. Unfortunately, Roger slipped in the shallow° puddle of soda and fell on top of Todd. Todd yelled, "I think my wrist is broken." Roger added, "I think mine is, too." They were both right. Now the boys have (10)_____*identical*_____ casts on their left wrists. They proved that arguing can be a difficult sport, too.

Scores Check 2 _____%	Word Work _____%	Synonyms and Antonyms _____%	Final Check _____%

Enter your scores above and in the **Vocabulary Performance Chart** on the inside back cover of the book.

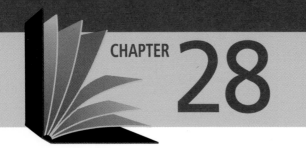

discard	mature
duration	miniature
essential	peer
exhibit	sanitary
juvenile	tragic

Ten Words in Context

In the space provided, write the letter of the meaning closest to that of each **boldfaced** word. Use the context of the sentences to help you figure out each word's meaning.

1 discard
(dĭ-skärd′)
- *verb*

- "Please don't **discard** your paper towel tubes," said the art teacher. "Save them and then bring them in for our projects."
- My uncle wishes he had the comic books he **discarded** when he was a boy. They would be worth quite a lot of money now.

B *Discard* means   A. to show.   B. to get rid of.   C. to keep.

2 duration
(dŏo-rā′shən)
- *noun*

- My little sister held her hands over her eyes for the **duration** of the horror movie.
- School was closed for the **duration** of the snowstorm.

A *Duration* means   A. a time period.   B. a place.   C. a memory.

3 essential
(ĭ-sĕn′shəl)
- *adjective*

- For the overnight trip, Eli packed only a few **essential** supplies, including his toothbrush, toothpaste, and a T-shirt to sleep in.
- On her desk, Holly kept **essential** study items: highlighting pens, index cards, and a dictionary.

B *Essential* means   A. expensive.   B. needed.   C. large.

4 exhibit
(ĭg-zĭb′ĭt)
- *verb*

- The science teacher **exhibited** her bug-eating plants at this year's flower show.
- Many parents **exhibit** their children's artwork on the refrigerator door.

C *Exhibit* means   A. to lose.   B. to hide.   C. to show.

5 juvenile
(jōo′və-nīl′)
- *adjective*

- Puppies, like most **juvenile** animals, are extremely cute. But be sure you know what that cute little puppy will grow into before you take it home.
- Some TV cartoon shows are not meant for **juvenile** audiences and are shown at night, when most children are in bed.

A *Juvenile* means   A. young.   B. difficult.   C. older.

6 mature
(mə-tyŏor′)
- *adjective*

- The largest living animal is the blue whale. A **mature** blue whale, when fully grown, can be over 100 feet long and weigh 300,000 pounds!
- Although Ravi is old enough to get his driver's license, his parents don't think he is **mature** enough to be a safe driver.

C *Mature* means   A. busy.   B. brave.   C. adult.

7 miniature
(mĭn′ē-ə-choŏr′)
- *adjective*

- It can take hours to play a regular game of golf, but **miniature** golf takes much less time because the course is so little.
- Grandma gave my little sister a **miniature** tea set, made up of a tiny teapot and four little cups.

B　*Miniature* means　　A. expensive.　　B. small-scale.　　C. ordinary.

8 peer
(pîr)
- *noun*

- In day care or nursery school, little children learn to share and play with their **peers**.
- Our history teacher is going to an education conference next week. "It's fun to meet and exchange ideas with my **peers** from other schools," she said.

A　*Peer* means　　A. an equal.　　B. an instructor.　　C. a lesson.

9 sanitary
(săn′ĭ-tĕr′ē)
- *adjective*

- "Don't let the puppy lick the baby's face!" said my sister, snatching her child away. "A dog's tongue isn't **sanitary**! The baby might get sick."
- To protect their patients, doctors and nurses don't wear ordinary street clothes in an operating room. They wear special **sanitary** clothing.

C　*Sanitary* means　　A. dry.　　B. new.　　C. clean.

10 tragic
(trăj′ĭk)
- *adjective*

- The January 2010 earthquake in Haiti had **tragic** results—the deaths of at least 230,000 people.
- The play *Romeo and Juliet* tells of the **tragic** deaths of two young lovers whose families were enemies.

B　*Tragic* means　　A. honest.　　B. terrible.　　C. failed.

Matching Words with Definitions

Following are definitions of the ten words. **Print** each word next to its definition. If you look closely at each word in context, you will be able to figure out its meaning.

1. _____exhibit_____　To present for others to see; display

2. _____duration_____　The time during which something exists or happens; the time remaining for something

3. _____miniature_____　Made on a small scale

4. _____discard_____　To throw away

5. _____juvenile_____　Young; not fully grown; like a child

6. _____tragic_____　Very sad; involving death, grief, or destruction

7. _____essential_____　Necessary

8. _____peer_____　A person who is on an equal level with another person, as in age or occupation; a member of the same group as others

9. _____sanitary_____　Free from dirt or germs

10. _____mature_____　Adult; fully developed; like an adult

CAUTION: Do not go any further until you are sure the above answers are correct. Then you can use the definitions to help you in the following practices. Your goal is eventually to know the words well enough so that you don't need to check the definitions at all.

Check 1

Using the answer lines, complete each item below with the correct word from the box.

| A. **discard** | B. **duration** | C. **essential** | D. **exhibit** | E. **juvenile** |
| F. **mature** | G. **miniature** | H. **peer** | I. **sanitary** | J. **tragic** |

___juvenile___ 1. Last year Maddie liked her dress with Winnie-the-Pooh on it, but now she thinks it makes her look too ___.

___sanitary___ 2. Before you put a bandage on that cut, wash it with soap and water to make the area as ___ as possible.

___miniature___ 3. At the bottom of our goldfish bowl lies a ___ pirate's ship.

___discard___ 4. Lewis likes to restore° old furniture, so he checks what his neighbors put outside in the trash. "You'd be surprised what people ___!" he says.

___peer___ 5. Mrs. Walker scolded her son for calling their elderly neighbor by her first name. "She's not a ___ of yours. Treat her with more respect."

___essential___ 6. For me, popcorn is an ___ part of the movie experience. I just don't enjoy a film without it.

___tragic___ 7. "Why do you look so sad?" my father said. "You only failed a test. That's not so ___. It's not as though someone died."

___exhibit___ 8. On Hobby Night, Joy ___ed her collection of coins from other countries.

___duration___ 9. Two rude women whispered throughout the ___ of my father's speech.

___mature___ 10. Lions live together in groups, with the ___ animals watching out for the younger ones.

NOTE: Now check your answers to these items by turning to page 241. Going over the answers carefully will help you prepare for the remaining practices, for which answers are not given.

Check 2

Using the answer lines, complete each item below with **two** words from the box. Use each word once.

___mature___
___duration___
1–2. When our family has a New Year's Eve party, the little kids have to go to bed at ten o'clock. But the more ___ ones can extend° their bedtime and stay up for the ___ of the party.

___discard___
___exhibit___
3–4. The movie star ___ed her first husband's love letters. Later, a reporter found them in her trash and ___ed them on TV.

___essential___
___sanitary___
5–6. "Before you begin cooking," said the TV chef, "it is ___ to make sure your work area is well scrubbed and ___."

___juvenile___
___tragic___
7–8. Recently, a ___ Siberian tiger died at the zoo. The loss of the baby tiger was ___ because there are only a few hundred Siberian tigers left in the world.

___miniature___
___peer___
9–10. Making ___ furniture for dollhouses is a popular activity with my third-grade niece and her ___s.

Word Work

A. Write each word next to the examples that best match it.

A. **duration**	B. **essential**	C. **exhibit**
D. **juvenile**	E. **sanitary**	

sanitary 1. Marta scrubbed the bathroom sink.
Before giving Randy an injection, the nurse wiped his arm with alcohol.
Jim washed the apple before he ate it.

juvenile 2. A newly hatched bird
Three little kittens
A kindergarten student

essential 3. A ball for playing soccer
Eggs to make an omelet
Wheels for a skateboard

duration 4. The movie lasted an hour and a half.
A week contains seven days.
The couple had been married for forty-seven years.

exhibit 5. Tack students' stories on the bulletin board
Hang a painting on the living-room wall
Place a statue of a queen in a museum

B. In the space provided, write the letter of the choice that best completes each item.

_B_ 6. Workers' **peers** include their
  A. children.   B. coworkers.   C. sports heroes.

_C_ 7. People **discard** items that they
  A. are very fond of.   B. know are valuable.   C. do not want anymore.

_A_ 8. Many people feel it would be **tragic** if the world's tigers
  A. died out.   B. had no stripes.   C. hunted for food.

_A_ 9. The nine-year-old is **mature** for his age. He
  A. reads as well as most twelve-year-olds.
  B. still sucks his thumb.
  C. enjoys computer games.

_B_ 10. Jack keeps his **miniature** cars in a
  A. garage.   B. shoebox.   C. parking lot.

Word Parts

A. The prefix *dis-* means "not," " lack of," "the opposite of," or "remove."

Examples:
disregard° — to not pay attention to   *dispute°* — the opposite of agreement
disorder — lack of order; confusion   *discard* — to remove from a group of items; throw away

On each answer line, write the word from the box that means the same as the *italicized* words.

A. **disagree**	B. **discourteous**	C. **dishonest**
D. **disloyal**	E. **displace°**	

_____displace_____   1. My bookcase is so full that if I buy a new book, I'll have to *remove from its place* one of the books I already have.

_____disloyal_____   2. I consider myself a true friend of Molly, but she thinks I was *not loyal* because I went to Disneyland with my family instead of to her birthday party.

_____dishonest_____   3. Brian paid for his purchase with a $20 bill, but the *not honest* cashier gave him change for $10 and kept the difference.

_____discourteous_____   4. When the restaurant manager heard a server being *the opposite of courteous* to a customer, she fired him on the spot.

_____disagree_____   5. My twin cousins love to argue. Sometimes I think they *do not agree* just for the fun of it.

B. The suffix *-ary* means "of," "connected with," or "relating to."

Examples:
imaginary — of the imagination   *dietary* — relating to diet
temporary° — connected with time   *sanitary* — relating to health

On each answer line, write the word from the box that best completes the item.

F. **complimentary**	G. **customary°**	H. **dietary**
I. **honorary**	J. **solitary°**	

_____dietary_____   6. Common ___ problems are skipping breakfast and getting too much sugar in beverages and foods.

_____complimentary_____   7. Even if you don't like someone's outfit, you can still make an honest ___ remark such as, "Your shirt is a pretty color."

_____customary_____   8. Although having a birthday cake is ___ in the United States, that's not the tradition in some other parts of the world.

_____honorary_____   9. Ms. Lopez never attended classes at the college, but it gave her an _____ degree to recognize her good work in building the children's hospital.

_____solitary_____   10. Dogs love the company of other dogs, but cats tend to be ___ animals, keeping pretty much to themselves.

Final Check

Read the passages carefully. Then fill in each blank with the word that best fits the context.

A. A Childish Collection

| A. **discard** | B. **exhibit** | C. **juvenile** | D. **mature** | E. **miniature** |

Have you ever had a collection? When I was younger, I collected (1)_____*miniature*_____ horses. They were so tiny that a dozen of them could inhabit° one bedroom shelf. No two of them were identical°; each one was different. I loved to (2)_____*exhibit*_____ them there, where my friends could admire the spectacle°. But when I was about 13, I decided to displace° them. I had the preconception° that my little horses were too (3)_____*juvenile*_____ for a teenager's bedroom. I couldn't bring myself to (4)_____*discard*_____ them entirely, though, so I wrapped them up carefully and put them away. Recently I found them again, and I felt sorry that I had hidden them away in a dark drawer. I decided that at my age, I should be (5)_____*mature*_____ enough not to care if anyone else thinks my horses are childish. I brought them out and arranged them once again on my bedroom shelf. And guess what? My very "grown-up" friends like to play with them.

B. Clara Barton

| F. **duration** | G. **essential** | H. **peer** | I. **sanitary** | J. **tragic** |

Clara Barton was born on Christmas Day, 1821. As a young girl, she was too shy to go to a regular school. So Clara was educated at home. Along with her lessons, her mother taught her to keep a house (6)_____*sanitary*_____ so that germs didn't spread there. Perhaps that is why Clara became a nurse.

When the Civil War began, in 1861, Clara learned that doctors on the battlefield did not have enough (7)_____*essential*_____ medical supplies, such as bandages. Clara thought it was (8)_____*tragic*_____ that soldiers were dying unnecessarily. She convinced° people to donate these crucial° supplies. Then she went to the battlefield herself to nurse wounded soldiers. She worked there for the (9)_____*duration*_____ of the entire war. After the war, she helped many families locate missing soldiers.

On a visit to Europe, Clara associated° with other nurses who had helped during wars. She learned that on the battlefield, her European (10)_____*peer*_____s wore red crosses to indicate° that they were neutral°; they treated anyone who was injured, no matter which side he fought for. Clara took the idea back home. In 1882, the once-shy girl founded the American Red Cross.

| Scores | Check 2 _____% | Word Work _____% | Word Parts _____% | Final Check _____% |

Enter your scores above and in the **Vocabulary Performance Chart** on the inside back cover of the book.

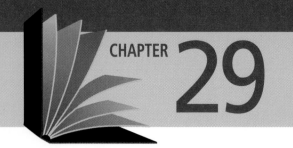

capability	magnify
content	postpone
duplicate	presentable
immense	realistic
industrious	stun

Ten Words in Context

In the space provided, write the letter of the meaning closest to that of each **boldfaced** word. Use the context of the sentences to help you figure out each word's meaning.

1 capability
(kā-pə-bĭl′ĭ-tē)
- *noun*

- Ellen has a great **capability** for science. She started taking college science courses when she was just 15.
- Some people don't have much **capability** for foreign languages. My father studied German for five years but can barely speak it.

<u>B</u> *Capability* means   A. fear.   B. talent.   C. place.

2 content
(kən-tĕnt′)
- *adjective*

- The cat is curled up and purring in the sunny window. Doesn't she look **content**?
- The children's story "The Fisherman's Wife" tells of a woman who was never **content**, no matter what wonderful things she had.

<u>B</u> *Content* means   A. busy.   B. pleased.   C. worried.

3 duplicate
(dōō′plĭ-kāt′)
- *verb*

- Wilson does a great imitation of Michael Jackson. He **duplicates** MJ's voice and dance moves perfectly.
- The vacuum-cleaner salesman said, "Many people have tried to **duplicate** our product, but they all failed! Only *this* vacuum cleaner is the real thing."

<u>A</u> *Duplicate* means   A. to copy.   B. to believe.   C. to enjoy.

4 immense
(ĭ-mĕns′)
- *adjective*

- An adult grizzly bear really is **immense**. It can be eight feet tall and weigh 850 pounds.
- We felt an **immense** sense of relief when the neighbor's missing child was found safe.

<u>C</u> *Immense* means   A. smart.   B. awful.   C. huge.

5 industrious
(ĭn-dŭs′trē-əs)
- *adjective*

- The phrase "busy as a beaver" comes from the fact that beavers are **industrious** builders.
- Feeling **industrious** last Saturday, I cleaned the house, did the laundry, and baked four loaves of bread.

<u>B</u> *Industrious* means   A. lonely.   B. ready to work.   C. playful.

6 magnify
(măg′nə-fī′)
- *verb*

- A microscope can **magnify** a blood cell hundreds of times, making it large enough for us to see.
- Somehow, the water **magnified** the fish at the end of my fishing line. Once I pulled the fish in, I was surprised how small it really was.

<u>C</u> *Magnify* means   A. to see.   B. to fool.   C. to make larger-looking.

7 postpone
(pōst-pōn′)
- *verb*

- Because of a snowstorm, our school's winter concert had to be **postponed** for a week.

- Can we **postpone** this conversation for just five minutes? Before we talk, I need to finish what I'm working on.

<u>A</u> *Postpone* means   A. to put off.   B. to begin.   C. to record.

8 presentable
(prĭ-zĕn′tə-bəl)
- *adjective*

- "We're leaving for Grandma's house in ten minutes, and I want you looking **presentable** by then!" the children's mother told them.

- In order to make the kitchen **presentable** in a hurry, I hid the dirty dishes under the sink.

<u>C</u> *Presentable* means   A. colorful.   B. comfortable.   C. fit to be seen.

9 realistic
(rē′ə-lĭs′tĭk)
- *adjective*

- To be **realistic**, I must admit that my weekend job at the grocery store will not ever allow me to buy a Cadillac.

- Doug says it takes a half-hour to get to his house, but forty-five minutes is more **realistic**.

<u>B</u> *Realistic* means   A. hopeful.   B. true-to-life.   C. different.

10 stun
(stŭn)
- *verb*

- The news that I had won a million dollars would probably **stun** me. I don't think I'd be able to speak at first.

- After a lifetime spent in the Midwest, my grandfather was **stunned** the first time he saw the ocean. "It's just unbelievable," he kept saying.

<u>B</u> *Stun* means   A. to teach.   B. to amaze.   C. to ruin.

Matching Words with Definitions

Following are definitions of the ten words. **Print** each word next to its definition. If you look closely at each word in context, you will be able to figure out its meaning.

1. _____duplicate_____   To make or perform an exact copy of; repeat

2. _____postpone_____   To delay until a future time

3. _____immense_____   Extremely large

4. _____capability_____   A talent or ability

5. _____realistic_____   Seeing or telling things as they are; based on things as they are

6. _____magnify_____   To make something appear larger than it really is

7. _____content_____   Satisfied; happy with what you have

8. _____stun_____   To shock; greatly surprise

9. _____presentable_____   In good enough condition to be shown to others

10. _____industrious_____   Hard-working; busy accomplishing something

CAUTION: Do not go any further until you are sure the above answers are correct. Then you can use the definitions to help you in the following practices. Your goal is eventually to know the words well enough so that you don't need to check the definitions at all.

Check 1

Using the answer lines, complete each item below with the correct word from the box.

A. **capability**	B. **content**	C. **duplicate**	D. **immense**	E. **industrious**
F. **magnify**	G. **postpone**	H. **presentable**	I. **realistic**	J. **stun**

postpone   1. When the guest of honor said that he'd be out of town that night, the surprise party had to be ___d until next week.

capability   2. Every day, you have the ___ to make someone else happy. Try using it!

magnify   3. Telescopes ___ objects that look small because they are far away.

duplicate   4. This year, the team will try to ___ its victory in last year's Super Bowl.

content   5. I offered to give Sue the comfortable chair I was sitting in, but she said, "No thanks; I'm ___ where I am."

presentable   6. Before she went to her job interview, Althea asked her sister if she could borrow some ___ shoes.

industrious   7. The principal stopped in to visit our busy classroom. "I'm glad to see your students looking so ___," she told the teacher.

immense   8. For Great-Grandma's ninetieth birthday party, we ordered an ___ cake. It was seven layers high and served sixty people.

stun   9. It would ___ Mom if my brother cleaned his room without being asked.

realistic   10. A long-term goal may not seem ___ at first, but you may reach it by taking one small step at a time.

NOTE: Now check your answers to these items by turning to page 241. Going over the answers carefully will help you prepare for the remaining practices, for which answers are not given.

Check 2

Using the answer lines, complete each item below with **two** words from the box. Use each word once.

stun
immense   1–2. I knew that seeing Mount Everest, the world's highest mountain, would ___ Rick. "I had no idea how ___ it really is," he said.

capability
magnify   3–4. My aunt no longer has the ___ to read without glasses. Her glasses ___ the print enough for her to read it easily.

content
realistic   5–6. People who feel they must have the best of everything are rarely ___. It's better to have more ___ ideas about what is important in life.

industrious
presentable   7–8. When Dad yelled, "Company's coming!" we were very ___ with the vacuum cleaner and dust cloth. By the time the guests arrived, the entire house looked ___. Even the bathroom was unusually sanitary°.

duplicate

postpone

9–10. To celebrate their anniversary, the couple wanted to ___ their first date. But they had to ___ the celebration because the restaurant where they'd eaten was closed for two weeks.

Word Work

A. In the space provided, write the letter of the choice that best completes each item.

_B_ 1. I prefer **realistic** movies, such as
    A. *Santa Claus versus the Martians.*
    B. *The Basketball Incident.*
    C. *The Little Mermaid.*

_A_ 2. Kiran looked quite **presentable** after he
    A. showered, shaved, and put on a nice outfit.
    B. came in from playing football on a muddy field.
    C. had been sick for several days.

_C_ 3. In school, the students learned to **magnify** items using a
    A. ruler.   B. calculator.   C. microscope.

_A_ 4. The rat was so **immense** that it
    A. looked more like a cat than a rat.
    B. ate hardly anything at all.
    C. could hide in tiny spaces.

_B_ 5. The baseball player pitched a no-hitter, then **duplicated** his performance in the next game by
    A. pitching poorly.
    B. pitching another no-hitter.
    C. being replaced.

B. In the space provided, write the letter of the word that most closely relates to the situation in each item.

_C_ 6. Andy dropped into his favorite chair, smiled happily, and said, "What a great day this has been."
    A. immense   B. realistic   C. content

_B_ 7. After school, the kids raked the leaves from the yard, took out the garbage, did the dishes, and tidied up the house.
    A. realistic   B. industrious   C. capability

_B_ 8. We delayed our family reunion by two weeks so that more people could attend.
    A. magnify   B. postpone   C. duplicate

_A_ 9. When he met the twin brother he'd never known he had, Rick was speechless with shock.
    A. stun   B. magnify   C. presentable

_B_ 10. Although he's never had a music lesson, Justin plays the piano very well.
    A. duplicate   B. capability   C. presentable

Synonyms and Antonyms

A. Synonyms. Write the letter of the word or phrase that most nearly means the **same** as each boldfaced word.

__B__ 1. **duplicate**

    A. fool   C. grow

    B. repeat   D. draw

__D__ 2. **realistic**

    A. lazy   C. strong

    B. quick   D. true-to-life

__A__ 3. **postpone**

    A. delay   C. encourage

    B. mail   D. rush

__B__ 4. **stun**

    A. annoy   C. dare

    B. surprise   D. burn

__C__ 5. **capability**

    A. weakness   C. power

    B. guilt   D. pride

B. Antonyms. Write the letter of the word or phrase that most nearly means the **opposite** of each boldfaced word.

__B__ 6. **content**

    A. happy   C. cozy

    B. unhappy   D. rude

__D__ 7. **immense**

    A. large   C. soothing

    B. sensible   D. tiny

__C__ 8. **industrious**

    A. simple   C. lazy

    B. frightened   D. hard-working

__B__ 9. **magnify**

    A. look up   C. show off

    B. make smaller   D. make larger

__B__ 10. **presentable**

    A. clean   C. generous

    B. messy   D. returnable

Final Check

Read the passages carefully. Then fill in each blank with the word that best fits the context.

A. From Poor Girl to College President

| A. **capability** | B. **content** | C. **industrious** | D. **presentable** | E. **realistic** |

Ruth Simmons grew up as a poor child living in a shack in Texas. The idea that she would even go to college, let alone become a college president, was simply not (1)_____realistic_____. Nevertheless°, in 1995, Dr. Simmons became president of Smith College. Five years later, Dr. Simmons was named president of Brown University. She became the first African American to lead an Ivy League school.

Ruth's father was a farmer, and her mother was a maid. They worked hard, but the family was so poor that for Christmas, each of the twelve children received only an apple, an orange, and ten nuts. Ruth had to wear hand-me-down clothing. But Ruth always had a great (2)_____capability_____ for learning. She says that when she first started school, "it was like waking up." When she won a scholarship to attend college, her high-school teachers were conscious° that Ruth's shabby clothing might make her seem inferior° to the other students. One teacher gave her clothes from her own closet so Ruth would look (3)_____presentable_____ on campus. Her brothers and sisters sent money when they could. Ruth justified° their faith in her. She excelled in college, acquired° advanced degrees, and held a series of increasingly significant° college jobs.

Today, Dr. Simmons is not (4)_____content_____ to enjoy her own triumph°. She wants to see other poor young people succeed as well. She tells them to work hard, as her parents did, and to be proud of being (5)_____industrious_____. According to Dr. Simmons, "Any work done out of love for one's family and out of duty is noble work."

B. Snowflakes

| F. **duplicate** | G. **immense** | H. **magnify** | I. **postpone** | J. **stun** |

You've probably heard the statement "No two snowflakes are alike." But can this be true? When you think of the (6)_____immense_____ amount of snow that falls each year, is it possible that nature never (7)_____duplicate_____s a snowflake? No, it probably isn't true. What is true is that no one has ever found two snowflakes that are identical°. A snowflake is made up of up to 100 million tiny fragments°. These pieces can be arranged in so many ways that it seems that no two snowflakes are alike.

Probably no one has ever cared more about snowflakes than a Vermont farmer named Wilson A. Bentley. In 1885, Mr. Bentley discovered that he could (8)_____magnify_____ a snowflake, to see it better, and then photograph it. After he saw the photo, he was amazed by the snowflake's beauty. He wrote, "It seemed a shame that this beauty should not be seen and appreciated. . . . When a snowflake melted, that design was forever lost." Bentley could not (9)_____postpone_____ the melting of snowflakes, but he did manage to keep and exhibit° a record of their beauty. He collected photographs of 2,400 snowflakes and published them in a book that would (10)_____stun_____ readers with the incredible° beauty and variety° of snowflakes. By the time he died in 1931, he was known as "Snowflake" Bentley.

Scores   Check 2 _____%   Word Work _____%   Synonyms and Antonyms _____%   Final Check _____%

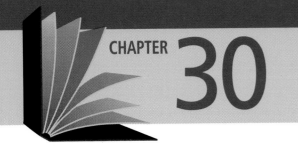

accurate	latter
bluff	modify
consist	toxic
discomfort	trifle
elementary	vanity

Ten Words in Context

In the space provided, write the letter of the meaning closest to that of each **boldfaced** word. Use the context of the sentences to help you figure out each word's meaning.

1 accurate
(ăk′yər-ĭt)
- *adjective*

● When you're measuring medicine, it's important to be **accurate**. Too much or too little can actually harm the patient.

● The spell checker program on my computer helps me make sure that my spelling is **accurate.**

_C_ *Accurate* means   A. generous.   B. healthy.   C. exactly right.

2 bluff
(blŭf)
- *verb*

● During her job interview, Lin didn't try to **bluff**. Instead of trying to suggest that she knew a lot about accounting, she simply said, "I will work hard to learn."

● A good card player knows how to **bluff**. If he or she has a bad hand, none of the other players knows it.

_A_ *Bluff* means   A. to pretend.   B. to tell the truth.   C. to leave.

3 consist
(kən-sĭst′)
- *verb*

● Middle schools usually **consist** of grades five through eight.

● "Egg creams" **consist** of milk, soda water, and syrup—but no egg and no cream.

_C_ *Consist of* means   A. to leave out.   B. to be like.   C. to include.

4 discomfort
(dĭs-kŭm′fərt)
- *noun*

● My nephews always suffer **discomfort** the day after Halloween. They eat far too much of the candy they collect.

● Jen felt such **discomfort** when she lied to her friend that she promised herself she'd never tell a lie again.

_A_ *Discomfort* means   A. physical or mental upset.   B. peace.   C. great danger.

5 elementary
(ĕl′ə-mĕn′tə-rē)
- *adjective*

● An **elementary** rule of science is this: What goes up must come down.

● In her first computer class, Wanda learned some **elementary** skills, such as how to start up the computer.

_C_ *Elementary* means   A. difficult.   B. false.   C. basic.

6 latter
(lăt′ər)
- *noun*

● When I was offered pumpkin pie or cherry pie, I chose the **latter**. Cherry pie has always been my favorite.

● When two things are mentioned, the first one is often called "the former" and the second is called "the **latter**."

_B_ *Latter* means   A. first one.   B. second one.   C. least.

7 modify
(mŏd′ə-fī′)
- *verb*

- A mechanic can **modify** a car so it can be driven by someone who can't use his or her legs.
- The dress Krystal made is like one she saw in a magazine, but she **modified** it by giving it long sleeves.

B *Modify* means   A. to buy.   B. to make different.   C. to harm.

8 toxic
(tŏk′sĭk)
- *adjective*

- After they learned that a company had dumped **toxic** waste nearby, Mr. and Mrs. Miller no longer wanted to buy the house they'd looked at.
- It's very dangerous to mix bleach with other household cleaners. The mixture can create **toxic** gas.

C *Toxic* means   A. a small amount of.   B. heavy.   C. unhealthy.

9 trifle
(trī′fəl)
- *verb*

- Alicia broke up with Ed because he **trifled** with her feelings. He would insult her in public and then say, "Why get upset? I was just kidding around."
- "Never **trifle** with the truth," my dad used to say. "Nobody respects a liar."

A *Trifle with* means   A. to play with.   B. to treat seriously.   C. to question.

10 vanity
(văn′ĭ-tē′)
- *noun*

- The wicked queen in "Snow White" was famous for her **vanity**. Every day, she asked a magic mirror who the most beautiful woman in the country was, and it said, "You are." One day, the mirror answered, "Snow White is more beautiful than you." That day, the queen decided Snow White had to die.
- Because of Mark's **vanity** about his expert piano playing, he refuses to play anything for others, even for fun, unless he's learned it perfectly.

B *Vanity* means   A. kindness.   B. too much pride.   C. concern for health.

Matching Words with Definitions

Following are definitions of the ten words. **Print** each word next to its definition. If you look closely at each word in context, you will be able to figure out its meaning.

1. _____consist_____   To be made up (of); be formed or composed (of)
2. _____trifle_____   To treat as if it has little value
3. _____latter_____   The second of two things or persons mentioned
4. _____modify_____   To change somewhat
5. _____discomfort_____   A feeling of pain or uneasiness; lack of comfort
6. _____toxic_____   Poisonous; very bad for one's health
7. _____vanity_____   A feeling of too much pride in one's appearance, ability, etc.
8. _____accurate_____   Correct; without errors; precise°
9. _____bluff_____   To pretend to know more or feel more confident than one really does
10. _____elementary_____   Basic; simple

CAUTION: Do not go any further until you are sure the above answers are correct. Then you can use the definitions to help you in the following practices. Your goal is eventually to know the words well enough so that you don't need to check the definitions at all.

Check 1

Using the answer lines, complete each item below with the correct word from the box.

| A. accurate | B. bluff | C. consist | D. discomfort | E. elementary |
| F. latter | G. modify | H. toxic | I. trifle | J. vanity |

__Vanity__ 1. "Why aren't you wearing your glasses?" I asked Eileen when I saw her at the formal° dance. "___," she answered. "I look better without them."

__accurate__ 2. Your addition here is not ___; 28 plus 73 is not 104.

__consist__ 3. My sister's new apartment ___s of just two rooms. Before she moved in, she had to discard° many things she possessed°, keeping only what was essential°.

__trifle__ 4. "Don't ___ with me," the movie detective told the suspect in a stern° tone of voice. "Tell me what you know, and tell it to me quickly."

__elementary__ 5. Here's an ___ fashion tip: Don't wear plaid pants with a striped shirt.

__discomfort__ 6. When the beggar asked for money, you could see ___ in people's faces.

__latter__ 7. January has thirty-one days, and February has only twenty-eight. But of the two months, the ___ always seems longer to me.

__modify__ 8. Dan ordered a tuna sandwich, but then he called the waitress back so he could ___ his order: "May I have that on rye instead of white bread?"

__toxic__ 9. A sign on the truck warned that it was carrying ___ materials.

__bluff__ 10. As I took my friend over to meet my neighbor, I realized I'd forgotten the neighbor's name. I tried to ___ by saying, "Why don't you two introduce yourselves to each other?"

NOTE: Now check your answers to these items by turning to page 241. Going over the answers carefully will help you prepare for the remaining practices, for which answers are not given.

Check 2

Using the answer lines, complete each item below with **two** words from the box. Use each word once.

__Vanity__
__toxic__ 1–2. ___ has led people to do dangerous things. For instance, women used to put drops of a ___ liquid in their eyes to make them brighter.

__elementary__
__bluff__ 3–4. Before you visit a foreign country, it's good to learn some ___ phrases, such as "Please" and "Thank you." Beyond that, don't try to ___. Just say, "I'm sorry; I don't speak the language."

__discomfort__
__accurate__ 5–6. When my father had stomach ___, his doctor ordered a test. "This test gives ___ results, so we'll know exactly what's the matter," the doctor asserted°.

__modify__
__latter__ 7–8. When my uncles Mike and Leonard came to this country, one of them decided to ___ his last name. The former kept the name Mike Barrenski, but the ___ is now known as Leonard Barr.

__trifle__
__consist__ 9–10. Because my brother has ___d with so many girls' feelings, his female friends now ___ of only my mom and my sister.

Word Work

A. In the space provided, write the letter of the choice that best completes each item.

_B_ 1. The **discomfort** Velma was feeling was due to

  A. the happy news she had just received.
  B. her new shoes, which pinched her feet.
  C. her fluffy, warm bathrobe.

_A_ 2. Dennis and Mitchell were talking when the **latter** suddenly became angry and pushed

  A. Dennis.   B. Mitchell.   C. both Dennis and Mitchell.

_C_ 3. A person who **trifles** with your feelings

  A. cares deeply for you.
  B. feels bad about what he or she is doing.
  C. is not concerned about your feelings.

_B_ 4. If the Weather Bureau's prediction of two feet of snow turns out to be **accurate**, our area will receive

  A. no snow at all.   B. two feet of snow.   C. less than a foot of snow.

_C_ 5. You might **modify** a recipe in order to

  A. share it with a friend.
  B. know where to find it easily the next time.
  C. make it lower in fat.

B. In the space provided, write the letter of the word that most closely relates to the situation in each item.

_C_ 6. "Of course I know how to multiply fractions! But it's pretty complicated, and it would take me too long to explain it or show it to you."

  A. latter   B. vanity   C. bluff

_B_ 7. That spider's bite is so poisonous that most victims die within four hours.

  A. latter   B. toxic   C. elementary

_C_ 8. New York City is made up of five boroughs: Manhattan, the Bronx, Queens, Brooklyn, and Staten Island.

  A. modify   B. vanity   C. consist

_A_ 9. Two plus two equals four. *Cat* is spelled C-A-T.

  A. elementary   B. latter   C. modify

_C_ 10. Many celebrities have face-lifts to make themselves look younger than they are.

  A. trifle   B. consist   C. vanity

Analogies

Each item below starts with a pair of words in CAPITAL LETTERS. For each item, figure out the relationship between these two words. Then decide which of the choices (A, B, C, or D) expresses a similar relationship. Write the letter of your choice on the answer line. (All the repeated words in these items are from this unit.)

__C__ 1. ACCURATE : WRONG ::

    A. magnify° : telescope   C. essential° : unimportant
    B. factual : story   D. identical° : same

__A__ 2. BLUFF : PRETEND ::

    A. duplicate° : copy   C. lie : truth
    B. play : poker   D. sprawl° : gather

__B__ 3. CONSIST OF : CONTAIN ::

    A. cook : recipe   C. create : destroy
    B. throw out : discard°   D. postpone° : date

__A__ 4. DISCOMFORT : PLEASURE ::

    A. poverty : wealth   C. flood : water
    B. happy : joy   D. exhibit° : paintings

__B__ 5. TOXIC : POISON ::

    A. realistic° : imagination   C. tragic° : funny
    B. sweet : sugar   D. magic : magician

__D__ 6. ELEMENTARY : ALPHABET ::

    A. large : immense°   C. childish : mature°
    B. school : classroom   D. green : grass

__C__ 7. LATTER : SECOND ::

    A. numbers : enumerate°   C. last : final
    B. before : after   D. stern° : teacher

__D__ 8. VANITY : MODESTY ::

    A. mirror : reflection   C. enforce° : law
    B. plane : pilot   D. strength : weakness

__C__ 9 TRIFLE WITH : TAKE SERIOUSLY ::

    A. emotion : anger   C. mistrust° : believe
    B. tell : secret   D. work : industrious°

__D__ 10. MODIFY : HAIRDO ::

    A. debate° : argue   C. truck : highway
    B. repair : fix   D. rewrite : paragraph

Final Check

Read the passages carefully. Then fill in each blank with the word that best fits the context.

A. Three Little Words

| A. **bluff** | B. **elementary** | C. **consist** | D. **discomfort** | E. **vanity** |

Three little words can make the world a better place. No, they're not "I love you." They are simply these: "I don't know." Although the words seem (1)___elementary___, many people find them difficult to say. They will do almost anything to evade° admitting they don't know something. For instance, a teacher might ask a student, "What were some of the causes of the Civil War?" Instead of saying, "I don't know," the student will try to (2)___bluff___ his way out of the situation by saying, "Well, there were a lot of them, but they're pretty hard to enumerate°." Or at a news conference, a reporter might ask a politician how she would reform° the banking system. The politician's (3)___vanity___ about being an expert won't allow her to say the fundamental° truth: "I don't know." So she spends ten minutes giving an answer that (4)___consist___s of nothing but hot air. The truth is that people respect someone who is honest enough to say, "I don't know." So the next time you're asked a question you can't answer, admit it—say you can't. The brief (5)___discomfort___ you may feel is less than the immense° trouble you'll avoid.

B. A Child-Safe Home

| F. **accurate** | G. **latter** | H. **modify** | I. **toxic** | J. **trifle** |

When Elena was expecting her first child, she wanted to do everything right. She saw her doctor regularly during the duration° of her pregnancy. She took special vitamins. She kept (6)___accurate___ records of her weight gains from week to week. She exercised and ate a balanced diet. She wouldn't think of smoking or drinking.

But Elena hadn't thought of everything. A few weeks before the baby was due, Elena's mother, Anna, came over for a visit. Elena and Anna sat and talked for a little while, and then the (7)___latter___ looked around the apartment. "You know, this isn't a child-safe home," Anna said in an anxious° tone of voice. "Look at all the dangers there are for a baby or a toddler. "

Elena was stunned°. She knew that her mother was right and that if they postponed° doing something about the problem, there could be tragic° results. The two spent the rest of the day doing a thorough° job of making the apartment safe for a baby. They took (8)___toxic___ household cleaners, such as bleach and ammonia, and locked them away on high shelves. They had to (9)___modify___ the doors on the cabinets so that little fingers could not seize° and open them. They fitted child-proof plugs into electrical outlets and put a baby gate across the top of the stairs. When they were finished, Elena was content°. "I'll take every precaution° I can to keep my baby safe," she said. "A child's health is much too important to (10)___trifle___ with."

| Scores | Check 2 _____% | Word Work _____% | Analogies _____% | Final Check _____% |

The box at the right lists twenty-five words from Unit Six. Using the clues at the bottom of the page, fill in these words to complete the puzzle that follows.

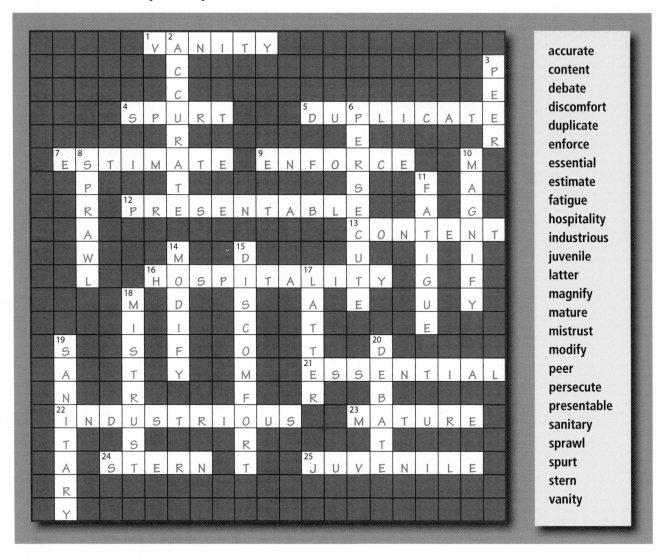

accurate
content
debate
discomfort
duplicate
enforce
essential
estimate
fatigue
hospitality
industrious
juvenile
latter
magnify
mature
mistrust
modify
peer
persecute
presentable
sanitary
sprawl
spurt
stern
vanity

ACROSS

1. Too much pride in one's appearance or ability

4. To flow out suddenly and with force

5. To make or perform an exact copy of; repeat

7. To make a guess at something's size, amount, or value

9. To make sure that a rule or law is obeyed

12. In good enough condition to be shown

13. Satisfied; happy with what you have

16. Generous, friendly treatment of guests

21. Necessary

22. Hard-working; busy accomplishing something

23. Adult; fully developed

24. Serious and strict

25. Young; not fully grown

DOWN

2. Correct; precise

3. A person who is on an equal level with another person

6. To harm again and again; treat cruelly

8. To sit or lie with arms and legs thrown outward

10. To make something appear larger than it really is

11. The state of being very tired

14. To change somewhat

15. A feeling of pain or uneasiness

17. The second of two things or persons mentioned

18. To have no trust in; to doubt

19. Free from dirt or germs

20. To discuss a question by looking at different points of view

PART A

Choose the word that best completes each item and write it in the space provided.

_____enforce_____ 1. Communities ___ their laws by using fines and jail time.

    A. estimate   B. enforce   C. magnify   D. mistrust

_____discard_____ 2. Instead of washing cloth diapers, most people now use diapers that they can ___.

    A. discard   B. enumerate   C. justify   D. exhibit

_____duration_____ 3. When they arrived at the party, Henry said something that made Irina angry. For the ___ of the party, Irina didn't speak to him.

    A. essential   B. fatigue   C. duration   D. toxic

_____consist_____ 4. Tomorrow's test will ___ of short essay and multiple-choice questions.

    A. postpone   B. consist   C. modify   D. persecute

_____estimate_____ 5. I ___ that the drive from here to Florida will take about twenty hours.

    A. trifle   B. displace   C. enumerate   D. estimate

_____Fatigue_____ 6. ___, cough, and fever are often signs that you have the flu.

    A. Fatigue   B. Hospitality   C. Peer   D. Vanity

_____flimsy_____ 7. Cheap clothing rarely lasts a long time; it's too ___.

    A. elementary   B. industrious   C. miniature   D. flimsy

_____identical_____ 8. To me, all chicken eggs look ___. Can a mother hen tell which are hers?

    A. content   B. essential   C. identical   D. stern

_____Immense_____ 9. ___ redwood trees line the "Avenue of the Giants" in northern California. Some are more than 360 feet high.

    A. Singular   B. Flimsy   C. Immense   D. Presentable

_____justify_____ 10. The shoplifter tried to ___ his stealing by saying, "The store's owner makes so much money, he'll never miss what I take."

    A. associate   B. enforce   C. persecute   D. justify

_____vanity_____ 11. We'd been lost for half an hour, but Dad's ___ wouldn't allow him to ask for directions. "I know exactly where we are!" he kept insisting.

    A. fatigue   B. hospitality   C. peer   D. vanity

(Continues on next page)

_____modify_____ 12. Aisha had planned on serving roast chicken with baked potatoes and salad for dinner. When she realized she had no potatoes, she had to quickly ___ her menu.

    A. modify   B. magnify   C. exhibit   D. enumerate

_____miniature_____ 13. On top of the wedding cake stood a ___ bride and groom, only about five inches tall.

    A. sanitary   B. miniature   C. mature   D. singular

PART B

Write **C** if the italicized word is used **correctly**. Write **I** if the word is used **incorrectly**.

_C_ 14. Since Marva wanted her checkbook to be *accurate*, she used a calculator to do the addition and subtraction.

_I_ 15. The kindergarten teacher's sweet smile and *stern* voice made even the shyest child feel relaxed.

_C_ 16. In the Spanish course for beginners, we learned to ask and answer a few *elementary* questions.

_I_ 17. Barry's favorite books are *realistic* ones about creatures from other planets that travel through time.

_I_ 18. You can sense our neighbor's *hospitality* as soon as you see the signs in his yard saying, "Beware of Dog," "No Trespassing," and "Go Away."

_I_ 19. Adding sweet-smelling, *toxic* oils to the water makes bathing a delightful treat.

_C_ 20. Sharing a toothbrush is not a very *sanitary* thing to do.

_C_ 21. Samuel *soothed* the frightened puppy by patting it and talking to it gently.

_C_ 22. "It's *essential* that Mrs. Peterson have her medicine every four hours," the doctor said. "Otherwise, she could become very ill."

_I_ 23. The high-school seniors were asked to read to their *peers* in kindergarten.

_I_ 24. "You won't believe what just happened!" Roberta cried. From the joyful look on her face, I could tell she had *tragic* news.

_C_ 25. *Mature* female animals have been known to take care of motherless babies in addition to their own.

Score	(Number correct) _____	x 4 = _____%

PART A

On the answer line, write the word from the box that completes each item below. Use each word once.

A. **associate**	B. **debate**	C. **discomfort**	D. **discredit**	E. **displace**
F. **industrious**	G. **juvenile**	H. **latter**	I. **mistrust**	J. **persecute**
K. **presentable**	L. **sprawl**	M. **trifle**		

_____trifle_____   1. I didn't like the woman who interviewed me. I asked her seriously when I might hear about the job, but she just ___d with me, laughing and saying, "Sooner or later."

_____discredit_____   2. Trying to ___ one of his coworkers, Jerry told the boss that the man had been caught stealing.

_____sprawl_____   3. The thoughtless man ___ed across the seat on the bus, taking up as much room as three other people.

_____presentable_____   4. "Can you wait for me to shower and shave?" Randall said. "I want to look ___ when we go out."

_____persecute_____   5. Cruel people on the block ___d the new family because of their race, sending them hateful letters.

_____latter_____   6. "Your money or your life!" the robber said. I preferred to save the ___, so I handed over the money.

_____mistrust_____   7. The shopkeeper ___s everyone. "Anyone will cheat you if you're not careful," she claims.

_____juvenile_____   8. Although a grown-up Dalmatian dog is white with black spots, a ___ Dalmatian is pure white.

_____industrious_____   9. The boss fired the lazy worker. "I need to find someone more ___," he said.

_____displace_____   10. "I can't find anything," Juan complained. "When Hal cleaned up the apartment, he ___d everything."

_____associate_____   11. Since her family moved across town, Sandy doesn't ___ with her old friends anymore.

_____debate_____   12. The two candidates for mayor are going to ___ about whether to raise taxes or not.

_____discomfort_____   13. I don't know if Sharon was embarrassed, angry, or sad at the meeting, but it was clear she was feeling some sort of ___.

(Continues on next page)

PART B

Write **C** if the italicized word is used **correctly**. Write **I** if the word is used **incorrectly**.

_C_ 14. At her interview, Janice *enumerated* all the reasons she should be given the job.

_I_ 15. Being able to speak three languages is a wonderful *barrier* to Francesca at her office, where she meets many people from other countries.

_I_ 16. After the rainstorm, puddles of water *spurted* quietly on the sidewalk.

_C_ 17. A fortuneteller claims to have the *capability* to see into the future.

_C_ 18. Some words that are well-known in the *singular*—such as "cactus"—are less well-known in the plural. More than one cactus would be "cacti."

_C_ 19. That instructor never gives the same exam twice, even though it would be easier for her to *duplicate* the questions on an old one.

_I_ 20. The couple upstairs are clearly *content* with each other. Their fights wake us up almost every night.

_I_ 21. Because he was ashamed of his poor report card, my brother *exhibited* it in the back of his desk drawer.

_C_ 22. Because he doesn't want to admit he is unemployed, Scott *bluffs* when he is asked what he does for a living. He says things like, "I'm doing a little bit of this and that right now."

_C_ 23. "I will introduce the graduates one by one," said the principal. "To save time, please *postpone* your applause until all the names have been called."

_I_ 24. At the street fair, an artist offered to write our names in an unusual way. She said she would *magnify* the letters so that the whole name could fit on a single grain of rice.

_I_ 25. When I came to the kitchen for breakfast, I was *stunned*—my father said, "Good morning," as usual.

Score   (Number correct) _____ x 4 = _____%

PART A: Synonyms

In the space provided, write the letter of the choice that is most nearly the **same** in meaning as the **boldfaced** word.

___C___ 1. **barrier**
- A. something that helps
- B. something that is similar
- C. something that gets in the way
- D. something that is different

___A___ 2. **bluff**   A. pretend   B. reject   C. realize   D. limit

___C___ 3. **capability**   A. action   B. excuse   C. talent   D. victim

___A___ 4. **consist of**   A. be made up of   B. be sure of   C. be missing   D. be worth

___D___ 5. **discomfort**   A. dishonesty   B. pleasure   C. ability   D. pain

___B___ 6. **displace**   A. name   B. move away   C. throw away   D. show

___A___ 7. **duplicate**   A. copy   B. erase   C. purchase   D. envy

___B___ 8. **duration**
- A. amount something weighs
- B. time something lasts
- C. value something is worth
- D. material something is made of

___A___ 9. **elementary**   A. basic   B. difficult   C. recent   D. complete

___D___ 10. **enforce**   A. ignore   B. suggest   C. release   D. carry out

___D___ 11. **enumerate**   A. give away   B. reduce   C. choose   D. list

___B___ 12. **estimate**   A. measure   B. guess   C. separate   D. confuse

___A___ 13. **industrious**   A. hard-working   B. badly made   C. tired   D. not honest

___C___ 14. **justify**   A. throw away   B. permit   C. give a reason for   D. listen

___D___ 15. **juvenile**   A. strange   B. large   C. happy   D. young

___A___ 16. **magnify**   A. make appear larger   B. make ready   C. shrink   D. hide

___A___ 17. **mistrust**   A. doubt   B. believe   C. know   D. blame

___B___ 18. **modify**   A. keep   B. change   C. scare   D. hurry

___A___ 19. **peer**   A. equal   B. enemy   C. boss   D. servant

___B___ 20. **persecute**   A. praise   B. harm   C. love   D. expect

___B___ 21. **realistic**   A. exciting   B. true to life   C. very large   D. accidental

___A___ 22. **sprawl**   A. spread out   B. repeat   C. regret   D. encourage

___B___ 23. **spurt**   A. loosen   B. flow suddenly   C. drip   D. fasten tightly

___B___ 24. **stun**   A. respect   B. surprise   C. forget   D. refuse

___B___ 25. **trifle**   A. put away   B. treat lightly   C. hide from   D. set up

(Continues on next page)

PART B: Antonyms

In the space provided, write the letter of the choice that is most nearly **opposite** in meaning to the **boldfaced** word.

__B__ 26. **accurate**   A. timid   B. full of mistakes   C. active   D. honest

__A__ 27. **associate**   A. stay away from   B. accept   C. copy   D. make fun of

__C__ 28. **content**   A. not wealthy   B. not fair   C. not satisfied   D. not honest

__C__ 29. **debate**   A. repeat   B. allow   C. agree   D. bore

__A__ 30. **discard**   A. keep   B. enter   C. notice   D. let

__B__ 31. **discredit**   A. agree   B. honor   C. cause pain   D. pretend

__C__ 32. **essential**   A. possible   B. expensive   C. not needed   D. borrowed

__A__ 33. **exhibit**   A. hide   B. chase   C. purchase   D. need

__B__ 34. **fatigue**   A. worry   B. peppiness   C. humor   D. sadness

__C__ 35. **flimsy**   A. funny   B. untrue   C. strong   D. colorful

__D__ 36. **hospitality**   A. blame   B. generosity   C. action   D. unfriendliness

__D__ 37. **identical**   A. common   B. famous   C. cheap   D. different

__A__ 38. **immense**   A. tiny   B. clever   C. pretty   D. noisy

__D__ 39. **latter**   A. best   B. easiest   C. lowest   D. first

__B__ 40. **mature**   A. stupid   B. young   C. smooth   D. active

__D__ 41. **miniature**   A. recent   B. lost   C. comical   D. large

__A__ 42. **postpone**   A. do earlier   B. do better   C. do again   D. do badly

__A__ 43. **presentable**   A. messy   B. careful   C. same   D. best

__C__ 44. **sanitary**   A. modern   B. cold   C. dirty   D. shiny

__A__ 45. **singular**   A. many   B. bright   C. careless   D. boring

__A__ 46. **soothe**   A. disturb   B. trust   C. hide   D. forget

__A__ 47. **stern**   A. friendly   B. worried   C. interested   D. strong

__C__ 48. **toxic**   A. sweet   B. dusty   C. harmless   D. simple

__C__ 49. **tragic**   A. unusual   B. long-lasting   C. happy   D. foolish

__A__ 50. **vanity**   A. modesty   B. honesty   C. confusion   D. agreement

Score   (Number correct) _____   x 2 = _____%

Enter your score above and in the **Vocabulary Performance Chart** on the inside back cover of the book.

Appendixes

A. Limited Answer Key

IMPORTANT NOTE: This answer key contains the answers for the "Check 1" activity that is on the third page of each chapter. You should not look at these answers until you have tried your best to pick the word that belongs in each sentence of this activity.

If you use the answer key correctly, it will help you learn and remember the words in the chapter. It will also help you prepare for the other activities and tests, for which the answers are not given. To make this key easier to use, parts of the titles of each chapter's readings are written after the chapter number.

Chapter 1 (Johnny Appleseed; Lovable Leech?)

Check 1

1. transform
2. fertile
3. preference
4. surplus
5. peculiar
6. solitary
7. principal
8. challenge
9. suitable
10. dependent

Chapter 2 (Finding Fault; What Hobbies Reveal)

Check 1

1. frustration
2. deliberate
3. Excessive
4. indicate
5. attitude
6. fragile
7. category
8. analyze
9. critical
10. contrast

Chapter 3 (Furniture; Barbara's Date)

Check 1

1. desperate
2. evident
3. accompany
4. improper
5. dispose of
6. rejection
7. preserve
8. determine
9. pursue
10. restore

Chapter 4 (The Salesman; Peace at Last)

Check 1

1. reduction
2. betray
3. exaggerate
4. abundant
5. neutral
6. comparison
7. demonstrate
8. distinct
9. inhabit
10. dispute

Chapter 5 (Study Skills; Training a Puppy)

Check 1

1. unstable
2. utilize
3. aggravate
4. considerable
5. obnoxious
6. intentional
7. coincide
8. interference
9. humane
10. cease

Chapter 6 (Toasters; A Mean Man)

Check 1

1. reliable
2. advise
3. minimum
4. penalize
5. originate
6. current
7. deprive
8. hesitate
9. objection
10. maintain

Chapter 7 (A Special Memory; Watch Manners!)

Check 1

1. endure
2. classify
3. recollect
4. astonish
5. exclaim
6. abrupt
7. eager
8. complex
9. horizontal
10. consent

Chapter 8 (Brothers and Sisters; Kevin's Date)

Check 1

1. potential
2. vanish
3. variety
4. appeal
5. wholesome
6. adequate
7. establish
8. customary
9. respond
10. awkward

Chapter 9 (Gym Program; Through Child's Eyes)

Check 1

1. discipline
2. ultimate
3. resort
4. vague
5. interpret
6. propose
7. eliminate
8. furthermore
9. emphasis
10. brutal

Chapter 10 (Knowing How to Argue; Change)

Check 1

1. linger
2. anticipate
3. occur
4. reluctant
5. version
6. particular
7. miserable
8. accustomed
9. misinterpret
10. revise

Chapter 11 (Coma; Doughnut Contest)

Check 1

1. internal
2. external
3. maximum
4. remedy
5. incredible
6. conscious
7. spectacle
8. protest
9. assume
10. verdict

Chapter 12 (People's Choice; Christmas Wars)

Check 1

1. triumph
2. artificial
3. counsel
4. frequency
5. complicate
6. conscience
7. temporary
8. represent
9. transparent
10. detect

Chapter 13 (What's Your Type?; What a Circus!)

Check 1

1. withdraw
2. energetic
3. strive
4. trait
5. foresight
6. tolerance
7. agonizing
8. interval
9. substance
10. prosper

Chapter 14 (Practicing Kindness; Stinking Rose)

Check 1

1. consistent
2. significant
3. evaluate
4. plea
5. random
6. cope
7. phrase
8. sole
9. practical
10. approximately

Chapter 15 (Modern Fairy Tale; Wolf Children)

Check 1

1. shallow
2. authentic
3. harsh
4. concept
5. disrupt
6. thrive
7. remote
8. confront
9. eligible
10. characteristic

Chapter 16 (Mismatched Couple; Campaign)

Check 1

1. transfer
2. burden
3. influence
4. extravagant
5. sympathize
6. apparent
7. fulfill
8. security
9. economical
10. automatic

Chapter 17 (Famous Detective; Why So Quiet?)

Check 1

1. outspoken
2. deceive
3. communicate
4. bewilder
5. theory
6. investigate
7. legible
8. earnest
9. fiction
10. emotion

Chapter 18 (Fear of Public Speaking; Magic?)

Check 1

1. humiliate
2. divert
3. assure
4. revive
5. impulse
6. crucial
7. perceive
8. hostile
9. frantic
10. extraordinary

Chapter 19 (Miracle Runner; One of Days)

Check 1

1. alert
2. primary
3. idle
4. theme
5. overcome
6. abandon
7. devote
8. circumstances
9. function
10. dominate

Chapter 20 (Common Cold; Criminal with Tail?)

Check 1

1. misleading
2. prey
3. exclude
4. hinder
5. severe
6. monotonous
7. obtain
8. excerpt
9. seize
10. disregard

Chapter 21 (Traveling; Saving Earth's Supplies)

Check 1

1. resources
2. unanimous
3. conflict
4. vicinity
5. possess
6. vary
7. procedure
8. convert
9. renew
10. stress

Chapter 22 (More Fat; Is Prison Effective?)

Check 1

1. precise
2. nevertheless
3. decay
4. expand
5. promote
6. vast
7. corrupt
8. reform
9. tendency
10. abolish

Chapter 23 (She Changed My Mind; So Sue Me)

Check 1

1. clarify
2. assert
3. rigid
4. evade
5. extend
6. preconception
7. resemble
8. senseless
9. precaution
10. vertical

Chapter 24 (My History Report; Mrs. Thornton)

Check 1

1. comprehend
2. inferior
3. impression
4. overwhelm
5. thorough
6. anxious
7. dramatic
8. frank
9. convince
10. illustrate

Chapter 25 (Wacky Weddings; Cost of Hatred)

Check 1

1. fragment
2. commitment
3. formal
4. acquire
5. spite
6. resent
7. precede
8. solemn
9. fundamental
10. symbolize

Chapter 26 (My Parents' Problem; The Hike)

Check 1

1. associate
2. estimate
3. justify
4. flimsy
5. barrier
6. persecute
7. fatigue
8. soothe
9. mistrust
10. hospitality

Chapter 27 (A Teacher's Lesson; Sports Heroes)

Check 1

1. debate
2. discredit
3. spurt
4. enforce
5. stern
6. identical
7. enumerate
8. singular
9. sprawl
10. displace

Chapter 28 (Childish Collection; Clara Barton)

Check 1

1. juvenile
2. sanitary
3. miniature
4. discard
5. peer
6. essential
7. tragic
8. exhibit
9. duration
10. mature

Chapter 29 (College President; Snowflakes)

Check 1

1. postpone
2. capability
3. magnify
4. duplicate
5. content
6. presentable
7. industrious
8. immense
9. stun
10. realistic

Chapter 30 (Three Little Words; Child-Safe)

Check 1

1. Vanity
2. accurate
3. consist
4. trifle
5. elementary
6. discomfort
7. latter
8. modify
9. toxic
10. bluff

B. Dictionary Use

It isn't always possible to figure out the meaning of a word from its context. That's where a dictionary comes in. Following is some basic information to help you use a dictionary.

How to Find a Word

A dictionary contains so many words that it can take a while to find the one you're looking for. But if you know how to use guidewords, you can find a word rather quickly. *Guidewords* are the two words at the top of each dictionary page. The first guideword tells what the first word is on the page. The second guideword tells what the last word is on that page. The other words on a page fall alphabetically between the two guidewords. So when you look up a word, find the two guidewords that alphabetically surround the word you're looking for.

● Which of the following pairs of guidewords would be on the page with the word *litigate*?

(liquid / litter)   **lodger / longhand**   **light / lily**

The answer to this question and the questions that follow are given on the next page.

How to Use a Dictionary Listing

A dictionary listing includes many pieces of information. Here is a typical listing. Note that it includes much more than just a definition.

> **thun•der** (thŭn′dər) *n.* **1.** The explosive sound following an electrical charge of lightning. **2.** Any loud, resounding noise. — *v.* **3.** To give forth thunder. **4.** To make a loud, resounding noise like thunder. **5.** To utter loudly or threateningly.

Key parts of a dictionary entry are listed and explained below.

Syllables. Dots separate dictionary entry words into syllables. Note that *thunder* has one dot, which breaks the word into two syllables.

● To practice seeing the syllable breakdown in a dictionary entry, write the number of syllables in each word below.

    out•pa•tient __3__   **Mis•sis•sip•pi** __4__   **re•frig•er•a•tor** __5__

Pronunciation guide. The information within parentheses after the entry word shows how to pronounce the entry word. This pronunciation guide includes two types of symbols: pronunciation symbols and accent marks.

Pronunciation symbols represent the consonant and vowel sounds in a word. The consonant sounds are probably very familiar to you, but you may find it helpful to review some of the sounds of the vowels—*a, e, i, o,* and *u.* Every dictionary has a key explaining the sounds of its pronunciation symbols, including the long and short sounds of vowels.

    Long vowels have the sound of their own names. For example, the *a* in *pay* and the *o* in *no* both have long vowel sounds. Long vowel sounds are shown by a straight line above the vowel: ā, ō.

    In many dictionaries, the *short vowels* are shown by a curved line above the vowel. Thus the *u* in the first syllable of *thunder* is a short *u* (ŭ). The pronunciation chart on the inside front cover of this book indicates that the short *u* has the sound of *u* in *up.* It also indicates that the short *a* has the sound of *a* in *apple,* that the short *e* has the sound of *e* in *end,* and so on.

● Which of the words below have a short vowel sound? Which has a long vowel sound?

    camp (kămp) __short__   **pie** (pī) __long__   **silk** (sĭlk) __short__

Another pronunciation symbol is the *schwa* (ə), which looks like an upside-down *e*. It stands for certain rapidly spoken, unaccented vowel sounds, such as the *a* in *above*, the *e* in *item*, the *i* in *easily*, the *o* in *gallop*, and the *u* in *circus*. More generally, it has an "uh" sound, like the "uh" a speaker says when hesitating. Here are three more words that include the schwa sound:

a•like (ə-līk′)   **an•swer** (ăn′sər)   **pro•nounce** (prə-nouns′)

● Which syllable in *thunder* contains the schwa sound, the first or the second? _____ *second* _____

Accent marks are small black marks that tell you which syllable to emphasize, or stress, as you say a word. An accent mark follows *thun* in the pronunciation guide for *thunder*. This mark tells you to stress the first syllable of *thunder*. Some syllables are in between, and they are marked with a lighter accent mark.

● Which syllable has the stronger accent in *automatic*? _____ *third* _____

au•to•mat•ic (ô′tə-măt′ĭk)

Parts of speech. After the pronunciation key and before each set of definitions, the entry word's parts of speech are given. The parts of speech are abbreviated as follows:

noun—*n.*   pronoun—*pron.*   adjective—*adj.*   adverb—*adv.*   verb—*v.*

● The listing for *thunder* shows that it can be two parts of speech. Write them below:

_____ *noun* _____   _____ *verb* _____

Definitions. Words often have more than one meaning. When they do, each meaning is usually numbered in the dictionary. You can tell which definition of a word fits a given sentence by looking at the *context*—the rest of the sentence. For example, the word *copy* has several definitions, including these two: **1.** To make a copy of. **2.** To imitate.

● Show with a check (✓) which definition (1 or 2) applies in each sentence below:

The boy learned to swear by *copying* his father.   1 ___   2 ✓

The students *copied* the homework assignment into their notebooks.   1 ✓   2 ___

Other information. After the definitions in a listing in a hardbound dictionary, you may find information about the *origin* of a word. This information, usually given in brackets ([ ]), explains which languages contain earlier forms of the word. And you may sometimes be given one or more synonyms or antonyms for the entry word. *Synonyms* are words that are similar in meaning to the entry word; *antonyms* are words that are opposite in meaning.

Which Dictionaries to Own

You will find it useful to own two recent dictionaries: a small paperback dictionary to carry to class and a hardbound dictionary, which contains more information than a small paperback version, to keep at home. Here are several good dictionaries that are published in both paperback and hardbound editions:

The American Heritage Dictionary
The Random House College Dictionary
Webster's New World Dictionary

Answers to the Dictionary Questions

Guide words: *liquid / litter*
Number of syllables: 3, 4, 5
Vowels: *camp, silk* (short)*; pie* (long)
Schwa: second syllable of *thunder*

Accent: stronger accent on third syllable *(mat)*
Parts of speech: noun and verb
Definitions: 2; 1

C. Topics for Discussion and Writing

NOTE: The first five items for each chapter are intended for discussion; the last two, for writing. Feel free, however, to either talk or write about any of the items.

Chapter 1 (Johnny Appleseed; The Lovable Leech?)

1. Everyone has some personal habits that might seem odd to others. For instance, one person might put all her books in alphabetical order, while another might constantly jingle the **surplus** change in his pocket. Describe something that you do, or that someone you know does, which might seem **peculiar** to other people.

2. If you could **transform** one room in your home, which one would it be—and how would you change it?

3. Think of a friend of yours and decide, from what you know of that person, what a **suitable** job would be for him or her. To do so, first think about the person's talents, likes, and dislikes.

4. Who is a person you feel is **dependent** upon you in some way? Describe the ways in which that person relies on you.

5. Some people feel strongly that they should have their dogs and cats "fixed" so that they are no longer **fertile**. Others think they should let their pets have babies at least once, or even many times. What is your opinion about letting pets reproduce?

6. Write about a **challenge** that you have faced and dealt with successfully. What was the **principal** reason that this challenge was difficult for you? How did you go about dealing with it?

7. When you are feeling blue or depressed, which is your **preference**: to cheer yourself up by being with other people, or to be **solitary** and have quiet time alone? Tell about a time that makes your preference clear.

Chapter 2 (Finding Fault; What Do Your Hobbies Reveal about You?)

1. What do your favorite leisure activities reveal about you? Tell about one or more of your principal° interests and what they **indicate** about your personality.

2. Many people feel that a positive, hopeful **attitude** is more likely to lead to success than a negative one. Do you agree? Explain your answer.

3. What are you most **critical** about in other people? What are you most critical about in yourself? Is your answer the same in both cases? Or is there a **contrast** between the faults you focus on in someone else and those you see in yourself?

4. What is your favorite **category** of reading material? If you don't like to read, what type of reading do you least dislike?

5. We are likely to think that if someone hurts us **deliberately**, it is worse than doing the same harm by accident. But why? Aren't we hurt just as much either way?

6. Write about something in your life that causes you **excessive frustration**. It might be a personal relationship, a chore you hate, or a problem that keeps coming up. Explain why it makes you feel so discouraged.

7. In a paper, **analyze** what makes learning easy or hard for you. Give examples to show what you mean.

Chapter 3 (Fixing Up Furniture; Barbara's Date with Her Cousin)

1. Do you own something special that you hope to **preserve** throughout your life? What is it, and how could you keep it in good condition?

2. What kind of items do you frequently use that other people **dispose** of, and what do you use them for? What would you have to do if such items were no longer available, and you **desperately** needed them?

3. If a visitor went shopping with you, what would become **evident** to him or her about your taste in clothes?

4. What career do you plan on **pursuing**? How did you **determine** your career choice? What ways can you pursue it in addition to going to school?

5. Who is the actor or actress you would most like to **accompany** to the Academy Awards ceremony? Why?

6. What is one goal in life that is important for you to **pursue**? When did it become **evident** to you that this was a meaningful goal for you? Write about that goal and its meaning in your life.

7. Write about a time when you experienced a feeling of **rejection**. How did you feel? What did you do afterward to **restore** your feeling of self-confidence?

Chapter 4 (The Vacuum-Cleaner Salesman; Peace at Last)

1. If you found out that someone you love very much had committed a crime, would you **betray** him or her and tell the police?

2. Imagine that you are working at a company that needs to save money. It gives you and your coworkers this choice: Everyone takes a **reduction** in pay, or half of the workers will lose their jobs. You don't know, of course, who will be fired and who won't. Would you take the cut in pay? Why or why not?

3. When something bad happens, do you tend to **exaggerate** it ("This is the end of the world!"), or do you tend to play it down ("It's no big deal")? Make a **comparison** between these two attitudes° toward trouble. Which one do you think is more helpful? Why?

4. Describe a **dispute** in which you felt strongly about one side, and another debate in which you felt **neutral**. Why did you have strong feelings about the first issue, but not about the second one?

5. Do you think human beings will ever **inhabit** another planet? Why or why not?

6. If you could make one thing on Earth more **abundant**, what would it be, and why? Write about your choice.

7. Write about how you would **demonstrate** to others something you know how to do very well, such as baking a cake or riding a bike. How would you give your audience a **distinct** idea of the process?

Chapter 5 (Study Skills to the Rescue!; Training a Puppy)

1. Think of several things that upset you, disturb you, or make you angry or annoyed. These things may happen in the world, in your community, or in your family. Now suppose that you can make one of them—but only one—**cease**. Which one would you stop, and why?

2. Have you ever experienced an interesting **coincidence**—two things that happened at the same time, as if they had been planned? For example, someone may have called you on the phone just as you were beginning to think of that person. Tell about an interesting coincidence in your life.

3. Have you ever been in a situation where telling a lie seemed more **humane** than telling the truth? Why was the lie kinder? In such a situation, is it all right to lie? Why or why not?

4. What do you think makes the difference between a solid, lasting relationship—in a marriage, for example—and an **unstable**, troubled one? Do you think one single thing is most important, or is it a combination of many things?

5. Recycling is an issue of **considerable** importance to many people today. Do you or your family members save and **utilize** anything out of the ordinary, something that other people might not have thought to put to use? If so, what is it, and how do you use it?

6. People sometimes **aggravate** an already bad situation by well-meant but harmful **interference**. Write about a time in your own experience when someone (perhaps even you!) made things worse, even though the harm wasn't **intentional**.

7. Everyone has faults, of course, but have you ever known someone whose fault or faults were especially **obnoxious**? Write about what it was like to know this person, and how you reacted to his or her unpleasant qualities.

Chapter 6 (Toasters; A Mean Man)

1. Does someone you know have a nickname? How did that nickname **originate**?

2. Who do you think is a **reliable** person in your life? Who is *not* reliable? Would you **maintain** a friendship with someone who is not trustworthy? Explain your answers.

3. Name one **current** song, movie, or TV show that you enjoy. Then explain why you like it.

4. What do you think should be the **minimum** legal age for people to drive? To buy alcohol? To vote? To serve in the military? Explain.

5. Is there a time when it was clear to you that a friend was making a mistake? Did you try to **advise** the friend to do things differently, or did you **hesitate** to interfere? Tell about what your friend was doing and what you did, if anything.

6. Write a paper about what you think are some proper ways to **penalize** children when they misbehave. For example, do you think it is ever right to punish a child by spanking? Or do you think a better punishment is to **deprive** children of something they want?

7. What movie have you seen recently that you strongly disliked? Explain your **objection** to the film. End your paper by telling what you would **advise** the filmmakers to do in order to improve the movie.

Chapter 7 (A Special Memory; Watch Your Manners!)

1. Scientists think there may once have been some kind of life on Mars—not little green men, but simple life forms. If this turns out to be true, would it **astonish** you? Why or why not?

2. Which do you find harder to **endure**: a heat wave in the summer, or bitter cold in the winter? When it's very hot or cold outside, how do you try to make yourself more comfortable?

3. Can you think of an **abrupt** event you have experienced—something that happened suddenly and without warning? It might have been something important, like the end of a relationship, or something minor, like a sudden rainstorm. Tell what it was like.

4. What things in your life would you **classify** as too **complex**? How could you make these things simpler for you?

5. Did you ever **exclaim** something without meaning to—in class, for instance, or on a bus, or at a movie? Can you **recollect** how it happened? Can you remember how you felt and what happened afterward?

6. Write about a time when, as a young child or later, you were **eager** to do something, but your parents wouldn't **consent** to it. Try to explain both points of view, yours and theirs. How do you feel now about what happened?

7. **Classifying** items helps to show the similarities and differences among them. Write a paper in which you classify something into two or three categories°. Explain the features of each group and how each member of the group fits in. For instance, you might divide your courses into those in which the teacher teaches the whole class for the entire period and those in which students work in small groups.

Chapter 8 (Big Brothers and Sisters; Kevin's First Date)

1. Have you and your parents ever disagreed about whether or not a person was a **wholesome** influence in your life? How did you see that person, and how did that differ from the way your parents saw him or her?

2. What holiday is celebrated in a big way in your family? What are some of the **customary** ways you have **established** to celebrate that holiday each year?

3. If a genie offered you just one wish before **vanishing** in a puff of smoke, how would you **respond**?

4. Think of someone you know who has the **potential** to develop a talent. Who is the person, and what is his or her special ability? How do you think he or she can develop that ability?

5. Do people on the street ever **appeal** to you for money? Does this make you feel **awkward**? What do you do when that happens?

6. Write about a time when you thought that you were doing an **adequate** job at home or in school, but someone else—perhaps a parent or a teacher—thought you weren't working up to your **potential**. How did you **respond** to the person who encouraged you to do better?

7. What are some **wholesome** activities that you enjoy? In what ways do they improve your mind, body, or character? Write about a **variety** of such activities and how they affect you.

Chapter 9 (Differences in a Gym Program; Through a Child's Eyes)

1. Have you ever watched someone acting in a **brutal** fashion—on TV, in a movie, or in real life? What did the person do? How did you feel about what was happening?

2. Think about some of the major problems of our society, such as drug abuse, unemployment, poverty, hunger, and crime. Which problem do you think it is most important to **eliminate**? Why did you choose the one you did?

3. Why might parents sometimes **resort** to spanking their children? **Furthermore**, do you think that spanking is a good way to **discipline** children? Why or why not?

4. What are some of your earliest, most **vague** memories? Why do you think you still remember these events?

5. What, for you, would be the **ultimate** vacation? Where would you go, and how would you spend your time there?

6. Write a paper describing a change you would like to **propose** in how your school, workplace, or household is run. Describe in detail—not **vaguely**—how your suggestion would work.

7. TV, movies, and magazines are constantly giving us messages about fashion, body image, and other things having to do with outward appearance. How do you think people **interpret** these messages? Write a paper about whether or not there is too much **emphasis** today on "looking good."

Chapter 10 (Knowing How to Argue; A Change of School, A Change of Heart)

1. Describe something that **occurs** regularly—perhaps every day, or every week, or every year—that you **anticipate** with pleasure. What makes you look forward to it?

2. Has a friend ever asked you for a favor that you were **reluctant** to do? Describe what he or she asked for and why you did not want to say yes. Did you end up doing what your friend asked you to do?

3. Have you ever read something and then seen a television or movie **version** of the same story? Which did you prefer? Why?

4. Tell about a time when someone **misinterpreted** something you did or said. What did you mean? What did the person *think* you meant?

5. What are some reasons why a student might **linger** after school instead of going straight home?

6. Write about something that **occurred** that made you feel **miserable**. What happened? Why did you feel so bad about it? Did you ever become **accustomed** to what happened, or does it still bother you?

7. Write a paper about the best or worst job (or class or teacher) you ever had. Provide plenty of details that make very clear to the reader just why that **particular** job (or class or teacher) was a good one or a bad one. **Revise** the paper at least once, adding even more details when you do so.

Chapter 11 (Coming Out of a Coma; The Office Doughnut Contest)

1. Describe a time when something **incredible**—but true—happened to you. Or tell of a time when something hard to believe happened to someone you know.

2. What is an interesting **spectacle** you recently witnessed? Describe what made it noticeable.

3. What do you think should be the **maximum** number of students in a sixth-grade class? A high-school writing class? A college lecture class? Why do you think this should be the largest number of students allowed?

4. Most families have a few of their own **remedies** for minor illnesses or injuries. Tell about some ways your family deals with bruises, sickness, or maybe even hurt feelings. Are these remedies applied **internally** or **externally**? How do they work?

5. When have you **assumed** that something was true and then became **conscious** that you were mistaken? For example, you might have assumed that two people were related and later found out they weren't. Or you may have believed that someone agreed with you on some point and then found out he or she did not. Explain your reaction.

6. Think of a disagreement that two of your friends have had. If they asked you to decide who was right, what would be your **verdict**? Why?

7. Write about a time when you **protested** against something you thought was wrong or unfair. Did you protest quietly, or did you do something to make a **spectacle** of yourself?

Chapter 12 (The People's Choice; The Christmas Wars)

1. Why do fans have a sense of **triumph** when their team wins? After all, the fans don't do any of the playing; they only watch and cheer. What might their team's victory **represent** to them?

2. How would you **counsel** a teenager who wanted to drop out of school? Can you think of anything special to say—something that doesn't just repeat the advice that kids usually hear?

3. People tend to think that something that is "artificial" is worse than something that is "natural." Can you think of an opposite example—a human-made product that is better than the natural thing?

4. When someone is lying to you, do you think you can usually **detect** it? If so, how? If not, why not?

5. **Transparent** objects have various advantages. One obvious benefit of a window, for example, is letting more light into a room. What are some other ways in which something transparent can be useful?

6. Henry David Thoreau wrote that our lives are too cluttered by detail, and he urged us to "Simplify, simplify." Write about some ways you might make your own life simpler by getting rid of activities that **complicate** it, or at least by reducing their **frequency**.

7. Write about a time you had to do something difficult because your **conscience** demanded that you do it. For instance, you may have had to say no to a friend in order to avoid doing something you felt was wrong. Explain the situation and the choices you faced. Then tell what you finally decided to do and why.

Chapter 13 (What's Your Type?; What a Circus!)

1. Do you know someone in your community who has **prospered** more than most of the people around him or her? How did this person manage to succeed? Do you think this success was a matter of luck, ability, **energetic** effort, or all three?

2. Think of a time in your past when you had to **strive** to achieve something difficult. What were you trying to do, and why did you succeed or fail?

3. Describe a time in your life when you demonstrated **tolerance** for another person's opinions or behavior. How were that person's thoughts or actions different from what you were accustomed° to? How did you show your acceptance?

4 Think of a close friend or family member, and describe several of that person's **traits**. Which of those qualities have influenced you the most?

5. Some people like waiting for something nice to happen. They are able to enjoy the **interval** between deciding to do something—for instance, buying some new clothes—and actually doing it. Others hate to wait. As soon as they decide to buy something new, they want to be at the store, buying it. Which kind of person are you? Can you patiently look ahead to a nice event? Or does waiting spoil your enjoyment of the experience?

6. What's the most **agonizing** physical pain you have experienced? Did a person, an event, or a **substance** cause this pain? Explain what caused it and what it was like.

7. Think of a situation in your life in which you wish you had shown more **foresight**. Describe what happened. Then explain how things might have turned out differently if you had planned ahead better. Or, instead, tell about a time when you were very glad that you *did* have foresight.

Chapter 14 (Practicing Kindness; The Stinking Rose)

1. How do you **cope** with tension? Are you someone who deals with pressure well, without becoming overly upset? Or do you "fall apart" and become helpless? Describe a tense situation in your life, and **evaluate** how you have coped (or are coping) with it.

2. Do you know someone who is very **practical**? Do you know someone else who is not so practical and often does not consider things realistically? Describe those two people, giving examples of how one is sensible and the other is not so sensible.

3. What is a **phrase** that you associate with a particular person in your life? Did a parent, a grandparent, or a friend have a saying that he or she repeated often? What was that phrase, and when was the person likely to say it?

4. **Approximately** how much free time do you have in a week? Do you have a **significant** amount of free time in your life, or only a small amount of free time? What are some of the things you prefer to do in your free time?

5. While your life may change from day to day, there are some parts of your life that are **consistent**, that you can depend on routinely. For example, you may wake up every day to the sound of your alarm clock, or you may have a relationship that you can always count on. What are some of your favorite things that happen regularly in your life?

6. What is one behavior that you'd really like to see someone change? Perhaps you wish that a parent would stop smoking, or that a friend would quit asking to borrow money from you. Write a **plea** to that person, asking him or her to change this particular° behavior and explaining why.

7. Some people believe that everyone has only one "perfect match"—that there is a **sole** romantic partner for each of us. Others think that people get together at **random** and that there are a number of people out there who would make a good life partner. Write about whether you believe in "just one true love" or in "lots of possibilities," and explain why you do.

Chapter 15 (A Modern Fairy Tale; Wolf Children)

1. Some words can be used to describe people as well as things. For example, a **shallow** person does not think deeply about things. People who are **authentic** say what they really mean and actually do what they say they will do. Describe someone you know who is **shallow** and someone else you know who is **authentic**.

2. Tell about a time you **confronted** another person about something he or she had done. What were you upset about? How did you express your feelings to that person?

3. Name a **remote** place, a spot hardly anyone else knows about, where you go to relax or study. Tell about that place, including what you like about it.

4. What are some common ways that students **disrupt** classroom activities? What are some of the more unusual classroom disruptions you have seen?

5. Tell about a time that you spoke to someone in a **harsh** way, then wished you had not. Why do you think you spoke so unpleasantly?

6. What qualities do you think are **characteristic** of a good friendship? Write a paper explaining your **concept** of friendship.

7. Imagine that you could design your own school—one in which you could truly **thrive**. How would it meet your mental, emotional, and physical needs? What subjects would be taught? How would they be taught? Would the teaching be done in classrooms, or in some other setting? Could just anyone attend your school, or would only certain people be **eligible**? Write a description of your ideal school.

Chapter 16 (A Mismatched Couple; A Campaign to Become Class President)

1. What gives you a sense of **security** at home or at school? What makes you feel insecure? If you had to **transfer** to a different school, would you feel less secure? If so, what could you do to feel more comfortable?

2. Once people had to do their laundry by hand. Now there are **automatic** washers to do it for them. What automatic machine do you wish someone would invent to help you with some other task?

3. Think of one person who has had a big **influence** on your life. Describe how he or she has affected you.

4. Have you ever made a promise that was difficult to **fulfill**, yet you kept it? What was it? Why was it difficult to keep this promise?

5. Describe one way that your family tries to be **economical**.

6. Write about a time when it was **apparent** that something was bothering a friend. What made it obvious to you that something was bothering him or her? How did you help your friend deal with that **burden**? Did you just **sympathize**, or did you assist in some more active way?

7. If you had one day in which you could be as **extravagant** as you liked, what would you do? What dreams would you **fulfill** during that day?

Chapter 17 (The Famous Detective; Why So Quiet?)

1. Which member of your family is most **outspoken**? Give an example of a time that person has boldly stated his or her opinion.

2. Think of a friend who has moved away, but with whom you have stayed in touch. In what ways do the two of you **communicate**?

3. Tell about a time when a person seemed to you to be **earnest**, but then did something that showed he or she was not sincere at all. How did that person **deceive** you, and how did you discover the truth?

4. Describe a work of **fiction** that you have read and enjoyed. What about it maintained° your interest?

5. Lots of television shows are based on police officers, private detectives, or even scientists who **investigate** crimes or unusual events. What is one such show that you've watched? How do the people in the show go about their work?

6. Have you ever been involved in a mystery that was never solved? It might be the disappearance of something that belonged to you, or a change in a friend's appearance or behavior that you never understood. What happened to **bewilder** you? Do you have any **theory** about what might have really happened?

7. Select a particular **emotion**, such as sadness, embarrassment, joy, fear, or another feeling. Write about a time when you experienced that emotion strongly. Tell what happened, how you felt, and why you felt that way.

Chapter 18 (Fear of Public Speaking; Do You Believe in Magic?)

1. Of all the friendships you've had, which one seems the most **crucial** to you? Why has that one friendship been so important to you?

2. Describe a person you know who often seems **hostile**. Is this person unfriendly to everyone or only to certain people? How does the person express his or her hostility?

3. When have you seen one person try to **humiliate** another? What did he or she do in order to embarrass the other person? Describe what the first person did and how the other person reacted.

4. Tell a story about a time when you spoke or acted because of an **impulse**. Did you feel OK later about what you had said or done? Or did you wish you had thought it through more carefully first?

5. When you were a child, what kind of situation made you feel **frantic**? Losing a favorite plaything? Getting lost? How did you behave when you were feeling so anxious? (If you can't remember, think of a young child you know, and describe what might make this child feel frantic and how he or she would act.)

6. Write about how and where you like to study. Where do you prefer to sit? What do you like to have around you? Do you like to have music playing and people nearby, or do those things **divert** your attention? When you get sleepy or bored as you study, what do you do to **revive** yourself?

7. Write about the trip that you take to reach school. What route do you follow? Do you walk, or do you travel in a car or bus? Describe some of the sights, smells, and sounds that you usually **perceive** in the course of your trip. What **extraordinary** things have you ever seen or experienced along the way?

Chapter 19 (The Miracle Runner; One of Those Days)

1. Have you ever wished you could **abandon** your responsibilities—school, family, work—and just take off somewhere? Explain what **circumstances** made you feel that way.

2. When you have free time, do you **devote** yourself to some activity, or do you prefer to be **idle**? Why?

3. Prisons are the topic of many arguments these days. What do you think the **function** of a prison should be? To help criminals become better citizens? To punish them? Or just to keep them where they can't do any more harm? Explain.

4. Has anyone ever tried to **dominate** you or someone you know by threats or bullying? What are some things a person could do to **overcome** this kind of abuse?

5. Have you ever been to a **theme** park? If so, what was the theme, and how was it carried out?

6. When you are bored or sleepy, what do you do to make yourself more **alert**? Do you drink tea, cola, or coffee? Go for a fast walk? Take a shower? Describe something that wakes you up when you need a lift.

7. Write about your **primary** goal in getting an education. Is it to prepare for a good job? To please your family? To gain self-respect? To learn more about things that interest you? Or something else?

Chapter 20 (The All-Too-Common Cold; A Criminal with a Tail?)

1. When have you **disregarded** the advice someone gave you, and later wished you had paid attention to it? Tell about what happened.

2. How do you feel about the previews that are shown in theaters before the feature? Do you think that the **excerpts** give a good idea of what those movies will be like? Or would you rather **exclude** them from the show? Explain your answers.

3. Tell about a time when you were trying to leave the house to get to work or school, but something **hindered** you. What was it that got in the way of your leaving?

4. Do you ever see advertisements for products or hear claims that you think are **misleading**? Describe one such ad or claim. In what way do you believe it might lead people to a mistaken conclusion?

5. What was the most **severe** weather you have ever experienced? How bad was it, and how did you deal with it?

6. What is the most **monotonous** thing that you have ever had to do? Did you make it more exciting by playing music? By watching TV? Describe the task and what was so boring about it. Then tell how you made it more fun for yourself.

7. How do you feel about hunting? Would you enjoy following your **prey**—perhaps a deer—and then shooting it? Do you think that hunting is an acceptable way to **obtain** food? Or are you bothered by the idea of hunting wild animals? Write about your attitude° toward hunting.

Chapter 21 (Traveling with Children; Saving Earth's Natural Supplies)

1. After you woke up this morning, what **procedure** did you go through to get ready for your day? Do you ever **vary** your routine? If so, when—and why?

2. How do you **renew** the food supplies in your cupboard and refrigerator? Are you very organized, writing lists for once-a-week shopping trips? Or do you do a little shopping every day?

3. Name a few of your favorite places in the **vicinity** of your home. Why are these your favorites?

4. Do you think juries should always have to reach a **unanimous** verdict° to convict someone of a crime? Why or why not?

5. The United States has abundant° natural **resources**. Should they be **converted** to practical° uses (for example, drilling for oil or cutting down trees for paper and building materials)? Or should some be preserved as natural parklands and forests? Explain your answers.

6. Write about a time that you were in **conflict** with one or more other people. What was the argument about? Did you experience a lot of **stress** as a result of the conflict? How was the conflict finally settled?

7. Write about a close friend. What traits° does your friend **possess** that make you like him or her so much?

Chapter 22 (More Fat, Anyone?; Is Prison Effective?)

1. Tell about a home or building that has started to **decay**. What were the causes of the problem, and what could have been done to avoid it? What do you think will become of that home or building?

2. If you could **expand** one room in your home, which would it be? How would you use the increased space?

3. Some people say that commercials for candy, fast food, and salty snacks should not be broadcast during Saturday morning cartoons, because they **promote** bad eating habits among kids. Do you agree? Or should television stations be allowed to schedule these ads whenever they choose?

4. Think of a process in which it is important to be **precise**. Why is it important to do this in an exact way? What would happen if you were *not* precise?

5. Do you believe that prison actually **reforms** criminals? Why or why not? Can you think of a better way to deal with people who have broken the law?

6. If you had unlimited power, what is one thing that you would **abolish** from the world? Write in a serious or humorous style about something you would get rid of if you had **vast** power.

7. Why do you think that some people grow up to be honest, while others become **corrupt**? Are there reasons why certain people have a **tendency** to commit dishonest acts? Write about why a person growing up may become an honest—or a dishonest—adult.

Chapter 23 (She Changed My Mind; So Sue Me)

1. What is one responsibility you have in your life—around the house, at school, or at work—that you would like to **evade**? What are some ways you could try to escape that responsibility?

2. In your opinion, do dreams have any meaning? Or would you **assert** that they are just **senseless** collections of pictures and sounds? Explain why you feel as you do.

3. What are some **precautions** that you take to keep from becoming a victim of crime? Explain how the things you do help keep you safe.

4. Describe a time when you formed a **preconception** of something—perhaps a particular job, course, or activity—that turned out to be incorrect. Where did you get the ideas that led to your first opinion? After you actually experienced this situation, did you **rigidly** hold on to your earlier belief, or did you change your opinion—either for the better or for the worse? Explain.

5. Who are the two people in your family (or a family you know) who **resemble** each other the most? In what ways are they alike? Are they similar only in looks, or also in the way that they act?

6. Most people are lucky if they can go away for one or two weeks of vacation in a year. Imagine that somehow you have been able to **extend** your vacation to last an entire year—and that you have plenty of money to spend on it. Write a description of how you would spend your year.

7. Pretend that you are a scientist from Mars who has been sent to study the planet Earth. Your assignment today is to look out one window and describe all the **vertical** objects that you see. Since your Martian boss has never visited Earth, you will have to **clarify** what each object is and what it does, so be sure to include plenty of details about each object.

Chapter 24 (My History Report; Mrs. Thornton's Condition)

1. Did you ever try to **convince** a friend to give up a bad habit? What was the habit, and what did you say or do to convince your friend to give it up?

2. Tell about a time when your first **impression** of a person turned out to be mistaken. What happened to make you **comprehend** what the person was really like?

3. Do you know people who seem to like to make other people feel **inferior** to them? How do they do it?

4. Talk about a time when work or other responsibilities **overwhelmed** you. How were you overwhelmed, and how did you react?

5. How might someone go about doing a very **thorough** job of studying the words in this chapter? Name specific steps that the person could take.

6. Write about a time when you were **frank** about your feelings, even though you knew that someone else might not like what you said. How did you feel about speaking out honestly? Did the experience make you feel **anxious**? How did other people respond°?

7. Write about a particular° quality of someone you know. First, give a brief definition of this quality. Then use an example to **illustrate** what you mean. For instance, you might first say what stubbornness is. Then you could describe one particular event that showed a person's stubbornness in a **dramatic** way.

Chapter 25 (Wacky Weddings; The Cost of Hatred)

1. Of all the things that you have **acquired** in your life, which one is the most meaningful? Where and how did you get it? Is it something that is valuable in terms of money, or does it have another kind of value to you? Is it **fundamental** to your sense of who you are?

2. Think of one **commitment** you have made. It could have been to study harder, to break a bad habit, or to get more exercise. What led you to make that promise? Were you able to live up to it?

3. Describe a **formal** ceremony that you have seen. During that ceremony, were people more excited, more relaxed, or more **solemn** than usual? Give examples.

4. Think of a time when you **resented** another person's words or behavior. What did he or she do that angered you? How did you respond°?

5. The world is full of things that **symbolize** other things or ideas. For example, a diamond ring on a woman's left hand may symbolize her engagement. What are some other common things that stand for something else?

6. Pretend that you are an archeologist a thousand years from now. You are digging up the area that used to be your bedroom and finding **fragments** of things you once owned. Write about what you find there. What would a scientist learn or guess about life today by studying your room?

7. Write about an experience that left you feeling full of **spite** toward someone. What happened to stir up that angry feeling? In the time that **preceded** the experience, had you liked or disliked the other person? Afterward, did you express your anger openly, or did you keep it to yourself?

Chapter 26 (My Parents' Problem; The Hike That Hurt)

1. If someone you know thought you had insulted him or her, what could you do to **soothe** that person's hurt feelings?

2. Have you ever met anyone whom you instantly **mistrusted**? What was it about that person that made you mistrustful? Do you think you were right to feel the way you did?

3. Are there people in your school who **persecute** others because of their race, religion, or other reasons? If so, give an example of their behavior. Why do you think that these people act this way?

4. Identify a goal that you have for your own life. What do you think might be the biggest **barrier** to your achieving that goal? Can you think of at least one way to overcome that barrier?

5. Tell about a time when you were shown great **hospitality**. Who treated you that way? Just what was done that made you feel so welcome?

6. How long would you **estimate** you have known your oldest friend? Why do you like to **associate** with that person? Answer these questions in a paper about this friend.

7. Write about a time you made a decision that made other people unhappy. What happened? How did you **justify** the decision? Do you feel now that you made the right choice?

Chapter 27 (A Teacher's Lesson; My Sports Heroes)

1. Would you enjoy having an **identical** twin? Why or why not?

2. What is a rule that you think should be put into effect at your school or workplace? How would you **enforce** that rule?

3. What is one topic that you hear people **debate** about? What is your opinion on that topic?

4. Have you ever admired someone—maybe a public figure—and then learned something that **discredited** that person in your eyes? If so, explain what you learned that changed your mind about the person.

5. Do you know of anyone who was **displaced** by losing a home to fire or as a result of family problems? Tell how that person dealt with the loss.

6. Write a paper in which you **enumerate** and explain three things that you like about one of the following: your school, your job, or a close friend.

7. Think about a time that someone had a **stern** talk with you, a talk that you've never forgotten. Describe what the talk was about and how you felt about it afterward.

Chapter 28 (A Childish Collection; Clara Barton)

1. Think about the things that you own. What is one possession that you plan never to **discard**? Why is that item so special to you?

2. If you were going to adopt a cat or dog, would you prefer to get a **juvenile** or an adult animal? What would be the advantages of each choice?

3. What do you **exhibit** in your bedroom (or another room)? A particular poster? A collection of, say, **miniature** animals or cars? Photographs? Explain what you've chosen to display and why.

4. We usually think of "**peer** pressure" as the pressure a person feels from his or her friends to do bad or unhealthy things. But can peer pressure be positive? If so, give some examples.

5. Imagine that you're going to live on a desert island for six months. Food, water, and shelter will be provided for you. You may bring along only one item. What would that item be, and why is it so **essential** to you?

6. Have you ever known someone who had to go through a **tragic** experience? In addition to causing pain, did the experience make that individual become more **mature** in some way? Write about what the person experienced, and how he or she responded.

7. Pretend you have an entire month—and all the money you need—to do anything you want. Write a paper describing what you would do for the **duration** of that month. Would you stay in one place and do one thing, or would you travel and do a variety of things?

Chapter 29 (From Poor Girl to College President; Snowflakes)

1. Think of someone you know who is **industrious**. Give examples that show why you chose that person.

2. If you could suddenly have the **capability** to do one thing extremely well, what would it be? Would you play a musical instrument, excel at a sport, speak a foreign language, or do something else? Why?

3. If you learned that very important guests were coming to visit in half an hour, what would you do in that time to make your home (or room) more **presentable**?

4. Think of a day in your life that was so enjoyable you'd like to **duplicate** it. What was so special about that day?

5. What qualities or possessions do people really need in their lives in order to be **content**? Why are these qualities or possessions so important?

6. Write about a time that an event or a piece of news **stunned** you. What was it about the event or news that caused you to feel such **immense** surprise?

7. In a paper, explain one goal you'd like to achieve during the next year—a **realistic** goal, not an unlikely one. Describe one or more steps you might take to reach your goal. Is there anything that might cause you to **postpone** taking these steps?

Chapter 30 (Three Little Words; A Child-Safe Home)

1. What do you feel is the most **elementary** rule about being a good friend? Why is this rule so basic to a good friendship?

2. What does your favorite meal **consist** of? Why do you like these foods so much?

3. Have you ever been bothered by the way a stranger was acting? Describe what was going on, and why you felt the **discomfort** you did.

4. Which would you rather be—rich, or talented? If you prefer the first choice, explain why. If you chose the **latter**, tell why it appeals to you more.

5. If you could **modify** just one thing about your home, what would it be, and why would you want to change it?

6. Do a thorough search of your bathroom, kitchen, or garage, and make an **accurate** list of all the **toxic** materials that you find there. What is the purpose of each one? Also, what can you do to use, store, and dispose° of these dangerous materials safely? Write a brief report on what you found.

7. **Vanity** sometimes causes us to try to **bluff** our way out of situations. In other words, our pride makes us pretend to know more than we really do. Write about a time you (or someone else) tried to bluff about something. Did you (or the other person) get away with it?

D. Word List

abandon, 142
abolish, 168
abrupt, 54
abundant, 28
accompany, 22
accurate, 224
accustomed, 72
acquire, 186
adequate, 60
advise, 48
aggravate, 34
agonizing, 98
alert, 142
analyze, 16
anticipate, 72
anxious, 180
apparent, 124
appeal, 60
approximately, 104
artificial, 92
assert, 174
associate, 200
assume, 86
assure, 136
astonish, 54
attitude, 16
authentic, 110
automatic, 124
awkward, 60
barrier, 200
betray, 28
bewilder, 130
bluff, 224
brutal, 66
burden, 124
capability, 218
category, 16
cease, 34
challenge, 10
characteristic, 110
circumstances, 142
clarify, 174
classify, 54
coincide, 34
commitment, 186

communicate, 130
comparison, 28
complex, 54
complicate, 92
comprehend, 180
concept, 110
conflict, 162
confront, 110
conscience, 92
conscious, 86
consent, 54
considerable, 34
consist, 224
consistent, 104
content, 218
contrast, 16
convert, 162
convince, 180
cope, 104
corrupt, 168
counsel, 92
critical, 16
crucial, 136
current, 48
customary, 60
debate, 206
decay, 168
deceive, 130
deliberate, 16
demonstrate, 28
dependent, 10
deprive, 48
desperate, 22
detect, 92
determine, 22
devote, 142
discard, 212
discipline, 66
discomfort, 224
discredit, 206
displace, 206
dispose, 22
dispute, 28
disregard, 148
disrupt, 110

distinct, 28
divert, 136
dominate, 142
dramatic, 180
duplicate, 218
duration, 212
eager, 54
earnest, 130
economical, 124
elementary, 224
eligible, 110
eliminate, 66
emotion, 130
emphasis, 66
endure, 55
energetic, 98
enforce, 206
enumerate, 206
essential, 212
establish, 60
estimate, 200
evade, 174
evaluate, 104
evident, 22
exaggerate, 29
excerpt, 148
excessive, 17
exclaim, 55
exclude, 148
exhibit, 212
expand, 168
extend, 174
external, 86
extraordinary, 136
extravagant, 124
fatigue, 200
fertile, 10
fiction, 130
flimsy, 200
foresight, 98
formal, 186
fragile, 17
fragment, 186
frank, 180
frantic, 136

261